THE COMPLETE WORKS

OF

JAMES WHITCOMB RILEY

IN SIX VOLUMES

Portrait by Steele

THE COMPLETE WORKS

OF

JAMES WHITCOMB RILEY

IN WHICH THE POEMS, INCLUDING A NUMBER HERETOFORE UNPUBLISHED,
ARE ARRANGED IN THE ORDER IN WHICH THEY WERE WRITTEN,
TOGETHER WITH PHOTOGRAPHS, BIBLIOGRAPHIC NOTES,
AND A LIFE SKETCH OF THE AUTHOR

COLLECTED AND EDITED BY

EDMUND HENRY EITEL

BIOGRAPHICAL EDITION
VOLUME THREE

INDIANAPOLIS
THE BOBBS-MERRILL COMPANY
PUBLISHERS

PRESS OF
BRAUNWORTH & CO.
BOOKBINDERS AND PRINTERS
BROOKLYN, N. Y.

CONTENTS

CONTENTS

CONTENTS

CONTENTS

CONTENTS

CONTENTS

CONTENTS

THE COMPLETE WORKS

OF

JAMES WHITCOMB RILEY

IN SIX VOLUMES

A FRUIT-PIECE

THE afternoon of summer folds
Its warm arms round the marigolds,

And, with its gleaming fingers, pets
The watered pinks and violets

That from the casement vases spill,
Over the cottage window-sill,

Their fragrance down the garden walks
Where droop the dry-mouthed hollyhocks.

How vividly the sunshine scrawls
The grape-vine shadows on the walls!

How like a truant swings the breeze
In high boughs of the apple-trees!

The slender "free-stone" lifts aloof,
Full languidly above the roof,

A hoard of fruitage, stamped with gold
And precious mintings manifold.

1

High up, through curled green leaves, a pear
Hangs hot with ripeness here and there.

Beneath the sagging trellisings,
In lush, lack-luster clusterings,

Great torpid grapes, all fattened through
With moon and sunshine, shade and dew,

Until their swollen girths express
But forms of limp deliciousness—

Drugged to an indolence divine
With heaven's own sacramental wine.

THE SOUTH WIND AND THE SUN

O THE South Wind and the Sun!
  How each loved the other one—
Full of fancy—full of folly—
  Full of jollity and fun!
  How they romped and ran about,
  Like two boys when school is out,
With glowing face, and lisping lip,
  Low laugh, and lifted shout!

  And the South Wind—he was dressed
  With a ribbon round his breast
That floated, flapped and fluttered
  In a riotous unrest,
  And a drapery of mist
  From the shoulder and the wrist
Flowing backward with the motion
  Of the waving hand he kissed.

And the Sun had on a crown
  Wrought of gilded thistle-down,
And a scarf of velvet vapor,
  And a raveled-rainbow gown;
  And his tinsel-tangled hair,
  Tossed and lost upon the air,
Was glossier and flossier
  Than any anywhere.

And the South Wind's eyes were two
  Little dancing drops of dew,
As he puffed his cheeks, and pursed his lips,
  And blew and blew and blew!
  And the Sun's—like diamond-stone,
  Brighter yet than ever known,
As he knit his brows and held his breath,
  And shone and shone and shone!

And this pair of merry fays
  Wandered through the summer days;
Arm in arm they went together
  Over heights of morning haze—
  Over slanting slopes of lawn
  Then went on and on and on,
Where the daisies looked like star-tracks
  Trailing up and down the dawn.

And where'er they found the top
  Of a wheat-stalk droop and lop
They chucked it underneath the chin
  And praised the lavish crop.

Till it lifted with the pride
Of the heads it grew beside,
And then the South Wind and the Sun
Went onward satisfied.

Over meadow-lands they tripped,
Where the dandelions dipped
In crimson foam of clover-bloom,
And dripped and dripped and dripped;
And they clinched the bumble-stings,
Gauming honey on their wings,
And bundling them in lily-bells,
With maudlin murmurings.

And the humming-bird, that hung
Like a jewel up among
The tilted honeysuckle-horns,
They mesmerized, and swung
In the palpitating air,
Drowsed with odors strange and rare,
And, with whispered laughter, slipped away,
And left him hanging there.

And they braided blades of grass
Where the truant had to pass;
And they wriggled through the rushes
And the reeds of the morass,
Where they danced, in rapture sweet,
O'er the leaves that laid a street
Of undulant mosaic for
The touches of their feet.

By the brook with mossy brink
Where the cattle came to drink,
They trilled and piped and whistled
With the thrush and bobolink,
Till the kine, in listless pause,
Switched their tails in mute applause,
With lifted heads, and dreamy eyes,
And bubble-dripping jaws.

And where the melons grew,
Streaked with yellow, green and blue,
These jolly sprites went wandering
Through spangled paths of dew;
And the melons, here and there,
They made love to, everywhere,
Turning their pink souls to crimson
With caresses fond and fair.

Over orchard walls they went,
Where the fruited boughs were bent
Till they brushed the sward beneath them
Where the shine and shadow blent;
And the great green pear they shook
Till the sallow hue forsook
Its features, and the gleam of gold
Laughed out in every nook.

And they stroked the downy cheek
Of the peach, and smoothed it sleek,
And flushed it into splendor;
And, with many an elfish freak,

Gave the russet's rust a wipe—
Prankt the rambo with a stripe,
And the wine-sap blushed its reddest
　　As they spanked the pippins ripe.

Through the woven ambuscade
That the twining vines had made,
They found the grapes, in clusters,
　　Drinking up the shine and shade—
Plumpt, like tiny skins of wine,
With a vintage so divine
That the tongue of fancy tingled
　　With the tang of muscadine.

And the golden-banded bees,
Droning o'er the flowery leas,
They bridled, reined, and rode away
　　Across the fragrant breeze,
Till in hollow oak and elm
They had groomed and stabled them
In waxen stalls that oozed with dews
　　Of rose and lily-stem.

Where the dusty highway leads,
High above the wayside weeds,
They sowed the air with butterflies
　　Like blooming flower-seeds,
Till the dull grasshopper sprung
Half a man's height up, and hung
Tranced in the heat, with whirring wings,
　　And sung and sung and sung!

And they loitered, hand in hand,
Where the snipe along the sand
Of the river ran to meet them
As the ripple meets the land,
Till the dragon-fly, in light
Gauzy armor, burnished bright,
Came tilting down the waters
In a wild, bewildered flight.

And they heard the killdee's call,
And afar, the waterfall,
But the rustle of a falling leaf
They heard above it all;
And the trailing willow crept
Deeper in the tide that swept
The leafy shallop to the shore,
And wept and wept and wept!

And the fairy vessel veered
From its moorings—tacked and steered
For the center of the current—
Sailed away and disappeared:
And the burthen that it bore
From the long-enchanted shore—
"Alas! the South Wind and the Sun!"
I murmur evermore.

For the South Wind and the Sun,
Each so loves the other one,
For all his jolly folly
And frivolity and fun,

That our love for them they weigh
  As their fickle fancies may,
And when at last we love them most,
  They laugh and sail away.

WHERE-AWAY

O THE Lands of Where-Away!
   Tell us—tell us—where are they?
Through the darkness and the dawn
We have journeyed on and on—
From the cradle to the cross—
From possession unto loss.—
Seeking still, from day to day,
For the Lands of Where-Away.

When our baby-feet were first
Planted where the daisies burst,
And the greenest grasses grew
In the fields we wandered through,—
On, with childish discontent,
Ever on and on we went,
Hoping still to pass, some day,
O'er the verge of Where-Away.

Roses laid their velvet lips
On our own, with fragrant sips;
But their kisses held us not,
All their sweetness we forgot;—

10

Though the brambles in our track
Plucked at us to hold us back—
"Just ahead," we used to say,
"Lie the Lands of Where-Away."

Children at the pasture-bars,
Through the dusk, like glimmering stars,
Waved their hands that we should bide
With them over eventide:
Down the dark their voices failed
Falteringly, as they hailed,
And died into yesterday—
Night ahead and—Where-Away?

Twining arms about us thrown—
Warm caresses, all our own,
Can but stay us for a spell—
Love hath little new to tell
To the soul in need supreme,
Aching ever with the dream
Of the endless bliss it may
Find in Lands of Where-Away!

THE SMITTEN PURIST

And the Charming Miss Smith's Effect Upon Him

THWEET Poethy! let me *lithp* forthwith,
That I may thhing of the name of Smith—
Which name, alath!
In Harmony hath
No adequate rhyme, letht you grant me thith,—
That the thimple thibillant thound of *eth*—
(Which to thave my thoul, I can not expreth!)
Thuth I may thhingingly,
Wooingly and winningly
Thu—thu—thound in the name of Smith.

O give me a name that will rhyme with Smith,—
For wild and weird ath the sthrange name ith,
I would sthrangle a sthrain
And a thad refrain
Faint and sthweet ath a whithpered kissth;
I would thhing thome thong for the mythtic
mitth
Who beareth the thingular name of Smith—
The dathzlingly brilli-ant,
Rarely rethilliant
Ap—pup—pellation of Smith!

12

O had I a name that would rhyme with Smith—
Thome rhythmical tincture of rethonant blith—
 Thome melody rare
 Ath the cherubth blare
On them little trumpeths they're foolin' with—
I would thit me down, and I'd thhing like thith
Of the girl of the thingular name of Smith—
 The sthrangely curiouth,
 Rich and luxuriouth
 Pup—patronymic of Smith!

CHRISTINE BRAIBRY

THE BEAUTIFUL DOLLY WHO COMES FROM
TENTOLEENA LAND
BRINGING A STRANGE LETTER

The Letter

THIS little Dolly's name is Christine Braibry.*
She was born in Tentoleena Land, where lilies
and red roses grow in the air, and humming-birds
and butterflies on stalks.

You must be kind to Christine, for everything
about her in your land will be very strange to her.
If she seems to stare in a bewildered way, and will
not answer when you ask her why, you must know
that she is simply dazed with the wonders that she
sees on every hand. It will doubtless be a long, long
while before Christine will cease to marvel at the
Sunshine of your strange country; for in Tentoleena Land there is never any shine but Moonshine,
and sometimes that gets so muddied up with shade
it soils the eyesight to gaze at it overmuch.

It will be trying, in your land, for Christine to
keep silent all the time, for, in your country, Dollies

*The terminal of this name is sounded short, as in "lovely."

14

can not walk and talk at all perfectly, because they only think they are dreaming all the time, and they dare not speak for fear their voices will awaken them, and they dare not move for fear of falling out of bed. So, you see, you should be very kind indeed to little Christine Braibry.

In Tentoleena Land the Dollies do not sleep long —they are always the first ones up at Moon-dawn— for Moon-dawn is the Dollies' morning. Then they go out in the fragrant grasses, where the big, ripe dewdrops grow—much nicer, purer dew than yours on earth, for in Tentoleena Land they gather it before it has been skimmed, and all the pearly cream that gathers on the surface of the drops they stir up with the rest and bathe in that; and this is why the Dollies always have such delicate complexions. Then, when the baths are over, they dress themselves, and waken their parents, and dress them— for in Tentoleena Land the parents are the children. Is not that odd?

Sometime Christine may get used to your strange land and all the wonders that she sees; and if she ever does, and smiles at you, and pulls your face down close to hers and kisses you, why, that will be the sign by which you'll know she's coming to again and wants to talk; and so the first thing you must ask of her is to sing this little song she made of Tentoleena Land. Only the words of it can be given here—(not half the beauty of the dainty song)—for when you *hear* it, in the marvelously faint, and low, and sweet, and tender, tinkling

tongue of Tentoleena Land, you will indeed be glad
that the gracious fairy Fortune ever sent you
Christine Braibry.

So, since all the sounds in the melodious utterance of Tentoleena Land are so exquisitely, so
chastely, rarely beautiful no earthly art may hope to
reproduce them, you must, as you here read the
words, just shut your eyes and *fancy* that you hear
little Christine Braibry singing this eery song of
hers :—

CHRISTINE'S SONG

UP in Tentoleena Land—
    Tentoleena! Tentoleena!
All the Dollies, hand in hand,
    Mina, Nainie, and Serena,
Dance the Fairy fancy dances,
With glad songs and starry glances,
Lisping roundelays; and, after,
Bird-like interludes of laughter
Strewn and scattered o'er the lawn
Their gilt sandals twinkle on
Through light mists of silver sand—
    Up in Tentoleena Land.

Up in Tentoleena Land—
    Tentoleena! Tentoleena!
Blares the eery Elfin band—
    Trumpet, harp and concertina—

Larkspur bugle—honeysuckle
Cornet, with a quickstep chuckle
In its golden throat; and, maybe,
Lilies-of-the-valley they be
Baby-silver-bells that chime
Musically all the time,
Tossed about from hand to hand—
    Up in Tentoleena Land.

Up in Tentoleena Land—
    Tentoleena! Tentoleena!
Dollies dark, and blond and bland—
    Sweet as musk-rose or verbena—
Sweet as moon-blown daffodillies,
Or wave-jostled water-lilies
Yearning to'rd the rose-mouths, ready
Leaning o'er the river's eddy,—
Dance, and glancing fling to you,
Through these lines you listen to,
Kisses blown from lip and hand
    Out of Tentoleena. Land!

DEAR HANDS

THE touches of her hands are like the fall
    Of velvet snowflakes; like the touch of down
The peach just brushes 'gainst the garden wall;
The flossy fondlings of the thistle-wisp
   Caught in the crinkle of a leaf of brown
The blighting frost hath turned from green to crisp.

Soft as the falling of the dusk at night,
The touches of her hands, and the delight—
   The touches of her hands!
The touches of her hands are like the dew
That falls so softly down no one e'er knew
The touch thereof save lovers like to one
Astray in lights where ranged Endymion.

O rarely soft, the touches of her hands,
As drowsy zephyrs in enchanted lands;
   Or pulse of dying fay; or fairy sighs;
Or—in between the midnight and the dawn,
When long unrest and tears and fears are gone—
   Sleep, smoothing down the lids of weary eyes.

18

WINTER FANCIES

I

WINTER without
 And warmth within;
The winds may shout
 And the storm begin;
The snows may pack
 At the window-pane,
And the skies grow black,
 And the sun remain
Hidden away
 The livelong day—
But here—in here is the warmth of May!

II

Swoop your spitefulest
 Up the flue,
 Wild Winds—do!
What in the world do I care for you?
 O delightfulest
 Weather of all,
 Howl and squall,
And shake the trees till the last leaves fall!

III

The joy one feels,
In an easy-chair,
Cocking his heels
In the dancing air
That wreathes the rim of a roaring stove
Whose heat loves better than hearts can love,
Will not permit
The coldest day
To drive away
The fire in his blood, and the bliss of it!

IV

Then blow, Winds, blow!
And rave and shriek,
And snarl and snow,
Till your breath grows weak—
While here in my room
I'm as snugly shut
As a glad little worm
In the heart of a nut!

"A BRAVE REFRAIN"

WHEN snow is here, and the trees look weird,
　　And the knuckled twigs are gloved with
　　　　frost;
When the breath congeals in the drover's beard,
　　And the old pathway to the barn is lost;
When the rooster's crow is sad to hear,
　　And the stamp of the stabled horse is vain,
And the tone of the cow-bell grieves the ear—
　　O then is the time for a brave refrain!

When the gears hang stiff on the harness-peg,
　　And the tallow gleams in frozen streaks;
And the old hen stands on a lonesome leg,
　　And the pump sounds hoarse and the handle
　　　　squeaks;
When the wood-pile lies in a shrouded heap,
　　And the frost is scratched from the window-pane
And anxious eyes from the inside peep—
　　O then is the time for a brave refrain!

When the ax-helve warms at the chimney-jamb,
　　And hobnailed shoes on the hearth below,
And the house-cat curls in a slumber calm,
　　And the eight-day clock ticks loud and slow;

21

When the harsh broom-handle jabs the ceil
  'Neath the kitchen-loft, and the drowsy brain
Sniffs the breath of the morning meal—
  O then is the time for a brave refrain!

Envoi

When the skillet seethes, and a blubbering hot
Tilts the lid of the coffee-pot,
And the scent of the buckwheat cake grows plain—
O then is the time for a brave refrain!

AS I SIT IN THE SILENCE

MANY pleasures of Youth have been buoyantly
    sung—
  And, borne on the winds of delight, may they
    beat
With their palpitant wings at the hearts of the
    Young,
  And in bosoms of Age find as warm a retreat!—
Yet sweetest of all of the musical throng,
  Though least of the numbers that upward aspire,
Is the one rising now into wavering song,
  As I sit in the silence and gaze in the fire.

'Tis a Winter long dead that beleaguers my door
  And muffles his steps in the snows of the past:
And I see, in the embers I'm dreaming before,
  Lost faces of love as they looked on me last:—
The round, laughing eyes of the desk-mate of old
  Gleam out for a moment with truant desire—
Then fade and are lost in a City of Gold,
  As I sit in the silence and gaze in the fire.

And then comes the face, peering back in my own,
  Of a shy little girl, with her lids drooping low,
As she faltering tells, in a far-away tone,
  The ghost of a story of long, long ago.—
Then her dewy blue eyes they are lifted again;
  But I see their glad light slowly fail and expire,
As I reach and cry to her in vain, all in vain!—
  As I sit in the silence and gaze in the fire.

Then the face of a Mother looks back, through the
      mist
    Of the tears that are welling; and, lucent with
      light,
I see the dear smile of the lips I have kissed
    As she knelt by my cradle at morning and night;
And my arms are outheld, with a yearning too wild
    For any but God in His love to inspire,
As she pleads at the foot of His throne for her
      child,—
    As I sit in the silence and gaze in the fire.

O pathos of rapture! O glorious pain!
  My heart is a blossom of joy overrun
With a shower of tears, as a lily with rain
    That weeps in the shadow and laughs in the sun
The blight of the frost may descend on the tree,
    And the leaf and the flower may fall and expire,
But ever and ever love blossoms for me,
    As I sit in the silence and gaze in the fire.

LONGFELLOW'S LOVE FOR THE CHILDREN

AWAKE, he loved their voices,
  And wove them into his rhyme;
And the music of their laughter
  Was with him all the time.

Though he knew the tongues of nations,
  And their meanings all were dear,
The prattle and lisp of a little child
  Was the sweetest for him to hear.

A SONG OF LONG AGO

A SONG of Long Ago:
   Sing it lightly—sing it low—
Sing it softly—like the lisping of the lips
   we used to know
When our baby-laughter spilled
From the glad hearts ever filled
With music blithe as robin ever trilled!

Let the fragrant summer breeze,
And the leaves of locust-trees,
And the apple-buds and -blossoms, and the
   wings of honey-bees,
All palpitate with glee,
Till the happy harmony
Brings back each childish joy to you and me.

Let the eyes of fancy turn
Where the tumbled pippins burn
Like embers in the orchard's lap of tangled
   grass and fern,—
There let the old path wind
In and out, and on behind
The cider-press that chuckles as we grind.

Blend in the song the moan
Of the dove that grieves alone,
And the wild whir of the locust, and the
    bumble's drowsy drone;
And the low of cows that call
Through the pasture-bars when all
The landscape fades away at evenfall.

Then, far away and clear,
Through the dusky atmosphere,
Let the wailing of the killdee be the only
    sound we hear:
O sad and sweet and low
As the memory may know
Is the glad-pathetic song of Long Ago!

UNLESS

WHO has not *wanted* does not guess
　　What plenty is.—Who has not groped
In depths of doubt and hopelessness
　　Has never truly hoped.—
Unless, sometimes, a shadow falls
　　Upon his mirth, and veils his sight,
　　And from the darkness drifts the light
Of love at intervals.

And that most dear of everything,
　　I hold, is love; and who can sit
With lightest heart and laugh and sing,
　　Knows not the worth of it.—
Unless, in some strange throng, perchance,
　　He feels how thrilling sweet it is,
　　One yearning look that answers his—
The troth of glance and glance.

Who knows not pain, knows not, alas!
　　What pleasure is.—Who knows not of
The bitter cup that will not pass,
　　Knows not the taste of love.

O souls that thirst, and hearts that fast,
　And natures faint with famishing,
　God lift and lead and safely bring
You to your own at last!

WHEN EARLY MARCH SEEMS MIDDLE MAY

WHEN country roads begin to thaw
　　In mottled spots of damp and dust,
And fences by the margin draw
　　Along the frosty crust
Their graphic silhouettes, I say,
The Spring is coming round this way.

When morning-time is bright with sun
　　And keen with wind, and both confuse
The dancing, glancing eyes of one
　　With tears that ooze and ooze—
And nose-tips weep as well as they,
The Spring is coming round this way.

When suddenly some shadow-bird
　　Goes wavering beneath the gaze,
And through the hedge the moan is heard
　　Of kine that fain would graze
In grasses new, I smile and say,
The Spring is coming round this way.

When knotted horse-tails are untied,
   And teamsters whistle here and there,
And clumsy mitts are laid aside
   And choppers' hands are bare,
And chips are thick where children play,
The Spring is coming round this way.

When through the twigs the farmer tramps,
   And troughs are chunked beneath the trees,
And fragrant hints of sugar-camps
   Astray in every breeze,—
When early March seems middle May,
The Spring is coming round this way.

When coughs are changed to laughs, and when
   Our frowns melt into smiles of glee,
And all our blood thaws out again
   In streams of ecstasy,
And poets wreak their roundelay,
The Spring is coming round this way.

THE MUSKINGUM VALLEY

THE Muskingum Valley!—How longin' the
    gaze
A feller throws back on its long summer days,
When the smiles of its blossoms and *my* smiles wuz
    one-
And-the-same, from the rise to the set o' the sun:
Wher' the hills sloped as soft as the dawn down to
    noon,
And the river run by like an old fiddle-tune,
And the hours glided past as the bubbles 'ud glide,
All so loaferin'-like, 'long the path o' the tide.

In the Muskingum Valley—it 'peared like the skies
Looked lovin' on me as my own mother's eyes,
While the laughin'-sad song of the stream seemed
    to be
Like a lullaby angels was wastin' on me—
Tel, swimmin' the air, like the gossamer's thread,
'Twixt the blue underneath and the blue overhead,
My thoughts went astray in that so-to-speak realm
Wher' Sleep bared her breast as a piller fer them.

In the Muskingum Valley, though far, far a-way,
I know that the winter is bleak there to-day—
No bloom ner perfume on the brambles er trees—
Wher' the buds ust to bloom, now the icicles
　　freeze.—
That the grass is all hid 'long the side of the road
Wher' the deep snow has drifted and shifted and
　　blowed—
And I feel in my life the same changes is there,—
The frost in my heart, and the snow in my hair.

But, Muskingum Valley! my memory sees
Not the white on the ground, but the green in the
　　trees—
Not the froze'-over gorge, but the current, as clear
And warm as the drop that has jes' trickled here;
Not the choked-up ravine, and the hills topped with
　　snow,
But the grass and the blossoms I knowed long ago
When my little bare feet wundered down wher' the
　　stream
In the Muskingum Valley flowed on like a dream.

SERENADE—TO NORA

THE moonlight is failin'—
  The sad stars are palin'—
The black wings av night are a-dhroopin' an'
      trailin';
    The wind's miserere
    Sounds lonesome an' dreary;
The katydid's dumb an' the nightingale's weary.

    Troth, Nora! I'm wadin'
    The grass an' paradin'
The dews at your dure, wid my swate serenadin',
    Alone and forsaken,
    Whilst you're never wakin'
To tell me you're wid me an' I am mistaken!

    Don't think that my singin'
    It's wrong to be flingin'
Forninst av the dreams that the Angels are bringin';
    For if your pure spirit
    Might waken and hear it,
You'd never be draamin' the Saints could come
      near it!

34

Then lave off your slaapin'—
The pulse av me's laapin'
To have the two eyes av yez down on me paapin'.
Och, Nora! It's hopin'
Your windy ye'll open
And light up the night where the heart av me's
gropin'.

THE LITTLE WHITE HEARSE

AS the little white hearse went glimmering by—
    The man on the coal-cart jerked his lines,
And smutted the lid of either eye,
    And turned and stared at the business signs;
        And the street-car driver stopped and beat
        His hands on his shoulders, and gazed up-street
        Till his eye on the long track reached the sky—
        As the little white hearse went glimmering by.

As the little white hearse went glimmering by—
    A stranger petted a ragged child
In the crowded walks, and she knew not why,
    But he gave her a coin for the way she smiled;
        And a boot-black thrilled with a pleasure
            strange
        As a customer put back his change
        With a kindly hand and a grateful sigh,
        As the little white hearse went glimmering by.

As the little white hearse went glimmering by—
    A man looked out of a window dim,
And his cheeks were wet and his heart was dry,
    For a dead child even was dear to him!
        And he thought of his empty life, and said:—
        "Loveless alive, and loveless dead—
        Nor wife nor child in earth or sky!"
        As the little white hearse went glimmering by.

A GLIMPSE OF PAN

I CAUGHT but a glimpse of him. Summer was
     here,
  And I strayed from the town and its dust and
     heat,
And walked in a wood, while the noon was near,
Where the shadows were cool, and the atmosphere
  Was misty with fragrances stirred by my feet
From surges of blossoms that billowed sheer
  Of the grasses, green and sweet.

And I peered through a vista of leaning trees,
  Tressed with long tangles of vines that swept
To the face of a river, that answered these
With vines in the wave like the vines in the breeze,
  Till the yearning lips of the ripples crept
And kissed them, with quavering ecstasies,
  And wistfully laughed and wept.

And there, like a dream in a swoon, I swear
  I saw Pan lying,—his limbs in the dew
And the shade, and his face in the dazzle and glare
Of the glad sunshine; while everywhere,
  Over, across, and around him blew
Filmy dragon-flies hither and there,   .
  And little white butterflies, two and two,
In eddies of odorous air.

THE GREAT GOD PAN

What was he doing, the great god Pan?
—Mrs. Browning

O PAN is the goodliest god, I wist,
  Of all of the lovable gods that be!—
For his two strong hands were the first to twist
From the depths of the current, through spatter
      and mist,
  The long-hushed reeds that he pressed in glee
To his murmurous mouth, as he chuckled and kissed
  Their souls into melody.

And the wanton winds are in love with Pan:
  They loll in the shade with him day by day;
And betimes as beast, and betimes as man,
They love him as only the wild winds can,—
  Or sleeking the coat of his limbs one way,
Or brushing his brow with the locks they fan
  To the airs he loves to play.

And he leans by the river, in gloom and gleam,
  Blowing his reeds as the breezes blow—
His cheeks puffed out, and his eyes in a dream,

And his hoof-tips, over the leaves in the stream,
  Tapping the time of the tunes that flow
As sweet as the drowning echoes seem
  To his rollicking wraith below.

HER LIGHT GUITAR

SHE twankled a tune on her light guitar—
    A low, sweet jangle of tangled sounds,
As blurred as the voices of the fairies are,
    Dancing in moondawn dales and downs;
        And the tinkling drip of the strange refrain
        Ran over the rim of my soul like rain.

The great blond moon in the midnight skies
    Paused and poised o'er the trellis eaves,
And the stars, in the light of her upturned eyes,
    Sifted their love through the rifted leaves
        Glittered and splintered in crystal mist
        Down the glittering string that her fingers
            kissed.

O the melody mad! O the tinkle and thrill
    Of the ecstasy of the exquisite thing!
The red rose dropped from the window-sill
    And lay in a long swoon quivering;
        While the dying notes of the strain divine
        Ripped in glee up my spell-bound spine.

THE ALL-GOLDEN

I

THROUGH every happy line I sing
  I feel the tonic of the Spring.
The day is like an old-time face
That gleams across some grassy place—
An old-time face—an old-time chum
Who rises from the grave to come
And lure me back along the ways
Of time's all-golden yesterdays.
Sweet day! to thus remind me of
The truant boy I used to love—
To set, once more, his finger-tips
Against the blossom of his lips,
And pipe for me the signal known
By none but him and me alone!

II

I see, across the schoolroom floor,
The shadow of the open door,
And dancing dust and sunshine blent
Slanting the way the morning went,

And beckoning my thoughts afar
Where reeds and running waters are;
Where amber-colored bayous glass
The half-drown'd weeds and wisps of grass,
Where sprawling frogs, in loveless key,
Sing on and on incessantly.
Against the green wood's dim expanse
The cattail tilts its tufted lance,
While on its tip—one might declare
The white "snake-feeder" blossomed there!

III

I catch my breath, as children do
In woodland swings when life is new,
And all the blood is warm as wine
And tingles with a tang divine.
My soul soars up the atmosphere
And sings aloud where God can hear,
And all my being leans intent
To mark His smiling wonderment.
O gracious dream, and gracious time,
And gracious theme, and gracious rhyme—
When buds of Spring begin to blow
In blossoms that we used to know
And lure us back along the ways
Of time's all-golden yesterdays!

THE WAY THE BABY CAME

O THIS is the way the baby came:
 Out of the night as comes the dawn
Out of the embers as the flame;
 Out of the bud the blossom on
The apple-bough that blooms the same
 As in glad summers dead and gone—
With a grace and beauty none could name—
O this is the way the baby came!

THE WAY THE BABY WOKE

AND this is the way the baby woke:
   As when in deepest drops of dew
The shine and shadows sink and soak,
   The sweet eyes glimmered through and
      through;
And eddyings and dimples broke
   About the lips, and no one knew
Or could divine the words they spoke—
And this is the way the baby woke.

THE WAY THE BABY SLEPT

THIS is the way the baby slept:
  A mist of tresses backward thrown
By quavering sighs where kisses crept
  With yearnings she had never known:
The little hands were closely kept
  About a lily newly blown—
And God was with her. And we wept.—
And this is the way the baby slept.

WHEN MAIMIE MARRIED

WHEN Maimie married Charley Brown,
　　Joy took possession of the town;
The young folks swarmed in happy throngs—
They rang the bells—they caroled songs—
They carpeted the steps that led
Into the church where they were wed;
And up and down the altar-stair
They scattered roses everywhere;
When, in her orange-blossom crown,
Queen Maimie married Charley Brown.

So beautiful she was, it seemed
Men, looking on her, dreamed they dreamed;
And he, the holy man who took
Her hand in his, so thrilled and shook,
The gargoyles round the ceiling's rim
Looked down and leered and grinned at him,
Until he half forgot his part
Of sanctity, and felt his heart
Beat worldward through his sacred gown—
When Maimie married Charley Brown.

The bridesmaids kissed her, left and right—
Fond mothers hugged her with delight—
Young men of twenty-seven were seen
To blush like lads of seventeen,
The while they held her hand to quote
Such sentiments as poets wrote.—
Yea, all the heads that Homage bends
Where bowed to her.—But O my friends,
My hopes went up—*my* heart went down—
When Maimie married—*Charley Brown!*

HER HAIR

THE beauty of her hair bewilders me—
　　Pouring adown the brow, its cloven tide
　Swirling about the ears on either side
And storming round the neck tumultuously:
Or like the lights of old antiquity
　　Through mullioned windows, in cathedrals wide,
　Spilled moltenly o'er figures deified
In chastest marble, nude of drapery.
And so I love it.—Either unconfined;
　　Or plaited in close braidings manifold;
Or smoothly drawn; or indolently twined
　　In careless knots whose coilings come unrolled
At any lightest kiss; or by the wind
　　Whipped out in flossy ravelings of gold.

A VISION OF SUMMER

'TWAS a marvelous vision of Summer.—
    That morning the dawn was late,
And came, like a long dream-ridden guest,
    Through the gold of the Eastern gate.

Languid it came, and halting
    As one that yawned, half roused,
With lifted arms and indolent lids
    And eyes that drowsed and drowsed.

A glimmering haze hung over
    The face of the smiling air;
And the green of the trees and the blue of
       the leas
    And the skies gleamed everywhere.

And the dewdrops' dazzling jewels,
    In garlands and diadems,
Lightened and twinkled and glanced and shot
    As the glints of a thousand gems:

Emeralds of dew on the grasses;
　The rose with rubies set;
On the lily, diamonds; and amethysts
　Pale on the violet.

And there were the pinks of the fuchsias,
　And the peony's crimson hue,
The lavender of the hollyhocks,
　And the morning-glory's blue:

The purple of the pansy bloom,
　And the passionate flush of the face
Of the velvet-rose; and the thick perfume
　Of the locust every place.

The air and the sun and the shadows
　Were wedded and made as one;
And the winds ran over the meadows
　As little children run:

And the winds poured over the meadows
　And along the willowy way
The river ran, with its ripples shod
　With the sunshine of the day:

O the winds flowed over the meadows
　In a tide of eddies and calms,
And the bared brow felt the touch of it
　As a sweetheart's tender palms.

And the lark went palpitating
  Up through the glorious skies,
His song spilled down from the blue profound
  As a song from Paradise.

And here was the loitering current—
  Stayed by a drift of sedge
And sodden logs—scummed thick with the
    gold
  Of the pollen from edge to edge.

The catbird piped in the hazel,
  And the harsh kingfisher screamed;
And the crane, in amber and oozy swirls,
  Dozed in the reeds and dreamed.

And in through the tumbled driftage
  And the tangled roots below,
The waters warbled and gurgled and lisped
  Like the lips of long ago.

And the senses caught, through the music,
  Twinkles of dabbling feet,
And glimpses of faces in coverts green,
  And voices faint and sweet.

And back from the lands enchanted,
  Where my earliest mirth was born,
The trill of a laugh was blown to me
  Like the blare of an elfin horn.

Again I romped through the clover;
  And again I lay supine
On grassy swards, where the skies, like eyes,
  Looked lovingly back to mine.

And over my vision floated
  Misty illusive things—
Trailing strands of the gossamer
  On heavenward wanderings:

Figures that veered and wavered,
  Luring the sight, and then
Glancing away into nothingness,
  And blinked into shape again.

From out far depths of the forest,
  Ineffably sad and lorn,
Like the yearning cry of a long-lost love,
  The moan of the dove was borne.

And through lush glooms of the thicket
  The flash of the redbird's wings
On branches of star-white blooms that shook
  And thrilled with its twitterings.

Through mossy and viny vistas,
  Soaked ever with deepest shade,
Dimly the dull owl stared and stared
  From his bosky ambuscade.

And up through the rifted tree-tops
   That signaled the wayward breeze,
I saw the hulk of the hawk becalmed
   Far out on the azure seas.

Then sudden an awe fell on me,
   As the hush of the golden day
Rounded to noon, as a May to June
   That a lover has dreamed away.

And I heard, in the breathless silence,
   And the full, glad light of the sun,
The tinkle and drip of a timorous shower—
   Ceasing as it begun.

And my thoughts, like the leaves and grasses,
   In a rapture of joy and pain,
Seemed fondled and petted and beat upon
   With a tremulous patter of rain.

WHILE CIGARETTES TO ASHES TURN

I

"HE smokes—and that's enough," says
       Ma—
"And cigarettes, at that!" says Pa.

"He must not call again," says she—
"He *shall* not call again!" says he.

They both glare at me as before—
Then quit the room and bang the door,—

While I, their wilful daughter, say,
"I guess I'll love him, anyway!"

II

At twilight, in his room, alone,
His careless feet inertly thrown

Across a chair, my fancy can
But worship this most worthless man!

54

I dream what joy it is to set
His slow lips round a cigarette,

With idle-humored whiff and puff—
Ah! this is innocent enough!

To mark the slender fingers raise
The waxen match's dainty blaze,

Whose chastened light an instant glows
On drooping lids and arching nose,

Then, in the sudden gloom, instead,
A tiny ember, dim and red,

Blooms languidly to ripeness, then
Fades slowly, and grows ripe again.

III

I lean back, in my own boudoir—
The door is fast, the sash ajar;

And in the dark, I smiling stare
At one wide window over there,

Where some one, smoking, pinks the gloom,
The darling darkness of his room!

I push my shutters wider yet,
And lo! I light a cigarette;

And gleam for gleam, and glow for glow,
Each pulse of light a word we know,

We talk of love that still will burn
While cigarettes to ashes turn.

THE LITTLE RED RIBBON

THE little red ribbon, the ring and the rose!
 The summer-time comes, and the summer-
    time goes—
And never a blossom in all of the land
As white as the gleam of her beckoning hand!

The long winter months, and the glare of the snows;
The little red ribbon, the ring and the rose!
And never a glimmer of sun in the skies
As bright as the light of her glorious eyes!

Dreams only are true; but they fade and are gone—
For her face is not here when I waken at dawn;
The little red ribbon, the ring and the rose
Mine only; *hers* only the dream and repose.

I am weary of waiting, and weary of tears,
And my heart wearies, too, all these desolate years,
Moaning over the one only song that it knows,—
The little red ribbon, the ring and the rose!

THE MAN IN THE MOON

SAID The Raggedy Man, on a hot afternoon:
　My!
　　Sakes!
　　　What a lot o' mistakes
Some little folks makes on The Man in the Moon!
But people that's be'n up to *see* him, like *me,*
And calls on him frequent and intimuttly,
Might drop a few facts that would interest you
　Clean!
　　Through!—
　　　If you wanted 'em to—
Some *actual* facts that might interest you!

O The Man in the Moon has a crick in his back;
　Whee!
　　Whimm!
　　　Ain't you sorry for him?
And a mole on his nose that is purple and black;
And his eyes are so weak that they water and run
If he dares to *dream* even he looks at the sun,—

58

So he jes' dreams of stars, as the doctors advise—
  My!
    Eyes!
      But isn't he wise—
To jes' dream of stars, as the doctors advise?

And The Man in the Moon has a boil on his ear—
  Whee!
    Whing!
      What a singular thing!
I know! but these facts are authentic, my dear,—
There's a boil on his ear; and a corn on his chin—
He calls it a dimple—but dimples stick in—
Yet it might be a dimple turned over, you know!
  Whang!
    Ho!
      Why, certainly so!—
It might be a dimple turned over, you know!

And The Man in the Moon has a rheumatic
      knee—
  Gee!
    Whizz!
      What a pity that is!
And his toes have worked round where his heels
      ought to be.—
So whenever he wants to go North he goes *South,*
And comes back with porridge-crumbs all round
      his mouth,

And he brushes them off with a Japanese fan,
  Whing!
    Whann!
      What a marvelous man!
What a very remarkably marvelous man!

And The Man in the Moon, sighed The Raggedy
    Man,
  Gits!
    So!
      Sullonesome, you know,—
Up there by hisse'f sence creation began!—
That when I call on him and then come away,
He grabs me and holds me and begs me to stay,—
Till—*Well!* if it wasn't fer *Jimmy-cum-jim,*
  Dadd!
    Limb!
      I'd go pardners with him—
Jes' jump my job here and be pardners with
    him!

A BAREFOOT BOY

A BAREFOOT boy! I mark him at his play—
 For May is here once more, and so is he,—
His dusty trousers, rolled half to the knee,
And his bare ankles grimy, too, as they:
Cross-hatchings of the nettle, in array
 Of feverish stripes, hint vividly to me
 Of woody pathways winding endlessly
Along the creek, where even yesterday
He plunged his shrinking body—gasped and shook—
 Yet called the water "warm," with never lack
Of joy. And so, half enviously I look
 Upon this graceless barefoot and his track,—
 His toe stubbed—ay, his big toe-nail knocked back
Like unto the clasp of an old pocketbook.

"THE PREACHER'S BOY"

I RICKOLLECT the little tad, back, years and
   years ago—
"The Preacher's Boy" that every one despised and
   hated so!
A meek-faced little feller, with white eyes and foxy
   hair,
And a look like he expected ser'ous trouble everywhere:
A sort o' fixed expression of suspicion in his glance;
His bare feet always scratched with briers; and
   green stains on his pants;
Molasses-marks along his sleeves; his cap-rim
   turned behind—
And so it is "The Preacher's Boy" is brought again
   to mind!

My fancy even brings the sly marauder back so
   plain,
I see him jump our garden-fence and slip off down
   the lane;
And I seem to holler at him and git back the old
   reply:
"Oh, no: your peaches is too green fer such a worm
   as I!"

Fer he scorned his father's phrases—every holy one
    he had—
"As good a man," folks put it, "as that boy of his
    was bad!"
And again from their old buggy-shed, I hear the
    "rod unspared"—
Of course that never "spoiled the child" for which
    nobody cared!

If any neighber ever found his gate without a latch,
Or rines around the edges of his watermelon-patch;
His pasture-bars left open; or his pump-spout
    chocked with clay,
He'd swear 'twas "that infernal Preacher's Boy,"
    right away!
When strings was stretched acrost the street at
    night, and some one got
An everlastin' tumble, and his nose broke, like as
    not,
And laid it on "The Preacher's Boy"—no powers,
    low ner high,
Could ever quite substantiate that boy's alibi!

And did *nobody* like the boy?—Well, all the *pets* in
    town
Would eat out of his fingers; and canaries would
    come down
And leave their swingin' perches and their fish-bone
    jist to pick
The little warty knuckles that the dogs would leap
    to lick.—

No little snarlin', snappin' fiste but what would leave
  his bone
To foller, ef *he* whistled, in that tantalizin' tone
That made a goods-box whittler blasphemeusly
  protest
"He couldn't tell, 'twixt dog and boy, which one
  was ornriest!"

'Twas such a little cur as this, onc't, when the crowd
  was thick
Along the streets, a drunken corner-loafer tried to
  kick,
When a sudden foot behind him tripped him up, and
  falling so
He "marked his man," and jerked his gun—drawed
  up and let 'er go!
And the crowd swarmed round the victim—holding
  close against his breast
The little dog unharmed, in arms that still, as they
  caressed,
Grew rigid in their last embrace, as with a smile of
  joy
He recognized the dog was saved. So died "The
  Preacher's Boy"!

When it appeared, before the Squire, that fatal
  pistol-ball
Was fired at "a dangerous beast," and not the boy at
  all,

And the facts set forth established,—it was like-
    befittin' then
To order out a possy of the "city councilmen"
To kill *the dog!* But, strange to tell, they searched
    the country round,
And never hide-ner-hair of that "said" dog was ever
    found!
And, somehow, *then* I sort o' thought—and half-
    way think, *to-day*—
The spirit of "The Preacher's Boy" had whistled
    him away.

WE TO SIGH INSTEAD OF SING

"RAIN and rain! and rain and rain!"
Yesterday we muttered
Grimly as the grim refrain
That the thunders uttered:
All the heavens under cloud—
All the sunshine sleeping;
All the grasses limply bowed
With their weight of weeping.

Sigh and sigh! and sigh and sigh!
Never end of sighing;
Rain and rain for our reply—
Hopes half drowned and dying;
Peering through the window-pane,
Naught but endless raining—
Endless sighing, and, as vain,
Endlessly complaining.

Shine and shine! and shine and shine!
Ah! to-day the splendor!—
All this glory yours and mine—
God! but God is tender!

We to sigh instead of sing,
Yesterday, in sorrow,
While the Lord was fashioning
This for our To-morrow!

NOTHIN' TO SAY

NOTHIN' to say, my daughter! Nothin' at all
    to say!
Gyrls that's in love, I've noticed, giner'ly has their
    way!
Yer mother did, afore you, when her folks objected
    to me—
Yit here I am and here you air! and yer mother—
    where is she?

You look lots like yer mother: purty much same in
    size;
And about the same complected; and favor about
    the eyes:
Like her, too, about livin' here, because *she* couldn't
    stay;
It'll 'most seem like you was dead like her!—but I
    hain't got nothin' to say!

She left you her little Bible—writ yer name acrost
    the page—
And left her ear-bobs fer you, ef ever you come of
    age;
I've alluz kep' 'em and gyuarded 'em, but ef yer
    goin' away—
Nothin' to say, my daughter! Nothin' at all to say!

You don't rickollect her, I reckon? No: you wasn't
    a year old then!
And now yer—how old *air* you? W'y, child, not
    "twenty"! When?
And yer nex' birthday's in Aprile? and you want to
    git married that day?
I wisht yer mother was livin'!—but I hain't got
    nothin' to say!

Twenty year! and as good a gyrl as parent ever
    found!
There's a straw ketched on to yer dress there—I'll
    bresh it off—turn round.
(Her mother was jes' twenty when us two run
    away.)
Nothin' to say, my daughter! Nothin' at all to say!

JACK-IN-THE-BOX

Grandfather, musing

IN childish days! O memory,
  You bring such curious things to me!—
Laughs to the lip—tears to the eye,
In looking on the gifts that lie
Like broken playthings scattered o'er
Imagination's nursery floor!
Did these old hands once click the key
That let "Jack's" box-lid upward fly,
And that blear-eyed, fur-whiskered elf
Leap, as though frightened at himself,
And quiveringly lean and stare
At me, his jailer, laughing there?

A child then! Now—I only know
They call me very old; and so
They will not let me have my way,—
But uselessly I sit all day
Here by the chimney-jamb, and poke
The lazy fire, and smoke and smoke,

And watch the wreaths swoop up the flue,
And chuckle—ay, I often do—
Seeing again, all vividly,
Jack-in-the-box leap, as in glee
To see how much he looks like me!

. . . . They talk. I can't hear what they
    say—
But I am glad, clean through and through
Sometimes, in fancying that they
Are saying, "Sweet, that fancy strays
In age back to our childish days!"

THE OLD TRUNDLE-BED

O THE old trundle-bed where I slept when a
  boy!
What canopied king might not covet the joy?
The glory and peace of that slumber of mine,
Like a long, gracious rest in the bosom divine:
The quaint, homely couch, hidden close from the
  light,
But daintily drawn from its hiding at night.
O a nest of delight, from the foot to the head,
Was the queer little, dear little, old trundle-bed!

O the old trundle-bed, where I wondering saw
The stars through the window, and listened with
  awe
To the sigh of the winds as they tremblingly crept
Through the trees where the robin so restlessly
  slept:
Where I heard the low, murmurous chirp of the
  wren,
And the katydid listlessly chirrup again,
Till my fancies grew faint and were drowsily led
Through the maze of the dreams of the old trundle-
  bed.

NOTHIN' TO SAY.

Nothin' to say, my daughter!
    Nothin' at all to say! —
Girls that's in love, I've noticed,
    Ginerly has their way —
Your mother did, afore you,
    When her folks objected to me —
And here I am, and here you air —
    And your mother — where is she?

You look lots like your mother —
    Purty much same in size,
And 'bout the same complected,
    And favor about the eyes —
Like her, too, 'bout livin' here,
    Because she couldn't stay —
It'll most surely like you was dead like her! —
    But I haint got nothin' to say!

She left you her little bible —
    Writ your name acrost the page;
And left her ear=bobs fer ye,
    Ef ever you 'come of age. —
I've allus kep' 'em, an' gyaurded 'em,
    But ef you're agoin' away —
Nothin' to say, my daughter —
    Nothin' at all to say!

You don't rickollect her, I reckon? —
    You wasn't a year old then, —
And now you're — How old air ye?
    W'y, child, not twenty? — When?
And your next birthday's in Aprile?
    And you want to git married that day?
I wisht your mother was livin'! —
    But I haint got nothin' to say!

Twenty years — and as good a girl
Th' parent ever found! —
There's a straw ketched onto your dress there—
I'll brush it off — turn' round! —
(Her mother was jes' twenty
When us two run away!)
Nothin' to say, my daughter —
Nothin' at all to say!

James Whitcomb Riley

O the old trundle-bed!   O the old trundle-bed!
With its plump little pillow, and old-fashioned
    spread;
Its snowy-white sheets, and the blankets above,
Smoothed down and tucked round with the touches
    of love;
The voice of my mother to lull me to sleep
With the old fairy stories my memories keep
Still fresh as the lilies that bloom o'er the head
Once bowed o'er my own in the old trundle-bed.

MY MARY

MY Mary, O my Mary!
   The simmer skies are blue:
The dawnin' brings the dazzle,
   An' the gloamin' brings the dew,—
The mirk o' nicht the glory
   O' the moon, an' kindles, too,
The stars that shift aboon the lift.—
   But naething brings me you!

Where is it, O my Mary,
   Ye are biding a' the while?
I ha' wended by your window—
   I ha' waited by the stile,
An' up an' down the river
   I ha' won for mony a mile,
Yet never found, adrift or drown'd,
   Your lang-belated smile.

Is it forgot, my Mary,
   How glad we used to be?—
The simmer-time when bonny bloomed
   The auld trysting-tree,—

How there I carved the name for you,
  An' you the name for me;
An' the gloamin' kenned it only
  When we kissed sae tenderly.

Speek ance to me, my Mary!—
  But whisper in my ear
As light as ony sleeper's breath,
  An' a' my soul will hear;
My heart shall stap its beating,
  An' the soughing atmosphere
Be hushed the while I leaning smile
  An' listen to you, dear!

My Mary, O my Mary!
  The blossoms bring the bees;
The sunshine brings the blossoms,
  An' the leaves on a' the trees;
The simmer brings the sunshine
  An' the fragrance o' the breeze,—
But O wi'out you, Mary,
  I care naething for these!

We were sae happy, Mary!
  O think how ance we said—
Wad ane o' us gae fickle,
  Or ane o' us lie dead,—
To feel anither's kisses
  We wad feign the auld instead,
An' ken the ither's footsteps
  In the green grass owerhead.

My Mary, O my Mary!
  Are ye dochter o' the air,
That ye vanish aye before me
  As I follow everywhere?—
Or is it ye are only
  But a mortal, wan wi' care,
Sin' I search through a' the kirkyird
  An' I dinna find ye there?

TWO SONNETS TO THE JUNE-BUG

I

YOU make me jes' a little nervouser
        Than any dog-gone bug I ever see!
    And you know night's the time to pester me—
When any tetch at all 'll rub the fur
Of all my patience back'ards! You're the myrrh
    And ruburb of my life! A bumblebee
    Cain't hold a candle to you; and a he
Bald hornet, with a laminated spur
In his hip-pocket, daresent even cheep
        When you're around! And, dern ye! you have
            made
Me lose whole ricks, and stacks, and piles of sleep,—
    And many of a livelong night I've laid
And never shut an eye, hearin' you keep
        Up that eternal buzzin' serenade!

II

And I've got up and lit the lamp, and clum
    On cheers and trunks and wash-stands and bu-
        reaus,
    And all such dangerous articles as those,

And biffed at you with brooms, and never come
In two feet of you,—maybe skeered you some,—
    But what does that amount to when it throws
    A feller out o' balance, and his nose
Gits barked ag'inst the mantel, while you hum
Fer joy around the room, and churn your head
    Ag'inst the ceilin', and draw back and butt
The plasterin' loose, and drop—behind the bed,
    Where never human-bein' ever putt
Harm's hand on you, or ever truthful said
    He'd choked your dern infernal wizzen shut!

ONE AFTERNOON

BELOW, cool grasses: over us
The maples waver tremulous.

A slender overture above,
Low breathing as a sigh of love

At first, then gradually strong
And stronger: 'tis the locust's song,

Swoln midway to a pæan of glee,
And lost in silence dwindlingly.

Not utter silence; nay, for hid
In ghosts of it, the katydid

Chirrs a diluted echo of
The loveless song he makes us love.

The low boughs are drugged heavily
With shade; the poem you read to me

Is not more gracious than the trill
Of birds that twitter as they will.

Half consciously, with upturned eyes,
I hear your voice—I see the skies,

Where, o'er bright rifts, the swallows glance
Like glad thoughts o'er a countenance;

And voices near and far are blent
Like sweet chords of some instrument

Awakened by the trembling touch
Of hands that love it overmuch.

Dear heart, let be the book a while!
I want your face—I want your smile!

Tell me how gladder now are they
Who look on us from Heaven to-day.

THE BEAUTIFUL CITY

THE Beautiful City! Forever
 Its rapturous praises resound;
We fain would behold it—but never
 A glimpse of its glory is found:
We slacken our lips at the tender
 White breasts of our mothers to hear
Of its marvelous beauty and splendor;—
 We see—but the gleam of a tear!

Yet never the story may tire us—
 First graven in symbols of stone—
Rewritten on scrolls of papyrus
 And parchment, and scattered and blown
By the winds of the tongues of all nations,
 Like a litter of leaves wildly whirled
Down the rack of a hundred translations,
 From the earliest lisp of the world.

We compass the earth and the ocean,
 From the Orient's uttermost light,
To where the last ripple in motion
 Lips hem of the skirt of the night,—

But the Beautiful City evades us—
   No spire of it glints in the sun—
No glad-bannered battlement shades us
   When all our long journey is done.

Where lies it?   We question and listen;
   We lean from the mountain, or mast,
And see but dull earth, or the glisten
   Of seas inconceivably vast:
The dust of the one blurs our vision,
   The glare of the other our brain,
Nor city nor island Elysian
   In all of the land or the main!

We kneel in dim fanes where the thunders
   Of organs tumultuous roll,
And the longing heart listens and wonders,
   And the eyes look aloft from the soul:
But the chanson grows fainter and fainter,
   Swoons wholly away and is dead;
And our eyes only reach where the painter
   Has dabbled a saint overhead.

The Beautiful City! O mortal,
   Fare hopefully on in thy quest,
Pass down through the green grassy portal
   That leads to the Valley of Rest;
There first passed the One who, in pity
   Of all thy great yearning, awaits
To point out the Beautiful City,
   And loosen the trump at the gates.

A LIFE TERM

SHE was false, and he was true,—
  Thus their lives were rent apart;
'Twas his dagger driven through
  A mad rival's heart.

He was shut away. The moon
  May not find him; nor the stars—
Nay, nor yet the sun of noon
  Pierce his prison bars.

She was left—again to sin—
  Mistress of all siren arts:
The poor, soulless heroine
  Of a hundred hearts!

Though she dare not think of him
  Who believed her lies, and so
Sent a ghost adown the dim
  Path she dreads to go,—

He, in fancy, smiling, sips
  Of her kisses, purer yet
Than the dew upon the lips
  Of the violet.

McFEETERS' FOURTH

IT was needless to say 'twas a glorious day,
  And to boast of it all in that spread-eagle way
That our Forefathers had since the hour of the birth
Of this most patriotic republic on earth!
But 'twas justice, of course, to admit that the sight
Of the old Stars-and-Stripes was a thing of delight
In the eyes of a fellow, however he tried
To look on the day with a dignified pride
That meant not to brook any turbulent glee
Or riotous flourish of loud jubilee!

So argued McFeeters, all grim and severe,
Who the long night before, with a feeling of fear,
Had slumbered but fitfully, hearing the swish
Of the sky-rocket over his roof, with the wish
That the boy-fiend who fired it were fast to the end
Of the stick to forever and ever ascend!
Or to hopelessly ask why the boy with the horn
And its horrible havoc had ever been born!
Or to wish, in his wakefulness, staring aghast,
That this Fourth of July were as dead as the last!

So, yesterday morning, McFeeters arose,
With a fire in his eyes, and a cold in his nose,
And a guttural voice in appropriate key
With a temper as gruff as a temper could be.
He growled at the servant he met on the stair,
Because he was whistling a national air,
And he growled at the maid on the balcony, who
Stood enrapt with the tune of "The Red-White-and-
     Blue"
That a band was discoursing like mad in the street,
With drumsticks that banged, and with cymbals that
     beat.

And he growled at his wife, as she buttoned his vest,
And applausively pinned a rosette on his breast
Of the national colors, and lured from his purse
Some change for the boys—for fire-crackers—or
     worse;
And she pointed with pride to a soldier in blue
In a frame on the wall, and the colors there, too;
And he felt, as he looked on the features, the glow
The painter found there twenty long years ago,
And a passionate thrill in his breast, as he felt
Instinctively round for the sword in his belt.

What was it that hung like a mist o'er the room?—
The tumult without—and the music—the boom
Of the cannon—the blare of the bugle and fife?—
No matter!—McFeeters was kissing his wife,
And laughing and crying and waving his hat

Like a genuine soldier, and crazy, at that!
—*Was* it needless to say 'twas a glorious day
And to boast of it all in that spread-eagle way
That our Forefathers had since the hour of the birth
Of this most patriotic republic on earth?

AT NINETY IN THE SHADE

H OT weather? Yes; but really not,
     Compared with weather twice as hot.
Find comfort, then, in arguing thus,
And you'll pull through victorious!—
For instance, while you gasp and pant
And try to cool yourself—and can't—
With soda, cream and lemonade,
The heat at ninety in the shade,—
Just calmly sit and ponder o'er
These same degrees, with ninety **more**
On top of them, and so concede
The weather now is cool indeed!
Think—as the perspiration dews
Your fevered brow, and seems to ooze
From out the ends of every hair—
Whole floods of it, with floods to spare—
Think, I repeat, the while the sweat
Pours down your spine—how hotter yet
Just ninety *more* degrees would be,
And bear *this* ninety patiently!
Think—as you mop your brow and hair,
With sticky feelings everywhere—
How ninety more degrees increase

Of heat like this would start the grease;
Or, think, as you exhausted stand,
A wilted "palm-leaf" in each hand—
When the thermometer has done
With ease the lap of ninety-one;
O think, I say, what heat might do
At one hundred and eighty-two—
Just twice the heat you now declare,
Complainingly, is hard to bear.
Or, as you watch the mercury
Mount, still elate, one more degree,
And doff your collar and cravat,
And rig a sponge up in your hat,
And ask Tom, Harry, Dick or Jim
If this is hot enough for him—
Consider how the sun would pour
At one hundred and eighty-four—
Just twice the heat that seems to be
Affecting you unpleasantly,
The very hour that you might find
As cool as dew, were you inclined.
But why proceed when none will heed
Advice apportioned to the need?
Hot weather? Yes; but really not,
Compared with weather twice as hot!

A SUDDEN SHOWER

BAREFOOTED boys scud up the street
  Or skurry under sheltering sheds;
And schoolgirl faces, pale and sweet,
  Gleam from the shawls about their heads.

Doors bang; and mother-voices call
  From alien homes; and rusty gates
Are slammed; and high above it all,
  The thunder grim reverberates.

And then, abrupt,—the rain! the rain!—
  The earth lies gasping; and the eyes
Behind the streaming window-pane
  Smile at the trouble of the skies.

The highway smokes; sharp echoes ring;
  The cattle bawl and cow-bells clank;
And into town comes galloping
  The farmer's horse, with steaming flank.

The swallow dips beneath the eaves
  And flirts his plumes and folds his wings;
And under the Catawba leaves
  The caterpillar curls and clings.

The bumblebee is pelted down
　　The wet stem of the hollyhock;
And sullenly, in spattered brown,
　　The cricket leaps the garden-walk.

Within, the baby claps his hands
　　And crows with rapture strange and
　　　　vague;
Without, beneath the rose-bush stands
　　A dripping rooster on one leg.

GOOD-BY ER HOWDY-DO

SAY good-by er howdy-do—
  What's the odds betwixt the two?
Comin'—goin', ev'ry day—
Best friends first to go away—
Grasp of hands you'd ruther hold
Than their weight in solid gold
Slips their grip while greetin' you.—
Say good-by er howdy-do!

Howdy-do, and then, good-by—
Mixes jes' like laugh and cry;
Deaths and births, and worst and best,
Tangled their contrariest;
Ev'ry jinglin' weddin'-bell
Skeerin' up some funer'l knell.—
Here's my song, and there's your sigh.—
Howdy-do, and then, good-by!

Say good-by er howdy-do—
Jes' the same to me and you;
'Taint worth while to make no fuss,
'Cause the job's put up on us!
Some One's runnin' this concern
That's got nothin' else to learn:
Ef *He's* willin', we'll pull through—
Say good-by er howdy-do!

91

WITH THE CURRENT

RAREST mood of all the year!
        Aimless, idle, and content—
Sky and wave and atmosphere
        Wholly indolent.

Little daughter, loose the band
        From your tresses—let them pour
Shadow-like o'er arm and hand
        Idling at the oar.

Low and clear, and pure and deep,
        Ripples of the river sing—
Water-lilies, half asleep,
        Drowsed with listening:

Tremulous reflex of skies—
        Skies above and skies below,—
Paradise and Paradise
        Blending even so!

Blossoms with their leaves unrolled
        Laughingly, as they were lips
Cleft with ruddy beaten gold
        Tongues of pollen-tips.

Rush and reed, and thorn and vine,
    Clumped with grasses lithe and tall—
With a web of summer-shine
        Woven round it all.

Back and forth, and to and fro—
    Flashing scale and wing as one,—
Dragon-flies that come and go,
        Shuttled by the sun.

Fairy lilts and lullabies,
    Fine as fantasy conceives,—
Echoes wrought of cricket-cries
        Sifted through the leaves.

O'er the rose, with drowsy buzz,
    Hangs the bee, and stays his kiss,
Even as my fancy does,
        Gipsy, over this.

Let us both be children—share
    Youth's glad voyage night and day,
Drift adown it, half aware,
        Anywhere we may.—

Drift and curve and deviate,
    Veer and eddy, float and flow,
Waver, swerve and undulate,
        As the bubbles go.

WET-WEATHER TALK

IT hain't no use to grumble and complane;
  It's jest as cheap and easy to rejoice.—
When God sorts out the weather and sends rain,
  W'y, rain's my choice.

Men ginerly, to all intents—
  Although they're apt to grumble some—
Puts most theyr trust in Providence,
  And takes things as they come—
    That is, the commonality
    Of men that's lived as long as me
    Has watched the world enugh to learn
    They're not the boss of this concern.

With *some,* of course, it's different—
  I've saw *young* men that knowed it all,
And didn't like the way things went
  On this terrestchul ball;—
    But all the same, the rain, some way,
    Rained jest as hard on picnic day;
    Er, when they railly *wanted* it,
    It mayby wouldn't rain a bit!

In this existunce, dry and wet
 Will overtake the best of men—
Some little skift o' clouds'll shet
 The sun off now and then.—
  And mayby, whilse you're wundern who
  You've fool-like lent your umbrell' to,
  And *want* it—out'll pop the sun,
  And you'll be glad you hain't got none!

It aggervates the farmers, too—
 They's too much wet, er too much sun,
Er work, er waitin' round to do
 Before the plowin' 's done:
  And mayby, like as not, the wheat,
  Jest as it's lookin' hard to beat,
  Will ketch the storm—and jest about
  The time the corn's a-jintin' out.

These-here *cy-clones* a-foolin' round—
 And back'ard crops!—and wind and rain!—
And yit the corn that's wallerd down
 May elbow up again!—
  They hain't no sense, as I can see,
  Fer mortuls, sich as us, to be
  A-faultin' Natchur's wise intents,
  And lockin' horns with Providence!

It hain't no use to grumble and complane;
 It's jest as cheap and easy to rejoice.—
When God sorts out the weather and sends rain,
  W'y, rain's my choice.

A POOR MAN'S WEALTH

A POOR man? Yes, I must confess—
No wealth of gold do I possess;
No pastures fine, with grazing kine,
Nor fields of waving grain are mine;
No foot of fat or fallow land
Where rightfully my feet may stand
The while I claim it as my own—
By deed and title, mine alone.

Ah, poor indeed! perhaps you say—
But spare me your compassion, pray!—
When I ride not—with you—I walk
In Nature's company, and talk
With one who will not slight or slur
The child forever dear to her—
And one who answers back, be sure,
With smile for smile, though I am poor.

And while communing thus, I count
An inner wealth of large amount,—
The wealth of honest purpose blent
With Penury's environment,—
The wealth of owing naught to-day
But debts that I would gladly pay,
With wealth of thanks still unexpressed
With cumulative interest.—

A wealth of patience and content—
For all my ways improvident;
A faith still fondly exercised—
For all my plans unrealized;
A wealth of promises that still,
Howe'er I fail, I hope to fill;
A wealth of charity for those
Who pity me my ragged clothes.

A poor man? Yes, I must confess—
No wealth of gold do I possess;
No pastures fine, with grazing kine,
Nor fields of waving grain are mine;
But ah, my friend! I've wealth, no end!
For millionairies might condescend
To bend the knee and envy me
This opulence of poverty.

'AUTOGRAPHIC

For an Album

I FEEL, if aught I ought to rhyme,
I ought 'a' thought a longer time,
And ought 'a' caught a higher sense,
Of autocratic eloquence.
I ought 'a' sought each haughty Muse
That taught a thought I ought to use,
And fought and fraught, and so devised
A poem *unmonotonized.*—
But since all this was vain, I thought
I ought to simply say,—I ought
To thank you, as I ought to do,
And ought to bow my best to you;
And ought to trust not to intrude
A rudely-wrought-up gratitude,
But ought to smile, and ought to laugh,
And ought to write—an autograph.

IN SWIMMING-TIME

CLOUDS above, as white as wool,
 Drifting over skies as blue
As the eyes of beautiful
 Children when they smile at you;
Groves of maple, elm, and beech,
 With the sunshine sifted through
Branches, mingling each with each,
 Dim with shade and bright with dew;
Stripling trees, and poplars hoar,
Hickory and sycamore,
And the drowsy dogwood bowed
Where the ripples laugh aloud,
And the crooning creek is stirred
 To a gaiety that now
Mates the warble of the bird
 Teetering on the hazel-bough;
Grasses long and fine and fair
As your schoolboy sweetheart's hair,
Backward roached and twirled and twined
By the fingers of the wind.
Vines and mosses, interlinked
 Down dark aisles and deep ravines,
Where the stream runs, willow-brinked,

Round a bend where some one leans
Faint and vague and indistinct
  As the like reflected thing
  In the current shimmering.
Childish voices farther on,
Where the truant stream has gone,
Vex the echoes of the wood
Till no word is understood,
Save that one is well aware
Happiness is hiding there.
There, in leafy coverts, nude
  Little bodies poise and leap,
Spattering the solitude
And the silence everywhere—
  Mimic monsters of the deep!
Wallowing in sandy shoals—
  Plunging headlong out of sight;
  And, with spurtings of delight,
Clutching hands, and slippery soles,
  Climbing up the treacherous steep
Over which the spring-board spurns
Each again as he returns.
  Ah! the glorious carnival!
    Purple lips and chattering teeth—
    Eyes that burn—but, in beneath,
  Every care beyond recall,
    Every task forgotten quite—
    And again, in dreams at night,
  Dropping, drifting through it all!

THE BEST IS GOOD ENOUGH

I QUARREL not with Destiny,
   But make the best of everything—
The best is good enough for me.

Leave Discontent alone, and she
Will shut her mouth and let *you* sing.
I quarrel not with Destiny.

I take some things, or let 'em be—
Good gold has always got the ring;
The best is good enough for me.

Since Fate insists on secrecy,
I have no arguments to bring—
I quarrel not with Destiny.

The fellow that goes "haw" for "gee"
Will find he hasn't got full swing.
The best is good enough for me.

One only knows our needs, and He
Does all of the distributing.
I quarrel not with Destiny:
The best is good enough for me.

HE CALLED HER IN

I

HE called her in from me and shut the door.
   And she so loved the sunshine and the
         sky!—
She loved them even better yet than I
That ne'er knew dearth of them—my mother
      dead,
Nature had nursed me in her lap instead:
And I had grown a dark and eery child
That rarely smiled,
Save when, shut all alone in grasses high,
Looking straight up in God's great lonesome sky
And coaxing Mother to smile back on me.
'Twas lying thus, this fair girl suddenly
Came on me, nestled in the fields beside
A pleasant-seeming home, with doorway wide—
The sunshine beating in upon the floor
Like golden rain.—
O sweet, sweet face above me, turn again
And leave me! I had cried, but that an ache
Within my throat so gripped it I could make
No sound but a thick sobbing. Cowering so,
I felt her light hand laid
Upon my hair—a touch that ne'er before

Had tamed me thus, all soothed and unafraid—
It seemed the touch the children used to know
When Christ was here, so dear it was—so dear,—
At once I loved her as the leaves love dew
In midmost summer when the days are new.
Barely an hour I knew her, yet a curl
Of silken sunshine did she clip for me
Out of the bright May-morning of her hair,
And bound and gave it to me laughingly,
And caught my hands and called me *"Little girl,"*
Tiptoeing, as she spoke, to kiss me there!
And I stood dazed and dumb for very stress
Of my great happiness.
She plucked me by the gown, nor saw how mean
The raiment—drew me with her everywhere:
Smothered her face in tufts of grasses green:
Put up her dainty hands and peeped between
Her fingers at the blossoms—crooned and talked
To them in strange, glad whispers, as we
    walked,—
Said *this* one was her angel mother—*this,*
Her baby-sister—come back, for a kiss,
Clean from the Good-World!—smiled and kissed
    them, then
Closed her soft eyes and kissed them o'er again.
And so did she beguile me—so we played,—
She was the dazzling Shine—I, the dark Shade—
And we did mingle like to these, and thus,
Together, made
The perfect summer, pure and glorious.
So blent we, till a harsh voice broke upon

Our happiness.—She, startled as a fawn,
Cried, "Oh, 'tis Father!"—all the blossoms gone
From out her cheeks as those from out her
　　grasp.—
Harsher the voice came:—She could only gasp
Affrightedly, "Good-by!—good-by! good-by!"
And lo, I stood alone, with that harsh cry
Ringing a new and unknown sense of shame
Through soul and frame,
And, with wet eyes, repeating o'er and o'er,—
"He called her in from me and shut the door!"

II

He called her in from me and shut the door!
And I went wandering alone again—
So lonely—O so very lonely then,
I thought no little sallow star, alone
In all a world of twilight, e'er had known
Such utter loneliness. But that I wore
Above my heart that gleaming tress of hair
To lighten up the night of my despair,
I think I might have groped into my grave
Nor cared to wave
The ferns above it with a breath of prayer.
And how I hungered for the sweet, sweet face
That bent above me in my hiding-place
That day amid the grasses there beside
Her pleasant home!—"Her *pleasant* home!" I
　　sighed,
Remembering;—then shut my teeth and feigned

The harsh voice calling *me,*—then clenched my
    nails
So deeply in my palms, the sharp wounds pained,
And tossed my face toward Heaven, as one who
    pales
In splendid martyrdom, with soul serene,
As near to God as high the guillotine.
And I had *envied* her? Not that—O no!
But I had longed for some sweet haven so!—
Wherein the tempest-beaten heart might ride
Sometimes at peaceful anchor, and abide
Where those that loved me touched me with their
    hands,
And looked upon me with glad eyes, and slipped
Smooth fingers o'er my brow, and lulled the
    strands
Of my wild tresses, as they backward tipped
My yearning face and kissed it satisfied.
Then bitterly I murmured as before,—
"He called her in from me and shut the door!"

III

He called her in from me and shut the door!
After long struggling with my pride and pain—
A weary while it seemed, in which the more
I held myself from her, the greater fain
Was I to look upon her face again;—
At last—at last—half conscious where my feet
Were faring, I stood waist-deep in the sweet
Green grasses there where she

First came to me.—
The very blossoms she had plucked that day,
And, at her father's voice, had cast away,
Around me lay,
Still bright and blooming in these eyes of mine;
And as I gathered each one eagerly,
I pressed it to my lips and drank the wine
Her kisses left there for the honey-bee.
Then, after I had laid them with the tress
Of her bright hair with lingering tenderness,
I, turning, crept on to the hedge that bound
Her pleasant-seeming home—but all around
Was never sign of her!—The windows all
Were blinded; and I heard no rippling fall
Of her glad laugh, nor any harsh voice call;—
But, clutching to the tangled grasses, caught
A sound as though a strong man bowed his head
And sobbed alone—unloved—uncomforted!—
And then straightway before
My tearless eyes, all vividly, was wrought
A vision that is with me evermore:—
A little girl that lies asleep, nor hears
Nor heeds not any voice nor fall of tears.—
And I sit singing o'er and o'er and o'er,—
"God called her in from him and shut the door!"

GIVE ME THE BABY

GIVE me the baby to hold, my dear—
   To hold and hug, and to love and kiss.
Ah! he will come to me, never a fear—
   Come to the nest of a breast like this,
As warm for him as his face with cheer.
Give me the baby to hold, my dear!

Trustfully yield him to my caress.
   "Bother," you say? What! "a bother" to
      me?—
To fill up my soul with such happiness
   As the love of a baby that laughs to be
Snuggled away where my heart can hear!
Give me the baby to hold, my dear!

Ah, but his hands are grimed, you say,
   And would soil my laces and clutch my hair.—
Well, what would pleasure me more, I pray,
   Than the touch and tug of the wee hands
      there?—
The wee hands there, and the warm face here—
Give me the baby to hold, my dear!

Give me the baby! (Oh, won't you see?
  . . . Somewhere, out where the green of
    the lawn
Is turning to gray, and the maple tree
  Is weeping its leaves of gold upon
A little mound, with a dead rose near. . . .)
Give me the baby to hold, my dear!

AN AUTUMNAL TONIC

WHAT mystery is it? The morning as rare
　　As the Indian Summer may bring!
A tang in the frost and a spice in the air
　　That no city poet can sing!
The crimson and amber and gold of the leaves,
　　As they loosen and flutter and fall
In the path of the park, as it rustlingly weaves
Its way through the maples and under the eaves
　　Of the sparrows that chatter and call.

What hint of delight is it tingles me through?—
　　What vague, indefinable joy?
What yearning for something divine that I knew
　　When a wayward and wood-roving boy?
Ah-ha! and Oho! but I have it, I say—
　　Oh, the mystery brightens at last,—
'Tis the longing and zest of the far, far away,
For a bountiful, old-fashioned dinner to-day,
　　With the hale harvest-hands of the past.

OUT OF THE HITHERWHERE

OUT of the hitherwhere into the YON—
The land that the Lord's love rests upon;
Where one may rely on the friends he meets,
And the smiles that greet him along the streets:
Where the mother that left you years ago
Will lift the hands that were folded so,
And put them about you, with all the love
And tenderness you are dreaming of.

Out of the hitherwhere into the YON—
Where all of the friends of your youth have gone,—
Where the old schoolmate that laughed with you,
Will laugh again as he used to do,
Running to meet you, with such a face
As lights like a moon the wondrous place
Where God is living, and glad to live,
Since He is the Master and may forgive.

Out of the hitherwhere into the YON !—
Stay the hopes we are leaning on—
You, Divine, with Your merciful eyes
Looking down from the far-away skies,—
Smile upon us, and reach and take
Our worn souls Home for the old home's sake.—
And so Amen,—for our all seems gone
Out of the hitherwhere into the YON.

A TINKLE OF BELLS

THE light of the moon on the white of the snow,
  And the answering twinkles along the street,
And our sleigh flashing by, in the glamour and
    glow
Of the glorious nights of the long ago,
  When the laugh of her lips rang clear and sweet
As the tinkle our horses shook out of the bells
    And flung and tossed back
    On our glittering track
In a shower of tremulous, murmuring swells
  Of the echoing, airy, melodious bells!—
  O the mirth of the bells!
  And the worth of the bells!
  Come tinkle again, in this dearth of the bells,
The laughter and love that I lack, yearning back
  For the far-away sound of the bells!

Ah! the bells, they were glad in the long ago!
And the tinkles they had, they have thrilled me so
I have said: "It is they and her songs and face
Make summer for me of the wintriest place!"
And now—but sobbings and sad farewells,
  As I peer in the night through the sleeted pane,
Hearing a clangor and wrangle of bells,
  And never a tinkle again!

The snow is a-swoon, and the moon dead-white,
And the frost is wild in the air to-night!
 Yet still will I linger and listen and pray
 Till the sound of her voice shall come this way,
  With a tinkle of bells,
   And the lisp-like tread
    Of the hooves of the sleigh,
  And the murmurs and swells
  Of the vows she said.
 And oh, I shall listen as madmen may,
Till the tinkling bells ring down this way!—
Till again the grasp of my hand entwines
The tensioned loops of the quivering lines,
And again we ride in the wake of the pride
And the strength of the coursers, side by side,
With our faces smitten again by the spray
Of the froth of our steeds as we gallop away
 In affright of the bells,
 And the might of the bells,
And the infinite glee and delight of the bells,
As they tinkle and tinkle and tinkle, till they
Are heard through the dawn where the mists are
  drawn,
And we canter and gallop and dash away
 Sheer into The Judgment Day!

THE OLD MAN

L O! steadfast and serene,
    In patient pause between
The seen and the unseen,
    What gentle zephyrs fan
Your silken silver hair,—
And what diviner air
Breathes round you like a prayer,
        Old Man?

Can you, in nearer view
Of Glory, pierce the blue
Of happy Heaven through;
    And, listening mutely, can
Your senses, dull to us,
Hear Angel-voices thus,
In chorus glorious—
        Old Man?

In your reposeful gaze
The dusk of Autumn days
Is blent with April haze,
    As when of old began

113

The bursting of the bud
Of rosy babyhood—
When all the world was good,
    Old Man.

And yet I find a sly
Little twinkle in your eye;
And your whisperingly shy
    Little laugh is simply an
Internal shout of glee
That betrays the fallacy
You'd perpetrate on me,
    Old Man!

So just put up the frown
That your brows are pulling down!
Why, the fleetest boy in town,
    As he bared his feet and ran,
Could read with half a glance—
And of keen rebuke, perchance—
Your secret countenance,
    Old Man!

Now, honestly, confess:
Is an old man any less
Than the little child we bless
    And caress when we can?
Isn't age but just a place
Where you mask the childish face
To preserve its inner grace,
    Old Man?

Hasn't age a truant day,
Just as that you went astray
In the wayward, restless way,
    When, brown with dust and tan,
Your roguish face essayed,
In solemn masquerade,
To hide the smile it made,
      Old Man?

Now, fair, and square, and true,
Don't your old soul tremble through,
As in youth it used to do
    When it brimmed and overran
With the strange, enchanted sights,
And the splendors and delights
Of the old "Arabian Nights,"
      Old Man?

When, haply, you have fared
Where glad Aladdin shared
His lamp with you, and dared
    The Afrite and his clan;
And, with him, clambered through
The trees where jewels grew—
And filled your pockets, too,
      Old Man?

Or, with Sinbad, at sea—
And in veracity
Who has sinned as bad as he,
    Or would, or will, or can?—

Have you listened to his lies,
With open mouth and eyes,
And learned his art likewise,
    Old Man?

And you need not deny
That your eyes were wet as dry,
Reading novels on the sly!
    And review them, if you can
And the same warm tears will fall—
Only faster, that is all—
Over Little Nell and Paul,
    Old Man!

Oh, you were a lucky lad—
Just as good as you were bad!
And the host of friends you had—
    Charley, Tom, and Dick, and Dan;
And the old School-Teacher, too,
Though he often censured you;
And the girls in pink and blue,
    Old Man.

And—as often you have leant,
In boyish sentiment,
To kiss the letter sent
    By Nelly, Belle, or Nan—
Wherein the rose's hue
Was red, the violet blue—
And sugar sweet—and you,
    Old Man,—

So, to-day, as lives the bloom,
And the sweetness, and perfume
Of the blossoms, I assume,
    On the same mysterious plan
The Master's love assures,
That the selfsame boy endures
In that hale old heart of yours,
    Old Man.

OUR KIND OF A MAN

I

THE kind of a man for you and me!
   He faces the world unflinchingly,
And smites, as long as the wrong resists,
With a knuckled faith and force like fists:
He lives the life he is preaching of,
And loves where most is the need of love;
His voice is clear to the deaf man's ears,
And his face sublime through the blind man's tears;
The light shines out where the clouds were dim,
And the widow's prayer goes up for him;
The latch is clicked at the hovel door
And the sick man sees the sun once more,
And out o'er the barren fields he sees
Springing blossoms and waving trees,
Feeling as only the dying may,
That God's own servant has come that way,
Smoothing the path as it still winds on
Through the golden gate where his loved have gone.

118

II

The kind of a man for me and you!
However little of worth we do
He credits full, and abides in trust
That time will teach us how more is just.
He walks abroad, and he meets all kinds
Of querulous and uneasy minds,
And, sympathizing, he shares the pain
Of the doubts that rack us, heart and brain;
And, knowing this, as we grasp his hand,
We are surely coming to understand!
He looks on sin with pitying eyes—
E'en as the Lord, since Paradise,—
Else, should we read, Though our sins should glow
As scarlet, they shall be white as snow?—
And, feeling still, with a grief half glad,
That the bad are as good as the good are bad,
He strikes straight out for the Right—and he
Is the kind of a man for you and me!

THE LITTLE COAT

HERE'S his ragged "roundabout." . .
 Turn the pockets inside out:
See; his penknife, lost to use,
Rusted shut with apple-juice;
Here, with marbles, top and string,
Is his deadly "devil-sling,"
With its rubber, limp at last
As the sparrows of the past!
Beeswax—buckles—leather straps—
Bullets, and a box of caps,—
Not a thing of all, I guess,
But betrays some waywardness—
E'en these tickets, blue and red,
For the Bible-verses said—
Such as this his mem'ry kept,—
                    "Jesus wept."

Here's a fishing-hook and -line,
Tangled up with wire and twine,
And dead angleworms, and some
Slugs of lead and chewing-gum,
Blent with scents that can but come
From the oil of rhodium.

120

Here—a soiled, yet dainty note,
That some little sweetheart wrote,
Dotting—"Vine grows round the stump,"
And—"My sweetest sugar-lump!"
Wrapped in this—a padlock key
Where he's filed a touch-hole—see!
And some powder in a quill
Corked up with a liver pill;
And a spongy little chunk
                    Of "punk."

Here's the little coat—but O
Where is he we've censured so?
Don't you hear us calling, dear?
Back! come back, and never fear.—
You may wander where you will,
Over orchard, field and hill;
You may kill the birds, or do
Anything that pleases you!
Ah, this empty coat of his!
Every tatter worth a kiss;
Every stain as pure instead
As the white stars overhead:
And the pockets—homes were they
Of the little hands that play
Now no more—but, absent, thus
                    Beckon us.

AN IMPROMPTU ON ROLLER SKATES

RUMBLE, tumble, growl and grate!
　　Skip, and trip, and gravitate!
Lunge, and plunge, and thrash the planks
With your blameless, shameless shanks,
In excruciating pain,
Stand upon your head again,
And, uncoiling kink by kink,
Kick the roof out of the rink!

In derisive bursts of mirth,
Drop ka-whop and jar the earth!
Jolt your lungs down in your socks,
Oh! tempestuous equinox
Of dismembered legs and arms!
Strew your ways with wild alarms;
Fameward skoot and ricochet
On your glittering vertebrae!

ME AND MARY

ALL my feelin's in the Spring
Gits so blame contrary,
I can't think of anything
    Only me and Mary!
"Me and Mary!" all the time,
"Me and Mary!" like a rhyme,
Keeps a-dingin' on till I'm
    Sick o' "Me and Mary!"

"Me and Mary! Ef us two
    Only was together—
Playin' like we used to do
    In the Aprile weather!"
All the night and all the day
I keep wishin' thataway
Till I'm gittin' old and gray
    Jes' on "Me and Mary!"

Muddy yit along the pike
    Sence the Winter's freezin',
And the orchard's back'ard-like
    Bloomin' out this season;

Only heerd one bluebird yit—
Nary robin ner tomtit;
What's the how and why of it?
    'Spect it's "Me and Mary!"

Me and Mary liked the birds—
    That is, *Mary* sort o'
Liked 'em first, and afterwards,
    W'y, I thought *I'd* ort 'o.
And them birds—ef Mary stood
Right here with me, like she should—
They'd be singin', them birds would,
    All fer me and Mary.

Birds er not, I'm hopin' some
    I can git to plowin'!
Ef the sun'll only come,
    And the Lord allowin',
Guess to-morry I'll turn in
And git down to work ag'in;
This here loaferin' won't win,
    Not fer me and Mary!

Fer a man that loves, like me,
    And's afeard to name it,
Till some other feller, he
    Gits the girl—dad-shame-it!
Wet er dry, er cloud er sun—
Winter gone er jes' begun—
Outdoor work fer me er none,
    No more "Me and Mary!"

WRITTEN IN BUNNER'S "AIRS FROM ARCADY"

O EVER gracious Airs from Arcady!
    What lack is there of any jocund thing
  In glancing wit or glad imagining
Capricious fancy may not find in thee?—
The laugh of Momus, tempered daintily
    To lull the ear and lure its listening;
  The whistled syllables the birds of spring
Flaunt ever at our guessings what they be;
The wood, the seashore, and the clanging town;
  The pets of fashion, and the ways of such;
The *robe de chambre,* and the russet gown;
  The lordling's carriage, and the pilgrim's crutch—
From hale old Chaucer's wholesomeness, clean
    down
  To our artistic Dobson's deftest touch!

A SONG

THERE is ever a song somewhere, my dear;
    There is ever a something sings always:
There's the song of the lark when the skies are
    clear,
    And the song of the thrush when the skies are
      gray.
The sunshine showers across the grain,
    And the bluebird trills in the orchard tree;
And in and out, when the eaves drip rain,
    The swallows are twittering ceaselessly.

There is ever a song somewhere, my dear,
    Be the skies above or dark or fair,
There is ever a song that our hearts may hear—
There is ever a song somewhere, my dear—
    There is ever a song somewhere!

There is ever a song somewhere, my dear,
    In the midnight black, or the midday blue:
The robin pipes when the sun is here,
    And the cricket chirrups the whole night through.
The buds may blow, and the fruit may grow,
    And the autumn leaves drop crisp and sear;
But whether the sun, or the rain, or the snow,
    There is ever a song somewhere, my dear.

There is ever a song somewhere, my dear,
  Be the skies above or dark or fair,
There is ever a song that our hearts may hear—
There is ever a song somewhere, my dear—
  There is ever a song somewhere!

NEVER TALK BACK

NEVER talk back! sich things is repperhensible;
    A feller only hurts hisse'f that jaws a man
        that's hot;
In a quarrel, ef you'll only keep your mouth shet
    and act sensible,
    The man that does the talkin' 'll git worsted every
        shot!

Never talk back to a feller that's abusin' you—
    Jes' let him carry on, and rip, and snort, and
        swear;
And when he finds his blamin' and defamin' 's jes'
    amusin' you,
    You've got him clean kaflummixed,—and you
        want to hold him there!

Never talk back, and wake up the whole community
    And call a man a liar, over Law, er Politics.—
You can lift and land him furder and with grace-
    fuller impunity
    With one good jolt of silence than a half a dozen
        kicks!

MY FRIEND

"HE is my friend," I said,—
          "Be patient!" Overhead
The skies were drear and dim;
And lo! the thought of him
Smiled on my heart—and then
The sun shone out again!

"He is my friend!" The words
Brought summer and the birds;
And all my winter-time
Thawed into running rhyme
And rippled into song,
Warm, tender, brave, and strong.

And so it sings to-day.—
So may it sing alway!
Though waving grasses grow
Between, and lilies blow
Their trills of perfume clear
As laughter to the ear,
Let each mute measure end
With "Still he is thy friend."

THE LITTLE FAT DOCTOR

HE seemed so strange to me, every way—
    In manner, and form, and size,
From the boy I knew but yesterday,—
    I could hardly believe my eyes!

To hear his name called over there,
    My memory thrilled with glee
And leaped to picture him young and fair
    In youth, as he used to be.

But looking, only as glad eyes can,
    For the boy I knew of yore,
I smiled on a portly little man
    I had never seen before!—

Grave as a judge in courtliness—
    Professor-like and bland—
A little fat doctor and nothing less,
    With his hat in his kimboed hand.

But how we talked old times, and "chaffed"
    Each other with "Minnie," and "Jim"—
And how the little fat doctor laughed,
    And how I laughed with him!

"And it's pleasant," I thought, "though I
    yearn to see
The face of the youth that was,
To know no boy could smile on me
    As the little fat doctor does!"

THE STRANGE YOUNG MAN

'TWAS a strange young man of the dreamy
      times
When bards made money, and bankers rhymes;
And drones made honey—and bees made naught;
And the bad sung hymns, and the good-folk fought;
And the merchants lurked in the shade all day
And pitched horseshoes in a listless way!
When the ticket-man at the station knew
If your trunk would go if you checked it through,
And if 2:30 meant half-past two,
And what in-the-name-of-the-land to do
If a man got left when he oughtn't to:
When the cabman wept as he took your fare,
And the street-car driver led in prayer—
And the cuss with the dyed mustache was there
That rode in town on a "jumper"-sled,
And got whipped twice for the things he said
To fellows that told him his hair was red.
And the strange young man (of which and whom
Our pencil offers to deign presume
To treat of now, in the days like these
When young men dress as they please to please)
Went round in a coat of pale pink-blue,

And a snow-white vest of a crimson hue,
And trousers purple, and gaiters gray—
All cut, as the French or the Dutch would say,—
La—macht nichts aus, oder—décolleté,—
Strange not only in dress, but in
The dimples he wore in cheek and chin—
All nailed over with scraps of tin,
Where he hadn't been shaved as he'd ought o'
    been;—
And his crape cravat, and the shape of that,
And the ear-tab over his diamond-pin.
And his friends all wondered, and used to say,—
"What a strange young man! Ah me! Hooray!
How sad he seems in his wild delight!
And how tickled indeed when he weeps outright!
What a comical man when he writhes in pain;
And how grieved he grows when he's glad again!"
And marveling still to remark new facts,
They said, "How slender and slim he acts!
And isn't it odd for a man to wear
A thumb-stall over his nose, and pare
His finger-nails with a carving-knife,
And talk of prunes to the landlord's wife?
It is patent to us—and, indeed, no doubt,
    Though as safely sealed as an oyster-can,—
Our interest in him must needs leak out,—
    Namely, that he is a strange young man!"

SCOTTY

SCOTTY'S dead.—Of course he is!
    Jes' that same old luck of his!—
Ever sence we went cahoots
He's be'n first, you bet yer boots!
When our schoolin' first begun,
Got two whippin's to my one:
Stold and smoked the first cigar:
Stood up first before the bar,
Takin' whisky-straight—and me
Wastin' time on "blackberry"!
Beat me in the Army, too,
And clean on the whole way through!—
In more scrapes around the camp,
And more troubles, on the tramp:
Fought and fell there by my side
With more bullets in his hide,
And more glory in the cause,—
That's the kind o' man *he* was!
Luck liked Scotty more'n me.—
I got married: Scotty, he
Never even would *apply*
Fer the pension-money I
Had to beg of "Uncle Sam"—

That's the kind o' cuss *I* am!—
Scotty allus first and best—
Me the last and ornriest!
Yit fer all that's said and done—
All the battles fought and won—
We hain't prospered, him ner me—
Both as pore as pore could be,—
Though we've allus, up tel now,
Stuck together anyhow—
Scotty allus, as I've said,
Luckiest—And now he's *dead!*

ON THE SUNNY SIDE

HI and whoop-hooray, boys!
　　Sing a song of cheer!
Here's a holiday, boys,
　　Lasting half a year!
Round the world, and half is
　　Shadow we have tried;
Now we're where the laugh is,—
　　On the sunny side!

Pigeons coo and mutter,
　　Strutting high aloof
Where the sunbeams flutter
　　Through the stable roof.
Hear the chickens cheep, boys,
　　And the hen with pride
Clucking them to sleep, boys,
　　On the sunny side!

Hear the clacking guinea;
　　Hear the cattle moo;
Hear the horses whinny,
　　Looking out at you!

136

On the hitching-block, boys,
  Grandly satisfied,
See the old peacock, boys,
  On the sunny side!

Robins in the peach tree;
  Bluebirds in the pear;
Blossoms over each tree
  In the orchard there!
All the world's in joy, boys,
  Glad and glorified
As a romping boy, boys,
  On the sunny side!

Where's a heart as mellow—
  Where's a soul as free—
Where is any fellow
  We would rather be?
Just ourselves or none, boys,
  World around and wide,
Laughing in the sun, boys,
  On the sunny side!

THE HARPER

LIKE a drift of faded blossoms
  Caught in a slanting rain,
His fingers glimpsed down the strings of
    his harp
  In a tremulous refrain:

Patter and tinkle, and drip and drip!
  Ah! but the chords were rainy sweet!
And I closed my eyes and I bit my lip,
  As he played there in the street.

Patter, and drip, and tinkle!
  And there was the little bed
In the corner of the garret,
  And the rafters overhead!

And there was the little window—
  Tinkle, and drip, and drip!—
The rain above, and a mother's love,
  And God's companionship!

THE BLOSSOMS ON THE TREES

BLOSSOMS crimson, white, or blue,
    Purple, pink, and every hue,
From sunny skies, to tintings drowned
    In dusky drops of dew,
I praise you all, wherever found,
    And love you through and through;—
        But, Blossoms on the Trees,
        With your breath upon the breeze,
There's nothing all the world around
    As half as sweet as you!

Could the rhymer only wring
    All the sweetness to the lees
Of all the kisses clustering
    In juicy Used-to-bes,
To dip his rhymes therein and sing
    The blossoms on the trees,—
"O Blossoms on the Trees,"
    He would twitter, trill, and coo,
"However sweet, such songs as these
    Are not as sweet as you:—
For you are *blooming* melodies
    The *eyes* may listen to!"

LAUGHTER HOLDING BOTH HIS SIDES

AY, thou varlet! Laugh away!
  All the world's a holiday!
Laugh away, and roar and shout
Till thy hoarse tongue lolleth out!
Bloat thy cheeks, and bulge thine eyes
Unto bursting; pelt thy thighs
With thy swollen palms, and roar
As thou never hast before!
Lustier! wilt thou! peal on peal!
Stiflest? Squat and grind thy heel—
Wrestle with thy loins, and then
Wheeze thee whiles, and whoop again!

IN STATE

IS it the martins or katydids?—
   Early morning or late at night?
A dream, belike, kneeling down on the lids
   Of a dying man's eyesight.

. . . .

Over and over I heard the rain—
   Over and over I waked to see
The blaze of the lamp as again and again
   Its stare insulted me.

. . . .

It is not the click of the clock I hear—
   It is the *pulse* of the clock,—and lo!
How it throbs and throbs on the quickened ear
   Of the dead man listening so!

I heard them whisper *"She* would not come;"
   But, being dead, I knew—I knew! . . .
Some hearts they love us alive, and some
   They love us dead—they do!

141

And *I* am dead—and I joy to be,—
  For here are my folded hands, so cold,
And yet blood-warm with the roses she
  Has given me to hold.

Dead—yea, dead!—But I hear the beat
  Of her heart, as her warm lips touch my
      brow—
And O how sweet—how *blinding* sweet
  To know that she loves me *now!*

THE DEAD LOVER

TIME is so long when a man is dead!
　　Some one sews; and the room is made
Very clean; and the light is shed
　　Soft through the window-shade.

Yesterday I thought: "I know
　　Just how the bells will sound, and how
The friends will talk, and the sermon go,
　　And the hearse-horse bow and bow!"

This is to-day; and I have no thing
　　To think of—nothing whatever to do
But to hear the throb of the pulse of a wing
　　That wants to fly back to you.

THE KIND OLD MAN

THE kind old man—the mild old man—
  Who smiled on the boys at play,
Dreaming, perchance, of his own glad youth
  When he was as blithe and gay!

And the larger urchin tossed the ball,
  And the lesser held the bat—
Though the kindly old man's eyes were blurred
  He could even notice that!

But suddenly he was shocked to hear
  Words that I dare not write,
And he hastened, in his kindly way,
  To curb them as he might!

And he said, "Tut! tut! you naughty boy
  With the ball! for shame!" and then,
"You boy with the bat, whack him over the
      head
  If he calls you that again!"

The kind old man—the mild old man—
  Who gazed on the boys at play,
Dreaming, perchance, of his own wild youth
  When he was as tough as they!

A SCRAWL

I WANT to sing something—but this is all—
  I try and I try, but the rhymes are dull
As though they were damp, and the echoes fall
    Limp and unlovable.

Words will not say what I yearn to say—
  They will not walk as I want them to,
But they stumble and fall in the path of the way
    Of my telling my love for you.

Simply take what the scrawl is worth—
  Knowing I love you as sun the sod
On the ripening side of the great round earth
    That swings in the smile of God.

AWAY

I CAN not say, and I will not say
  That he is dead.—He is just away!

With a cheery smile, and a wave of the hand,
He has wandered into an unknown land,

And left us dreaming how very fair
It needs must be, since he lingers there.

And you—O you, who the wildest yearn
For the old-time step and the glad return,—

Think of him faring on, as dear
In the love of There as the love of Here;

And loyal still, as he gave the blows
Of his warrior-strength to his country's foes.—

Mild and gentle, as he was brave,—
When the sweetest love of his life he gave

To simple things:—Where the violets grew
Blue as the eyes they were likened to,

The touches of his hands have strayed
As reverently as his lips have prayed:

When the little brown thrush that harshly chirred
Was dear to him as the mocking-bird;

And he pitied as much as a man in pain
A writhing honey-bee wet with rain.—

Think of him still as the same, I say:
He is not dead—he is just away!

A MONUMENT FOR THE SOLDIERS

A MONUMENT for the Soldiers!
  And what will ye build it of?
Can ye build it of marble, or brass, or bronze,
  Outlasting the Soldiers' love?
Can ye glorify it with legends
  As grand as their blood hath writ
From the inmost shrine of this land of thine
  To the outermost verge of it?

And the answer came: We would build it
  Out of our hopes made sure,
And out of our purest prayers and tears,
  And out of our faith secure:
We would build it out of the great white truths
  Their death hath sanctified,
And the sculptured forms of the men in arms,
  And their faces ere they died.

And what heroic figures
  Can the sculptor carve in stone?
Can the marble breast be made to bleed,
  And the marble lips to moan?

Can the marble brow be fevered?
  And the marble eyes be graved
To look their last, as the flag floats past,
  On the country they have saved?

And the answer came: The figures
  Shall all be fair and brave,
And, as befitting, as pure and white
  As the stars above their grave!
The marble lips, and breast and brow
  Whereon the laurel lies,
Bequeath us right to guard the flight
  Of the old flag in the skies!

A monument for the Soldiers!
  Built of a people's love,
And blazoned and decked and panoplied
  With the hearts ye build it of!
And see that ye build it stately,
  In pillar and niche and gate,
And high in pose as the souls of those
  It would commemorate!

OUT TO OLD AUNT MARY'S

WASN'T it pleasant, O brother mine,
  In those old days of the lost sunshine
Of youth—when the Saturday's chores were
      through,
And the "Sunday's wood" in the kitchen, too,
And we went visiting, "me and you,"
      Out to Old Aunt Mary's?—

"Me and you"—And the morning fair,
With the dewdrops twinkling everywhere;
  The scent of the cherry-blossoms blown
  After us, in the roadway lone,
  Our capering shadows onward thrown—
      Out to Old Aunt Mary's!

It all comes back so clear to-day!
Though I am as bald as you are gray,—
  Out by the barn-lot and down the lane
  We patter along in the dust again,
  As light as the tips of the drops of the rain,
      Out to Old Aunt Mary's.

The few last houses of the town;
Then on, up the high creek-bluffs and down;
  Past the squat toll-gate, with its well-sweep pole;

The bridge, and "the old 'babtizin'-hole,' "
Loitering, awed, o'er pool and shoal,
    Out to Old Aunt Mary's.

We cross the pasture, and through the wood,
Where the old gray snag of the poplar stood,
    Where the hammering "red-heads" hopped awry,
    And the buzzard "raised" in the "clearing"-sky
    And lolled and circled, as we went by
       Out to Old Aunt Mary's.

Or, stayed by the glint of the redbird's wings,
Or the glitter of song that the bluebird sings,
    All hushed we feign to strike strange trails,
    As the "big braves" do in the Indian tales,
    Till again our real quest lags and fails—
       Out to Old Aunt Mary's.—

And the woodland echoes with yells of mirth
That make old war-whoops of minor worth! . . .
    Where such heroes of war as we?—
    With bows and arrows of fantasy,
    Chasing each other from tree to tree
       Out to Old Aunt Mary's!

And then in the dust of the road again;
And the teams we met, and the countrymen;
    And the long highway, with sunshine spread
    As thick as butter on country bread,
    Our cares behind, and our hearts ahead
       Out to Old Aunt Mary's.—

For only, now, at the road's next bend
To the right we could make out the gable-end
   Of the fine old Huston homestead—not
   Half a mile from the sacred spot
   Where dwelt our Saint in her simple cot—
      Out to Old Aunt Mary's.

Why, I see her now in the open door
Where the little gourds grew up the sides and o'er
   The clapboard roof!—And her face—ah, me!
   Wasn't it good for a boy to see—
   And wasn't it good for a boy to be
      Out to Old Aunt Mary's?—

The jelly—the jam and the marmalade,
And the cherry and quince "preserves" she made!
   And the sweet-sour pickles of peach and pear,
   With cinnamon in 'em, and all things rare!—
   And the more we ate was the more to spare,
      Out to Old Aunt Mary's!

Ah! was there, ever, so kind a face
And gentle as hers, or such a grace
   Of welcoming, as she cut the cake
   Or the juicy pies that she joyed to make
   Just for the visiting children's sake—
      Out to Old Aunt Mary's!

The honey, too, in its amber comb
One only finds in an old farm-home;
   And the coffee, fragrant and sweet, and ho!

So hot that we gloried to drink it so,
With spangles of tears in our eyes, you know—
        Out to Old Aunt Mary's.

And the romps we took, in our glad unrest!—
Was it the lawn that we loved the best,
    With its swooping swing in the locust trees,
    Or was it the grove, with its leafy breeze,
    Or the dim haymow, with its fragrancies—
        Out to Old Aunt Mary's.

Far fields, bottom-lands, creek-banks—all,
We ranged at will.—Where the waterfall
    Laughed all day as it slowly poured
    Over the dam by the old mill-ford,
    While the tail-race writhed, and the mill-wheel
        roared—
        Out to Old Aunt Mary's.

But home, with Aunty in nearer call,
That was the best place, after all!—
    The talks on the back porch, in the low
    Slanting sun and the evening glow,
    With the voice of counsel that touched us so,
        Out to Old Aunt Mary's.

And then, in the garden—near the side
Where the beehives were and the path was wide,—
    The apple-house—like a fairy cell—
    With the little square door we knew so well,
    And the wealth inside but our tongues could tell—
        Out to Old Aunt Mary's.

And the old spring-house, in the cool green gloom
Of the willow trees,—and the cooler room
   Where the swinging shelves and the crocks were
      kept,
   Where the cream in a golden languor slept,
   While the waters gurgled and laughed and
      wept—
         Out to Old Aunt Mary's.

And as many a time have you and I—
Barefoot boys in the days gone by—
   Knelt, and in tremulous ecstasies
   Dipped our lips into sweets like these,—
   Memory now is on her knees
         Out to Old Aunt Mary's.—

For, O my brother so far away,
This is to tell you—she waits *to-day*
   To welcome us:—Aunt Mary fell
   Asleep this morning, whispering, "Tell
   The boys to come." . . . And all is well
         Out to Old Aunt Mary's.

IN THE AFTERNOON

YOU in the hammock; and I, near by,
  Was trying to read, and to swing you, too;
And the green of the sward was so kind to the eye,
  And the shade of the maples so cool and blue,
  That often I looked from the book to you
To say as much, with a sigh.

You in the hammock. The book we'd brought
  From the parlor—to read in the open air,—
Something of love and of Launcelot
  And Guinevere, I believe, was there—
  But the afternoon, it was far more fair
Than the poem was, I thought.

You in the hammock; and on and on
  I droned and droned through the rhythmic stuff—
But, with always a half of my vision gone
  Over the top of the page—enough
  To caressingly gaze at you, swathed in the fluff
Of your hair and your odorous "lawn."

You in the hammock—and that was a year—
   Fully a year ago, I guess—
And what do we care for their Guinevere
   And her Launcelot and their lordliness!—
   You in the hammock still, and—Yes—
Kiss me again, my dear!

UNINTERPRETED

SUPINELY we lie in the grove's shady greenery,
  Gazing, all dreamy-eyed, up through the
      trees,—
And as to the sight is the heavenly scenery,
  So to the hearing the sigh of the breeze.

We catch but vague rifts of the blue through the
      wavering
  Boughs of the maples; and, like undefined,
The whispers and lisps of the leaves, faint and
      quavering,
  Meaningless falter and fall on the mind.

The vine, with its beauty of blossom, goes rioting
  Up by the casement, as sweet to the eye
As the trill of the robin is restful and quieting
  Heard in a drowse with the dawn in the sky.

And yet we yearn on to learn more of the mystery—
  We see and we hear, but forever remain
Mute, blind and deaf to the ultimate history
  Born of a rose or a patter of rain.

BILLY'S ALPHABETICAL ANIMAL SHOW

A WAS an elegant Ape
　　Who tied up his ears with red tape,
　　　　And wore a long veil
　　　　Half revealing his tail
Which was trimmed with jet bugles and
　　　　crape.

B was a boastful old Bear
　　Who used to say,—"Hoomh! I declare
　　　　I can eat—if you'll get me
　　　　The children, and let me—
Ten babies, teeth, toe-nails and hair!"

C was a Codfish who sighed
　　When snatched from the home of his
　　　　　pride,
　　　　But could he, embrined,
　　　　Guess this fragrance behind,
How glad he would be to have died!

D was a dandified Dog
　　Who said,—"Though it's raining like a
　　　　frog
　　　　I wear no umbrellah,
　　　　Me boy, for a fellah
Might just as well travel incog!"

158

E was an elderly Eel
  Who would say,—"Well, I really feel—
    As my grandchildren wriggle
    And shout 'I should giggle'—
A trifle run down at the heel!"

F was a Fowl who conceded
  Some hens might hatch more eggs than
    she did,—
    But she'd children as plenty
    As eighteen or twenty,
And that was quite all that she needed.

G was a gluttonous Goat
  Who, dining one day, *table d'hôte,*
    Ordered soup-bone, *au fait,*
    And fish, *papier-mâché,*
And a *filet* of Spring overcoat.

H was a high-cultured Hound
  Who could clear forty feet at a bound,
    And a coon once averred
    That his howl could be heard
For five miles and three-quarters around.

I was an Ibex ambitious
  To dive over chasms auspicious;
    He would leap down a peak
    And not light for a week,
And swear that the jump was delicious.

J was a Jackass who said
He had such a bad cold in his head,
If it wasn't for leaving
The rest of us grieving,
He'd really rather be dead.

K was a profligate Kite
Who would haunt the saloons every night;
And often he ust
To reel back to his roost
Too full to set up on it right.

L was a wary old Lynx
Who would say,—"Do you know wot I
thinks?—
I thinks ef you happen
To ketch me a-nappin'
I'm ready to set up the drinks!"

M was a merry old Mole,
Who would snooze all day in his hole,
Then—all night, a-rootin'
Around and galootin'—
He'd sing "Johnny, Fill up the Bowl!"

N was a caustical Nautilus
Who sneered, "I suppose, when they've
caught all us,
Like oysters they'll serve us,
And can us, preserve us,
And barrel, and pickle, and bottle us!"

O was an autocrat Owl—
  Such a wise—such a wonderful fowl!
    Why, for all the night through
    He would hoot and hoo-hoo,
And hoot and hoo-hooter and howl!

P was a Pelican pet,
  Who gobbled up all he could get;
    He could eat on until
    He was full to the bill,
And there he had lodgings to let!

Q was a querulous Quail,
  Who said: "It will little avail
    The efforts of those
    Of my foes who propose
To attempt to put salt on my tail!"

R was a ring-tailed Raccoon,
  With eyes of the tinge of the moon,
    And his nose a blue-black,
    And the fur on his back
A sad sort of sallow maroon.

S is a Sculpin—you'll wish
  Very much to have one on your dish,
    Since all his bones grow
    On the outside, and so
He's a very desirable fish.

T was a Turtle, of wealth,
  Who went round with particular stealth,
    "Why," said he, "I'm afraid
    Of being waylaid
When I even walk out for my health!"

U was a Unicorn curious,
  With one horn, of a growth so *luxurious,*
    He could level and stab it—
    If you didn't grab it—
Clean through you, he was so blamed
      furious!

V was a vagabond Vulture
  Who said: "I don't want to insult yer,
    But when you intrude
    Where in lone solitude
I'm a-preyin', you're no man o' culture!"

W was a wild *W*oodchuck,
  And you just bet that he *could* "chuck"—
    He'd eat raw potatoes,
    Green corn, and tomatoes,
And tree roots, and call it all *"good* chuck!"

X was a kind of X-cuse
  Of some-sort-o'-thing that got loose
    Before we could name it,
    And cage it, and tame it,
And bring it in general use.

Y is a Yellowbird,—bright
　　As a petrified lump of starlight,
　　　Or a handful of lightning-
　　　Bugs, squeezed in the tight'ning
Pink fist of a boy, at night.

Z is the Zebra, of course!—
　　A kind of a clown-of-a-horse,—
　　　Each other despising,
　　　Yet neither devising
A way to obtain a divorce!

& here is the famous—what-is-it?
　　Walk up, Master Billy, and quiz it:
　　　You've seen the *rest* of 'em—
　　　Ain't this the *best* of 'em,
Right at the end of your visit?

THE PIXY PEOPLE

IT was just a very
   Merry fairy dream!—
All the woods were airy
   With the gloom and gleam;
Crickets in the clover
   Clattered clear and strong,
And the bees droned over
   Their old honey-song!

In the mossy passes,
   Saucy grasshoppers
Leaped about the grasses
   And the thistle-burs;
And the whispered chuckle
   Of the katydid
Shook the honeysuckle-
   Blossoms where he hid.

Through the breezy mazes
   Of the lazy June,
Drowsy with the hazes
   Of the dreamy noon,

Little Pixy people
 Winged above the walk,
Pouring from the steeple
 Of a mullein-stalk.

One—a gallant fellow—
 Evidently King,—
Wore a plume of yellow
 In a jeweled ring
On a pansy bonnet,
 Gold and white and blue,
With the dew still on it,
 And the fragrance, too.

One—a dainty lady,—
 Evidently Queen—
Wore a gown of shady
 Moonshine and green,
With a lace of gleaming
 Starlight that sent
All the dewdrops dreaming
 Everywhere she went.

One wore a waistcoat
 Of rose-leaves, out and in;
And one wore a faced-coat
 Of tiger-lily-skin;
And one wore a neat coat
 Of palest galingale;
And one a tiny street-coat,
 And one a swallow-tail.

And Ho! sang the King of them,
  And Hey! sang the Queen;
And round and round the ring of them
  Went dancing o'er the green;
And Hey! sang the Queen of them,
  And Ho! sang the King—
And all that I had seen of them
  —Wasn't anything!

It was just a very
  Merry fairy dream!—
All the woods were airy
  With the gloom and gleam;
Crickets in the clover
  Clattered clear and strong,
And the bees droned over
  Their old honey-song!

THE TOWN KARNTEEL

THE town Karnteel!—It's who'll reveal
　　Its praises jushtifiable?
For who can sing av anything
　　So lovely and reliable?
Whin Summer, Spring, or Winter lies
　　From Malin's Head to Tipperary,
There's no such town for interprise
　　Bechuxt Youghal and Londonderry!

There's not its likes in Ireland—
　　For twic't the week, be-gorries!
They're playing jigs upon the band,
And joomping there in sacks—and—and—
　　And racing, wid wheelborries!

Karnteel—it's there, like any fair,
　　The purty gurrls is plinty, sure!—
And, man-alive! at forty-five
　　The legs av me air twinty, sure!
I lave me cares, and hoein', too,
　　Behint me, as is sinsible,
And it's Karnteel I'm goin' to,
　　To cilebrate in principle!

167

For there's the town av all the land!
And twic't the week, be-gorries!
They're playing jigs upon the band,
And joomping there in sacks—and—and—
And racing, wid wheelborries!

And whilst I feel for owld Karnteel
That I've no phrases glorious,
It stands above the need av love
That boasts in voice uproarious!—
Lave that for Cork, and Dublin, too,
And Armagh and Killarney, thin,—
And Karnteel won't be troublin' you
Wid any jilous blarney, thin!

For there's the town av all the land!
Where twic't the week, be-gorries!
They're playing jigs upon the band,
And joomping there in sacks—and—and—
And racing, wid wheelborries!

DONN PIATT OF MAC-O-CHEE

I

DONN PIATT—of Mac-o-chee,—
    Not the one of History,
Who, with flaming tongue and pen,
Scathes the vanities of men;
Not the one whose biting wit
Cuts pretense and etches it
On the brazen brow that dares
Filch the laurel that it wears:
Not the Donn Piatt whose praise
Echoes in the noisy ways
Of the faction, onward led
By the statesman!—But, instead,
Give the simple man to me,—
Donn Piatt of Mac-o-chee!

II

Donn Piatt of Mac-o-chee!
Branches of the old oak tree,
Drape him royally in fine
Purple shade and golden shine!
Emerald plush of sloping lawn
Be the throne he sits upon!
And, O Summer Sunset, thou

Be his crown, and gild a brow
Softly smoothed and soothed and calmed
By the breezes, mellow-palmed
As Erata's white hand agleam
On the forehead of a dream.—
So forever rule o'er me,
Donn Piatt of Mac-o-chee!

III

Donn Piatt of Mac-o-chee!
Through a lilied memory
Plays the wayward little creek
Round thy home at hide-and-seek—
As I see and hear it, still
Romping round the wooded hill,
Till its laugh and babble blends
With the silence while it sends
Glances back to kiss the sight,
In its babyish delight,
Ere it strays amid the gloom
Of the glens that burst in bloom
Of the rarest rhyme for thee,
Donn Piatt of Mac-o-chee!

IV

Donn Piatt of Mac-o-chee!
What a darling destiny
Has been mine—to meet him there—
Lolling in an easy chair

On the terrace, while he told
Reminiscences of old—
Letting my cigar die out,
Hearing poems talked about;
And entranced to hear him say
Gentle things of Thackeray,
Dickens, Hawthorne, and the rest,
Known to him as host and guest—
Known to him as he to me—
Donn Piatt of Mac-o-chee!

HERR WEISER

HERR WEISER!—Threescore years and
    ten,—
A hale white rose of his countrymen,
Transplanted here in the Hoosier loam,
And blossomy as his German home—
As blossomy and as pure and sweet
As the cool green glen of his calm retreat,
Far withdrawn from the noisy town
Where trade goes clamoring up and down,
Whose fret and fever, and stress and strife,
May not trouble his tranquil life!

Breath of rest, what a balmy gust!—
Quit of the city's heat and dust,
Jostling down by the winding road,
Through the orchard ways of his quaint abode.—
Tether the horse, as we onward fare
Under the pear trees trailing there,
And thumping the wooden bridge at night
With lumps of ripeness and lush delight,
Till the stream, as it maunders on till dawn,
Is powdered and pelted and smiled upon.

Herr Weiser, with his wholesome face,
And the gentle blue of his eyes, and grace
Of unassuming honesty,
Be there to welcome you and me!
And what though the toil of the farm be stopped
And the tireless plans of the place be dropped,
While the prayerful master's knees are set
In beds of pansy and mignonette
And lily and aster and columbine,
Offered in love, as yours and mine?—

What, but a blessing of kindly thought,
Sweet as the breath of forget-me-not!—
What, but a spirit of lustrous love
White as the aster he bends above!—
What, but an odorous memory
Of the dear old man, made known to me
In days demanding a help like his,—
As sweet as the life of the lily is—
As sweet as the soul of a babe, bloom-wise
Born of a lily in Paradise.

FROM DELPHI TO CAMDEN

I

FROM Delphi to Camden—little Hoosier
      towns,—
But here were classic meadows, blooming dales and
      downs;
And here were grassy pastures, dewy as the leas
Trampled over by the trains of royal pageantries!

And here the winding highway loitered through the
      shade
Of the hazel covert, where, in ambuscade,
Loomed the larch and linden, and the greenwood-
      tree
Under which bold Robin Hood loud hallooed to me!

Here the stir and riot of the busy day
Dwindled to the quiet of the breath of May;
Gurgling brooks, and ridges lily-marged and
      spanned
By the rustic bridges found in Wonderland!

II

From Delphi to Camden,—from Camden back
    again !—
And now the night was on us, and the lightning and
    the rain ;
And still the way was wondrous with the flash of
    hill and plain,—
The stars like printed asterisks—the moon a murky
    stain !

And I thought of tragic idyl, and of flight and hot
    pursuit,
And the jingle of the bridle and cuirass and spur on
    boot,
As our horses' hooves struck showers from the
    flinty boulders set
In freshet-ways of writhing reed and drowning
    violet.

And we passed beleaguered castles, with their
    battlements a-frown ;
Where a tree fell in the forest was a turret toppled
    down ;
While my master and commander—the brave knight
    I galloped with
On this reckless road to ruin or to fame was—Dr.
    Smith !

A NOON INTERVAL

A DEEP, delicious hush in earth and sky—
  A gracious lull—since, from its wakening,
 The morn has been a feverish, restless thing
In which the pulse of Summer ran too high
And riotous, as though its heart went nigh
  To bursting with delights past uttering:
  Now, as an o'erjoyed child may cease to sing
All falteringly at play, with drowsy eye
  Draining the pictures of a fairy tale
To brim his dreams with—there comes o'er the day
  A loathful silence, wherein all sounds fail
Like loitering tones of some faint roundelay . . .
  No wakeful effort longer may avail—
The wand waves, and the dozer sinks away.

Eugene Field, James Whitcomb Riley, Bill Nye

AT MADAME MANICURE'S

DAINTIEST of Manicures!
   What a cunning hand is yours;
And how awkward, rude and great
Mine, as you manipulate!
Wonderfully cool and calm
Are the touches of your palm
To my fingers, as they rest
In their rosy, cozy nest,
While your own, with deftest skill,
Dance and caper as they will,—
Armed with instruments that seem
Gathered from some fairy dream—
Tiny spears. and simitars
Such as pixy armorers
Might have made for jocund fays
To parade on holidays,
And flash round in dewy dells,
Lopping down the lily-bells;
Or in tilting, o'er the leas,
At the clumsy bumblebees,
Splintering their stings perchance
As the knights in old romance
Snapped the spears of foes that fought

In the jousts at Camelot!
Smiling? Dainty Manicure?—
'Twould delight me, but that you're
Simply smiling, as I see,
At my nails and not at me!
Haply this is why they glow
And light up and twinkle so!

JOHN McKEEN

JOHN McKEEN, in his rusty dress,
  His loosened collar, and swarthy throat,
His face unshaven, and none the less,
His hearty laugh and his wholesomeness,
  And the wealth of a workman's vote!

Bring him, O Memory, here once more,
  And tilt him back in his Windsor chair
By the kitchen stove, when the day is o'er
And the light of the hearth is across the floor,
  And the crickets everywhere!

And let their voices be gladly blent
  With a watery jingle of pans and spoons,
And a motherly chirrup of sweet content,
And neighborly gossip and merriment,
  And old-time fiddle-tunes!

Tick the clock with a wooden sound,
  And fill the hearing with childish glee
Of rhyming riddle, or story found
In the Robinson Crusoe, leather-bound
  Old book of the Used-to-be!

John McKeen of the Past! Ah, John,
    To have grown ambitious in worldly ways!—
To have rolled your shirt-sleeves down, to don
A broadcloth suit, and, forgetful, gone
    Out on election days!

John, ah, John! did it prove your worth
    To yield you the office you still maintain?—
To fill your pockets, but leave the dearth
Of all the happier things on earth
    To the hunger of heart and brain?

Under the dusk of your villa trees,
    Edging the drives where your blooded span
Paw the pebbles and wait your ease,—
Where are the children about your knees,
    And the mirth, and the happy man?

The blinds of your mansion are battened to;
    Your faded wife is a close recluse;
And your "finished" daughters will doubtless do
Dutifully all that is willed of you,
    And marry as you shall choose!—

But O for the old-home voices, blent
    With the watery jingle of pans and spoons,
And the motherly chirrup of glad content,
And neighborly gossip and merriment,
    And the old-time fiddle-tunes!

THE BOY-FRIEND

CLARENCE, my boy-friend, hale and strong!
  O he is as jolly as he is young;
And all of the laughs of the lyre belong
  To the boy all unsung:

So I want to sing something in his behalf—
  To clang some chords, for the good it is
To know he is near, and to have the laugh
  Of that wholesome voice of his.

I want to tell him in gentler ways
  Than prose may do, that the arms of rhyme,
Warm and tender with tuneful praise,
  Are about him all the time.

I want him to know that the quietest nights
  We have passed together are yet with me,
Roistering over the old delights
  That were born of his company.

I want him to know how my soul esteems
  The fairy stories of Andersen,
And the glad translations of all the themes
  Of the hearts of boyish men.

Want him to know that my fancy flows,
 With the lilt of a dear old-fashioned tune,
Through "Lewis Carroll's" poemly prose,
 And the tale of "The Bold Dragoon."

O this is the Prince that I would sing—
 Would drape and garnish in velvet line,
Since courtlier far than any king
 Is this brave boy-friend of mine.

WHEN BESSIE DIED

"If from your own the dimpled hands had slipped,
And ne'er would nestle in your palm again;
If the white feet into the grave had tripped"——

WHEN Bessie died—
    We braided the brown hair, and tied
It just as her own little hands
Had fastened back the silken strands
A thousand times—the crimson bit
Of ribbon woven into it
That she had worn with childish pride—
Smoothed down the dainty bow—and cried—
        When Bessie died.

When Bessie died—
We drew the nursery blinds aside,
And, as the morning in the room
Burst like a primrose into bloom,
Her pet canary's cage we hung
Where she might hear him when he sung—
And yet not any note he tried
Though she lay listening folded-eyed.

When Bessie died—
We writhed in prayer unsatisfied:
We begged of God, and He did smile
In silence on us all the while;
And we did see Him, through our tears,
Enfolding that fair form of hers,
She laughing back against His love
The kisses we had nothing of—
And death to us He still denied,
When Bessie died—
            When Bessie died.

THE RIVALS; OR THE SHOWMAN'S RUSE

A TRAGI-COMEDY, IN ONE ACT

PERSONS REPRESENTED

BILLY MILLER ⎱
JOHNNY WILLIAMS ⎰   The Rivals

TOMMY WELLS   Conspirator

TIME—Noon. SCENE—Country Town—*Rear view
of the* Miller Mansion, *showing Barn, with
practical loft-window opening on alley-way,
with colored-crayon poster on wall beneath, an-
nouncing:*—"BILLY MILLER'S Big Show and
Monstur Circus and Equareum! A shour-bath
fer Each and All fer 20 pins. This Afternoon!
Don't fer git the Date!" *Enter* TOMMY WELLS
and JOHNNY WILLIAMS, *who gaze a while at
poster,* TOMMY *secretly smiling and winking at*
BILLY MILLER, *concealed at loft-window above.*

TOMMY [*To* JOHNNY]

Guess 'at Billy hain't got back,—
Can't see nothin' through the crack—
Can't hear nothin' neether—No!
. . . Thinks he's got the dandy show,
Don't he?

185

JOHNNY [*Scornfully*]

'Course! but what *I* care?—
He hain't got no show in there!—
What's *he* got in there but that
Old hen, cooped up with a cat
An' a turkle, an' that thing
'At he calls his "circus-ring"?
What a "circus-ring"! I'd *quit!*
Bet *mine's* twic't as big as it!

TOMMY

Yes, but *you* got no machine
W'at you bathe with, painted green,
With a string to work it, guess!

JOHNNY [*Contemptuously*]

Folks don't *bathe* in *circuses!*—
Ladies comes to *mine,* you bet!
I' got seats where *girls* can set;
An' a dressin'-room, an' all,
Fixed up in my pony's stall—
Yes, an' I got *carpet,* too,
Fer the tumblers, an' a blue
Center-pole!

TOMMY

Well, Billy, he's
Got a tight-rope an' trapeze,

An' a hoop 'at he jumps through
Head-first!

JOHNNY

    Well, what's *that* to do—
Lightin' on a pile o' hay?
Hain't no *actin'* thataway!

TOMMY

Don't care what you say, he draws
Bigger crowds than you do, 'cause
Sence he started up, I know
All the fellers says his show
Is the best-un!

JOHNNY

    Yes, an' he
Better not tell things on me!
His old circus hain't no good!—
'Cause he's got the neighborhood
Down on me he thinks 'at I'm
Goin' to stand it all the time;
Thinks ist 'cause my Pa don't 'low
Me to fight, he's got me now,
An' can say I lie, an' call
Me ist anything at all!
Billy Miller thinks I am
'Feard to say 'at he says *"dam"*—
Yes, an' *worser* ones! an' I'm

Goin' to tell his folks sometime!—
An' ef he don't shet his head
I'll tell worse 'an *that* he said
When he fighted Willie King—
An' got licked like ever'thing!—
Billy Miller better shin
Down his Daddy's lane ag'in,
Like a cowardy-calf, an' climb
In fer home another time!
Better—

[*Here* BILLY *leaps down from the loft upon his un-
suspecting victim; and two minutes later,*
JOHNNY, *with the half of a straw hat, a bleeding nose, and a straight rent across one trou-
sers-knee, makes his inglorious—exit.*]

THE CHRIST.

"FATHER!" (so The Word) He cried,—
　　"Son of Thine, and yet denied;
By my brothers dragged and tried,
Scoffed and scourged, and crucified,
With a thief on either side—
Brothers mine, alike belied,—
Arms of mercy open wide,
Father! Father!" So He died.

TO HEAR HER SING

To hear her sing—to hear her sing—
It is to hear the birds of Spring
In dewy groves on blooming sprays
Pour out their blithest roundelays.

It is to hear the robin trill
At morning, or the whippoorwill
At dusk, when stars are blossoming—
To hear her sing—to hear her sing!

To hear her sing—it is to hear
The laugh of childhood ringing clear
In woody path or grassy lane
Our feet may never fare again.

Faint, far away as Memory dwells,
It is to hear the village bells
At twilight, as the truant hears
Them, hastening home, with smiles and tears.

Such joy it is to hear her sing,
We fall in love with everything—
The simple things of every day
Grow lovelier than words can say.

The idle brooks that purl across
The gleaming pebbles and the moss
We love no less than classic streams—
The Rhines and Arnos of our dreams.

To hear her sing—with folded eyes,
It is, beneath Venetian skies,
To hear the gondoliers' refrain,
Or troubadours of sunny Spain.—

To hear the bulbul's voice that shook
The throat that trilled for Lalla Rookh:
What wonder we in homage bring
Our hearts to her—to hear her sing!

FROM THE HEADBOARD OF A GRAVE
IN PARAGUAY

A TROTH, and a grief, and a blessing,
   Disguised them and came this way,—
And one was a promise, and one was a doubt,
   And one was a rainy day.

And they met betimes with this maiden,—
   And the promise it spake and lied,
And the doubt it gibbered and hugged itself,
   And the rainy day—she died.

A CANARY AT THE FARM

FOLKS has be'n to town, and Sahry
   Fetched 'er home a pet canary,—
And of all the blame', contrary,
    Aggervatin' things alive!
I love music—that's I love it
When it's *free*—and plenty of it;—
But I kind o' git above it,
    At a dollar-eighty-five!

Reason's plain as I'm a-sayin',—
Jes' the idy, now, o' layin'
Out yer money, and a-payin'
    Fer a willer-cage and bird,
When the medder-larks is wingin'
Round you, and the woods is ringin'
With the beautifullest singin'
    That a mortal ever heard!

Sahry's sot, tho'.—So I tell her
He's a purty little feller,
With his wings o' creamy-yeller,
    And his eyes keen as a cat;

193

And the twitter o' the critter
'Pears to absolutely glitter!
Guess I'll haf to go and git her
    A high-priceter cage 'n that!

SEPTEMBER DARK

I

THE air falls chill;
    The whippoorwill
Pipes lonesomely behind the hill:
The dusk grows dense,
The silence tense;
And, lo, the katydids commence.

II

Through shadowy rifts
Of woodland, lifts
The low, slow moon, and upward drifts,
While left and right
The fireflies' light
Swirls eddying in the skirts of Night.

III

O Cloudland, gray
And level, lay
Thy mists across the face of Day!
At foot and head,
Above the dead,
O Dews, weep on uncomforted!

ANSELMO

YEARS did I vainly seek the good Lord's
      grace,—
  Prayed, fasted, and did penance dire and dread;
Did kneel, with bleeding knees and rainy face,
  And mouth the dust, with ashes on my head;
Yea, still with knotted scourge the flesh I flayed,
  Rent fresh the wounds, and moaned and shrieked
     insanely;
And froth oozed with the pleadings that I made,
  And yet I prayed on vainly, vainly, vainly!

A time, from out of swoon I lifted eye,
  To find a wretched outcast, gray and grim,
Bathing my brow, with many a pitying sigh,
  And I did pray God's grace might rest on him.—
Then, lo! a gentle voice fell on mine ears—
  "Thou shalt not sob in suppliance hereafter;
Take up thy prayers and wring them dry of tears,
  And lift them, white and pure with love and
     laughter!"

    So is it now for all men else I pray;
    So is it I am blest and glad alway.

TIME OF CLEARER TWITTERINGS

I

TIME of crisp and tawny leaves,
  And of tarnished harvest sheaves,
And of dusty grasses—weeds—
Thistles, with their tufted seeds
Voyaging the Autumn breeze
Like as fairy argosies:
Time of quicker flash of wings,
And of clearer twitterings
In the grove or deeper shade
Of the tangled everglade,—
Where the spotted water-snake
Coils him in the sunniest brake;
And the bittern, as in fright,
Darts, in sudden, slanting flight,
Southward, while the startled crane
Films his eyes in dreams again.

II

Down along the dwindled creek
We go loitering. We speak
Only with old questionings
Of the dear remembered things

Of the days of long ago,
When the stream seemed thus and so
In our boyish eyes:—The bank
Greener then, through rank on rank
Of the mottled sycamores,
Touching tops across the shores:
Here, the hazel thicket stood—
There, the almost pathless wood
Where the shellbark hickory tree
Rained its wealth on you and me.
Autumn! as you loved us then,
Take us to your heart again!

III

Season halest of the year!
How the zestful atmosphere
Nettles blood and brain and smites
Into life the old delights
We have wasted in our youth,
And our graver years, forsooth!
How again the boyish heart
Leaps to see the chipmunk start
From the brush and sleek the sun's
Very beauty, as he runs!
How again a subtle hint
Of crushed pennyroyal or mint
Sends us on our knees, as when
We were truant boys of ten—
Brown marauders of the wood,
Merrier than Robin Hood!

VI

Ah! will any minstrel say,
In his sweetest roundelay,
What is sweeter, after all,
Than black haws, in early Fall?—
Fruit so sweet the frost first sat,
Dainty-toothed, and nibbled at!
And will any poet sing
Of a lusher, richer thing
Than a ripe May-apple, rolled
Like a pulpy lump of gold
Under thumb and finger-tips,
And poured molten through the lips?
Go, ye bards of classic themes,
Pipe your songs by classic streams!
I would twang the redbird's wings
In the thicket while he sings!

THE BOYS

WHERE are they?—the friends of my child-
        hood enchanted—
The clear, laughing eyes looking back in my own,
And the warm, chubby fingers my palms have so
        wanted,
        As when we raced over
                Pink pastures of clover,
And mocked the quail's whir and the bumblebee's
        drone?

Have the breezes of time blown their blossomy faces
        Forever adrift down the years that are flown?
Am I never to see them romp back to their places,
        Where over the meadow,
                In sunshine and shadow,
The meadow-larks trill, and the bumblebees drone?

Where are they? Ah! dim in the dust lies the clover;
        The whippoorwill's call has a sorrowful tone,
And the dove's—I have wept at it over and over;—
        I want the glad luster
                Of youth, and the cluster
Of faces asleep where the bumblebees drone!

LINCOLN

A PEACEFUL life;—just toil and rest—
   All his desire;—
To read the books he liked the best
   Beside the cabin fire—
God's word and man's;—to peer sometimes
   Above the page, in smoldering gleams,
And catch, like far heroic rhymes,
   The on-march of his dreams.

A peaceful life;—to hear the low
   Of pastured herds,
Or woodman's ax that, blow on blow,
   Fell sweet as rhythmic words.
And yet there stirred within his breast
   A fateful pulse that, like a roll
Of drums, made high above his rest
   A tumult in his soul.

A peaceful life! . . . They haled him even
   As One was haled
Whose open palms were nailed toward Heaven
   When prayers nor aught availed.

And, lo, he paid the selfsame price
  To lull a nation's awful strife
And will us, through the sacrifice
  Of self, his peaceful life.

THE BLIND GIRL

IF I might see his face to-day!—
   He is so happy now!—To hear
His laugh is like a roundelay—
   So ringing-sweet and clear!
His step—I heard it long before
He bounded through the open door
To tell his marriage.—Ah! so kind—
So good he is!—And I—so blind!

But thus he always came to me—
   Me, first of all, he used to bring
His sorrow to—his ecstasy—
   His hopes and everything;
And if I joyed with him or wept,
It was not long *the music* slept,—
And if he sung, or if I played—
Or both,—we were the braver made.

I grew to know and understand
   His every word at every call,—
The gate-latch hinted, and his hand
   In mine confessed it all:

He need not speak one word to me—
He need not sigh—I need not see,—
But just the one touch of his palm,
And I would answer—song or psalm.

He wanted recognition—name—
   He hungered so for higher things,—
The altitudes of power and fame,
   And all that fortune brings:
Till, with his great heart fevered thus,
And aching as impetuous,
I almost wished sometimes that *he*
Were blind and patient made, like me.

But he has won!—I knew he would.—
   Once in the mighty Eastern mart,
I knew his music only could
   Be sung in every heart!
And when he proudly sent me this
From out the great metropolis,
I bent above the graven score
And, weeping, kissed it o'er and o'er.—

And yet not blither sing the birds
   Than this glad melody,—the tune
As sweetly wedded with the words
   As flowers with middle-June;
Had he not *told* me, I had known
It was composed of love alone—
His love for *her*.—And she can see
His happy face eternally!—

While *I*—O God, forgive, I pray!—
  Forgive me that I did so long
To look upon his face to-day!—
  I know the wish was wrong.—
Yea, I am thankful that my sight
Is shielded safe from such delight:—
I can pray better, with this blur
Of blindness—both for him and her.

THE KING

THEY rode right out of the morning sun—
    A glimmering, glittering cavalcade
Of knights and ladies, and every one
       In princely sheen arrayed;
And the king of them all, O he rode ahead,
With a helmet of gold, and a plume of red
That spurted about in the breeze and bled
       In the bloom of the everglade.

And they rode high over the dewy lawn,
    With brave, glad banners of every hue
That rolled in ripples, as they rode on
       In splendor, two and two;
And the tinkling links of the golden reins
Of the steeds they rode rang such refrains
As the castanets in a dream of Spain's
       Intensest gold and blue.

And they rode and rode; and the steeds they neighed
    And pranced, and the sun on their glossy hides
Flickered and lightened and glanced and played
       Like the moon on rippling tides;

And their manes were silken, and thick and
    strong,
And their tails were flossy, and fetlock-long,
And jostled in time to the teeming throng,
    And their knightly song besides.

Clank of scabbard and jingle of spur,
    And the fluttering sash of the queen went wild
In the wind, and the proud king glanced at her
    As one at a wilful child,—
And as knight and lady away they flew,
And the banners flapped, and the falcon, too,
And the lances flashed and the bugle blew,
    He kissed his hand and smiled.—

And then, like a slanting sunlit shower,
    The pageant glittered across the plain,
And the turf spun back, and the wild-weed flower
    Was only a crimson stain.
And a dreamer's eyes they are downward cast,
As he blends these words with the wailing blast:
"It is the King of the Year rides past!"
    And Autumn is here again.

A LIZ-TOWN HUMORIST

SETTIN' round the stove, last night,
Down at Wess's store, was me
And Mart Strimples, Tunk, and White,
And Doc Bills, and two er three
Fellers o' the Mudsock tribe
No use tryin' to describe!
And says Doc, he says, says he,—
"Talkin' 'bout good things to eat,
Ripe mushmillon's hard to beat!"

I chawed on. And Mart he 'lowed
Wortermillon beat the mush.—
"Red," he says, "and juicy—Hush!—
I'll jes' leave it to the crowd!"
Then a Mudsock chap, says he,—
"Punkin's good enough fer me—
Punkin pies, I mean," he says,—
"Them beats millons!—What say, Wess?"

I chawed on. And Wess says,—"Well,
You jes' fetch that wife of mine
All yer wortermillon-*rine,*—
And she'll bile it down a spell—

In with sorghum, I suppose,
And what else, Lord only knows!—
But I'm here to tell all hands
Them p'serves meets my demands!"

I chawed on. And White he says,—
"Well, I'll jes' stand in with Wess—
I'm no hog!" And Tunk says,—"I
Guess I'll pastur' out on pie
With the Mudsock boys!" says he;
"Now what's yourn?" he says to me:
I chawed on—fer—quite a spell—
Then I speaks up, slow and dry,—
"Jes' tobacker!" I-says-I.—
And you'd ort o' heerd 'em yell!

LIKE HIS MOTHER USED TO MAKE

"Uncle Jake's Place," St. Jo, Missouri, 1874.

"I WAS born in Indiany," says a stranger, lank
    and slim,
As us fellers in the restarunt was kind o' guyin'
    him,
And Uncle Jake was slidin' him another punkin pie
And a' extry cup o' coffee, with a twinkle in his
    eye,—
"I was born in Indiany—more'n forty year' ago—
And I hain't be'n back in twenty—and I'm workin'
    back'ards slow ;
But I've et in ever' restarunt 'twixt here and Santy
    Fee,
And I want to state this coffee tastes like gittin'
    home, to me !

"Pour us out another, Daddy," says the feller,
    warmin' up,
A-speakin' 'crost a saucerful, as Uncle tuk his cup,—
"When I seed yer sign out yander," he went on, to
    Uncle Jake,—
" 'Come in and git some coffee like yer mother used
    to make'—

I thought of *my* old mother, and the Posey County
    farm,
And me a little kid ag'in, a-hangin' in her arm,
As she set the pot a-bilin', broke the eggs and
    poured 'em in"—
And the feller kind o' halted, with a trimble in his
    chin:

And Uncle Jake he fetched the feller's coffee back,
    and stood
As solemn, fer a minute, as a' undertaker would;
Then he sort o' turned and tiptoed to'rds the kitchen
    door—and nex',
Here comes his old wife out with him, a-rubbin' of
    her specs—
And she rushes fer the stranger, and she hollers out,
    "It's him!—
Thank God we've met him comin'!—Don't you
    know yer mother, Jim?"
And the feller, as he grabbed her, says,—"You bet I
    hain't forgot—
But," wipin' of his eyes, says he, "yer coffee's
    mighty hot!"

A GOLDEN WEDDING

DECEMBER—1884

YOUR Golden Wedding!—fifty years
   Of comradeship, through smiles and tears!
Through summer sun, and winter sleet,
You walked the ways with willing feet;
For, journeying together thus,
Each path held something glorious.
No winter wind could blow so chill
But found you even warmer still
In fervor of affection—blest
In knowing all was for the best;
And so, content, you faced the storm
And fared on, smiling, arm in arm.

But why this moralizing strain
Beside a hearth that glows again
As on your *Wooden* wedding-day?—
When butter-prints and paddles lay
Around in dough-bowls, tubs and churns,
And all such "woodenish" concerns;
And "woodenish" they are—for now
Who can afford to keep a cow

212

And pestle some old churn, when you
Can buy good butter—"golden," too—
Far cheaper than you can afford
To make it and neglect the Lord!

And round your hearth the faces gleam
That may recall, as in a dream,
The brightness of a time when *Tin*
Came glittering and clanging in
And raising noise enough to seize
And settle any swarm of bees!
But those were darling times, no doubt,—
To see the mother pouring out
The "tins" of milk, and tilting up
The coffee-pot above each cup;
Or, with the ladle from the wall,
Dipping and serving mush for all.

And *all* the "weddings," as they came,—
The *"Glass,"* the *"China,"*—still the same
You see them, till the last ere this,—
The *"Silver,"*—and your wedded bliss
Abated not!—for love appears
Just silvered over with the years:—
Silver the grandchild's laugh you hear—
Silver his hopes, and silver-clear
Your every prayer for him,—and still
Silver your hope, through good and ill—
Silver and silver everywhere,
Bright as the silver of your hair!

But on your *Golden* Wedding!—Nay—
What can I give to you to-day
Who am too very poor indeed
To offer what I so much need?
If gold I gave, I fear, alack!
I'd needs provide you gave it back,
To stay me, the long years before
I'd stacked and heaped five dollars more!
And so, in lieu—and little worse—
I proffer you this dross of verse—
The merest tinsel, I admit,—
But take it—I have more of it.

HIS CHRISTMAS SLED

I

I WATCH him with his Christmas sled;
    He hitches on behind
A passing sleigh, with glad hooray,
    And whistles down the wind;
He hears the horses champ their bits,
    And bells that jingle-jingle—
You Woolly Cap! you Scarlet Mitts!
    You miniature "Kriss Kringle"!

I almost catch your secret joy—
    Your chucklings of delight,
The while you whiz where glory is
    Eternally in sight!
With you I catch my breath, as swift
    Your jaunty sled goes gliding
O'er glassy track and shallow drift,
    As I behind were riding!

II

He winks at twinklings of the frost,
    And on his airy race,
Its tingles beat to redder heat
    The rapture of his face:—

The colder, keener is the air,
  The less he cares a feather.
But, there! he's gone! and I gaze on
  The wintriest of weather!

Ah, Boy! still speeding o'er the track
  Where none returns again,
To sigh for you, or cry for you,
  Or die for you were vain.—
And so, speed on! the while I pray
  All nipping frosts forsake you—
Ride still ahead of grief, but may
  All glad things overtake you!

A NEW YEAR'S TIME AT WILLARDS'S

I

THE HIRED MAN TALKS

THERE'S old man Willards; an' his wife;
 An' Marg'et—S'repty's sister;—an'
There's me—an' I'm the hired man;
An' Tomps McClure, you bet yer life!

Well, now, old Willards hain't so bad,
Considerin' the chance he's had.
Of course, he's rich, an' sleeps an' eats
 Whenever he's a mind to: Takes
An' leans back in the Amen-seats
 An' thanks the Lord fer all he makes.—
That's purty much all folks has got
Ag'inst the old man, like as not!
But there's his woman—jes' the turn
Of them-air two wild girls o' hern—
 Marg'et an' S'repty—allus in
Fer any cuttin'-up concern—
 Church festibals, an' foolishin'

Round Christmas-trees, an' New Year's sprees—
   Set up to watch the Old Year go
An' New Year come—sich things as these;
   An' turkey-dinners, don't you know!
S'repty's younger, an' more gay,
   An' purtier, an' finer dressed
   Than Marg'et is—but, lawsy-day!
   She hain't the independentest!—
"Take care!" old Willards used to say,
"Take care!—Let Marg'et have her way,
An' S'repty, you go off an' play
On your melodeum!"—But, best
   Of all, comes Tomps! An' I'll be bound,
Ef he hain't jes' the beatin'est
   Young chap in all the country round!
     Ef you know Tomps you'd like him, shore!
   They hain't no man on top o' ground
     Walks into my affections more!—
An' all the Settlement'll say
That Tomps was liked jes' thataway
   By ever'body, till he tuk
     A shine to S'repty Willards.—Then
   You'd ort 'o see the old man buck
An' h'ist hisse'f, an' paw the dirt,
     An' hint that "common workin'-men
That didn't want their feelin's hurt
     'Ud better hunt fer 'comp'ny' where
     The folks was pore an' didn't care!"—
The pine-blank facts is,—the old man,
   Last Christmas was a year ago,

Found out some *presents* Tomps had got
  Fer S'repty, an' hit made him hot—
Set down an' tuk his pen in hand
  An' writ to Tomps an' told him so
  On legal cap, in white an' black,
An' give him jes' to understand
  "No Christmas-gifts o' 'lily-white'
  An' bear's-ile could fix matters right,"
    An' wropped 'em up an' sent 'em back!
Well, S'repty cried an' snuffled round
  Consid'able. But Marg'et she
Toed out another sock, an' wound
  Her knittin' up, an' drawed the tea,
  An' then set on the supper-things,
An' went up in the loft an' dressed—
An' through it all you'd never guessed
  What she was up to! An' she brings
Her best hat with her an' her shawl,
An' gloves, an' redicule, an' all,
An' injirubbers, an' comes down
An' tells 'em she's a-goin' to town
  To he'p the Christmas goin's-on
Her Church got up. An' go she does—
The best hosswoman ever was!
"An' what'll WE do while you're gone?"
The old man says, a-tryin' to be
Agreeable. "Oh! *you?*" says she,—
"*You* kin jaw S'repty, like you did,
An' slander Tomps!" An' off she rid!

Now, this is all *I'm* goin' to tell
    Of this-here story—that is, I
        Have done my very level best
As fur as this, an' here I "dwell,"
    As auctioneers says, winkin' sly:
        Hit's old man Willards tells the rest.

II

THE OLD MAN TALKS

Adzackly jes' one year ago,
    This New Year's day, Tomps comes to me—
        In my own house, an' whilse the folks
        Was gittin' dinner,—an' he pokes
His nose right in, an' says, says he:
"I got yer note—an' read it *slow!*
    You don't like *me,* ner I don't *you,*"
He says,—"we're even there, you know!
    But you've said, furder, that no gal
    Of yourn kin marry me, er shall,
An' I'd best shet off *comin',* too!"
An' then he says,—"Well, them's YOUR views;—
    But, havin' talked with S'repty, *we*
    Have both agreed to disagree
With your peculiar notions—some;
An', *that's* the reason, I refuse
    To quit a-comin' here, but come—
    Not fer to threat, ner raise no skeer
    An' spile yer turkey-dinner here,—
But, jes' fer *S'repty's* sake, to sheer
    Yer New Year's. Shall I take a cheer?"

Well, blame-don! ef I ever see
  Sich impidence! I couldn't say
Not nary word! But Mother she
  Sot out a cheer fer Tomps, an' they
Shuk hands an' turnt their back on me.
Then I riz—mad as mad could be!—
  But Marg'et says,—"Now, Pap! you set
  Right where you're settin'!—Don't you fret!
An', Tomps—*you* warm yer feet!" says she,
  "An' throw yer mitts an' comfert on
The bed there! Where is S'repty gone?—
  The cabbage is a-scortchin'! Ma,
  Stop cryin' there an' stir the slaw!"
Well!—what was *Mother cryin'* fer?—
  I half riz up—but Marg'et's chin
  Hit squared—an' I set down ag'in—
I allus *was* afeard o' her,
I was, by jucks! So there I set,
Betwixt a sinkin'-chill an' sweat,
An' scuffled with my wrath, an' shet
My teeth to mighty tight, you bet!
  An' yit, fer all that I could do,
I *eeched* to jes' git up an' whet
  The carvin'-knife a rasp er two
  On Tomps's ribs—an' so would you!—
Fer he had riz an' faced around,
  An' stood there, smilin', as they brung
The turkey in, all stuffed an' browned—
  Too sweet fer nose er tooth er tongue!
    With sniffs o' sage, an' p'r'aps a dash

Of old burnt brandy, steamin'-hot,
    Mixed kind o' in with apple-mash
An' mince-meat, an' the Lord knows what!
Nobody was a-talkin' then,
    To 'filiate my awk'ardness—
    No noise o' any kind but jes'
The rattle o' the dishes when
They'd fetch 'em in an' set 'em down,
An' fix an' change 'em round an' round,
    Like women does—till Mother says,—
"Vittels is ready; Abner, call
    Down S'repty—she's up-stairs, I guess."—
And Marg'et *she* says, "Ef you bawl
Like that, she'll not come down at all!
Besides, we needn't wait till *she*
Gits down! Here, Tomps, set down by me,
    An' Pap: say grace!" . . . Well, there I was!—
What *could* I do! I drapped my head
Behind my fists an' groaned, an' said:—
    "Indulgent Parent! in Thy cause
    We bow the head an' bend the knee,
An' break the bread, an' pour the wine,
    Feelin' "—(The stair-door suddenly
    Went bang! an' S'repty flounced by me)—
"Feelin'," I says, "this feast is Thine—
    This New Year's feast"—an' *rap-rap-rap!*
    Went Marg'et's case-knife on her plate—
    An' next, I heerd a sasser drap,—
    Then I looked up, an', strange to state,
There S'repty set in Tomps's lap—
    An' huggin' him, as shore as fate!

An' Mother kissin' him k-slap!—
An' Marg'et—she chips in to drap
  The ruther peert remark to me:—
    "That 'grace' o' yourn," she says, "won't 'gee'—
This hain't no *'New Year's* feast,'" says she,—
"This is a' INFAIR-Dinner, Pap!"

An' so it was!—be'n married fer
Purt' nigh a week!—'Twas Marg'et planned
    The whole thing fer 'em, through an'
      through
  I'm rickonciled; an', understand,
I take things jes' as they occur,—
    Ef *Marg'et* liked Tomps, Tomps 'ud do!—
But I-says-I, a-holt his hand,—
  "I'm glad you didn't marry HER—
'Cause *Marg'et's* my *guardeen*—yes-*sir!*—
    An' S'repty's good enough fer you!"

WHATEVER THE WEATHER MAY BE

"WHATEVER the weather may be," says
he—
"Whatever the weather may be,
It's plaze, if ye will, an' I'll say me say,—
Supposin' to-day was the winterest day,
Wud the weather be changing because ye cried,
Or the snow be grass were ye crucified?
The best is to make yer own summer," says he,
"Whatever the weather may be," says he—
"Whatever the weather may be!

"Whatever the weather may be," says he—
"Whatever the weather may be,
It's the songs ye sing, an' the smiles ye wear,
That's a-makin' the sun shine everywhere;
An' the world of gloom is a world of glee,
Wid the bird in the bush, an' the bud in the tree,
An' the fruit on the stim o' the bough," says he,
"Whatever the weather may be," says he—
"Whatever the weather may be!

"Whatever the weather may be," says he—
  "Whatever the weather may be,
Ye can bring the Spring, wid its green an' gold,
An' the grass in the grove where the snow lies cold;
An' ye'll warm yer back, wid a smiling face,
As ye sit at yer heart, like an owld fireplace,
An' toast the toes o' yer sowl," says he,
"Whatever the weather may be," says he—
  "Whatever the weather may be!"

A LEAVE-TAKING

SHE will not smile;
  She will not stir;
I marvel while
  I look on her.
    The lips are chilly
      And will not speak;
    The ghost of a lily
      In either cheek.

Her hair—ah me!
  Her hair—her hair!
How helplessly
  My hands go there!
    But my caresses
      Meet not hers,
    O golden tresses
      That thread my tears!

I kiss the eyes
  On either lid,
Where her love lies
  Forever hid.
    I cease my weeping
      And smile and say:
    I will be sleeping
      Thus, some day!

DOWN ON WRIGGLE CRICK

Best time to kill a hog's when he's fat
        —OLD SAW

MOSTLY, folks is law-abidin'
        Down on Wriggle Crick,—
Seein' they's no Squire residin'
    In our bailywick;
No grand juries, no suppeenies,
    Ner no vested rights to pick
Out yer man, jerk up and jail ef
    He's outragin' Wriggle Crick!

Wriggle Crick hain't got no lawin',
    Ner no suits to beat;
Ner no court-house gee-and-hawin'
    Like a County-seat;
Hain't no waitin' round fer verdicks,
    Ner non-gittin' witness-fees;
Ner no thiefs 'at gits "new hearin's,"
    By some lawyer slick as grease!

Wriggle Crick's leadin' spirit
    Is old Johnts Culwell,—
Keeps post-office, and right near it
    Owns what's called "The Grand Hotel"—

(Warehouse now)—buys wheat and ships it;
　　Gits out ties, and trades in stock,
And knows all the high-toned drummers
　　'Twixt South Bend and Mishawauk.

Last year comes along a feller—
　　Sharper 'an a lance—
Stovepipe-hat and silk umbreller,
　　And a boughten all-wool pants,—
Tinkerin' of clocks and watches;
　　Says a trial's all he wants—
And rents out the tavern-office
　　Next to Uncle Johnts.

Well.—He tacked up his k'dentials,
　　And got down to biz.—
Captured Johnts by cuttin' stenchils
　　Fer them old wheat-sacks o' his.—
Fixed his clock, in the post-office—
　　Painted fer him, clean and slick,
'Crost his safe, in gold-leaf letters,
　　"J. Culwells's, Wriggle Crick."

Any kind o' job you keered to
　　Resk him with, and bring,
He'd fix fer you—jes' appeared to
　　Turn his hand to anything!—
Rings, er earbobs, er umbrellers—
　　Glue a cheer er chany doll,—
W'y, of all the beatin' fellers,
　　He jes' beat 'em all!

Made his friends, but wouldn't stop there,—
   One mistake he learnt,
That was, sleepin' in his shop there.—
   And one Sund'y night it burnt!
Come in one o' jes' a-sweepin'
   All the whole town high and dry—
And that feller, when they waked him,
   Suffocatin', mighty nigh!

Johnts he drug him from the buildin',
   He'pless—*'peared* to be,—
And the women and the childern
   Drenchin' him with sympathy!
But I noticed Johnts helt on him
   With a' extry lovin' grip,
And the men-folks gathered round him
   In most warmest pardnership!

That's the whole mess, grease-and-dopin'!
   Johnts's safe was saved,—
But the lock was found sprung open,
   And the inside caved.
Was no trial—ner no jury—
   Ner no jedge ner court-house-click.—
Circumstances alters cases
   Down on Wriggle Crick!

LORD BACON

WRITTEN AS A JOKE AND ASCRIBED TO A VERY PRAC-
TICAL BUSINESS MAN, AMOS J. WALKER

MASTER of masters in the days of yore,
  When art met insult, with no law's redress;
When Law itself insulted Righteousness,
And Ignorance thine own scholastic lore,
And thou thine own judicial office more,—
  What master living now canst love thee less,
  Seeing thou didst thy greatest art repress
And leave the years its riches to restore
To us, thy long neglectors. Yield us grace
  To make becoming recompense, and dawn
On us thy poet-smile; nor let us trace,
  In fancy, where the old-world myths have gone,
The shade of Shakespeare, with averted face,
  Withdrawn to uttermost oblivion.

230

MY FIRST WOMERN

I BURIED my first womern
  In the spring; and in the fall
I was married to my second,
  And hain't settled yit at all!—
Fer I'm allus thinkin'—thinkin'
  Of the first one's peaceful ways,
A-bilin' soap and singin'
  Of the Lord's amazin' grace.

And I'm thinkin' of her, constant,
  Dyin' carpet-chain and stuff,
And a-makin' up rag carpets,
  When the *floor* was good enough!
And I mind her he'p a-feedin'
  And I riccollect her now
A-drappin' corn, and keepin'
  Clos't behind me and the plow!

And I'm allus thinkin' of her
  Reddin' up around the house;
Er cookin' fer the farm-hands;
  Er a-drivin' up the cows.—

And there she lays out yonder
  By the lower medder fence,
Where the cows was barely grazin',
  And they're usin' ever sence.

And when I look acrost there—
  Say it's when the clover's ripe,
And I'm settin', in the evenin',
  On the porch here, with my pipe,
And the *other'n* hollers "Henry!"—
  W'y they ain't no sadder thing
Than to think of my first womern
  And her funeral last spring
    Was a year ago—

THE QUEST

I AM looking for Love.   Has he passed this way,
With eyes as blue as the skies of May,
And a face as fair as the summer dawn?—
You answer back, but I wander on,—
For you say: "Oh, yes; but his eyes were gray,
And his face as dim as a rainy day."

Good friends, I query, I search for Love;
His eyes are as blue as the skies above,
And his smile as bright as the midst of May
When the truce-bird pipes: Has he passed this way?
And one says: "Ay; but his face, alack!
Frowned as he passed, and his eyes were black."

O who will tell me of Love? I cry!
His eyes are as blue as the mid-May sky,
And his face as bright as the morning sun;
And you answer and mock me, every one,
That his eyes were dark, and his face was wan,
And he passed you frowning and wandered on.

But stout of heart will I onward fare,
Knowing *my* Love is beyond—somewhere,—
The Love I seek, with the eyes of blue,
And the bright, sweet smile unknown of you;
And on from the hour his trail is found
I shall sing sonnets the whole year round.

TO AN IMPORTUNATE GHOST

GET gone, thou most uncomfortable ghost!
Thou really dost annoy me with thy thin
    Impalpable transparency of grin;
And the vague, shadowy shape of thee almost
Hath vexed me beyond boundary and coast
    Of my broad patience. Stay thy chattering chin,
    And reel the tauntings of thy vain tongue in,
Nor tempt me further with thy vaporish boast
    That I am *helpless* to combat thee! Well,
Have at thee, then! Yet if a doom most dire
    Thou wouldst escape, flee whilst thou canst!—
        Revile
Me not, Miasmic Mist!—Rank Air! *Retire!*
    One instant longer an thou haunt'st me, I'll
Inhale thee, O thou wraith despicable!

WHO BIDES HIS TIME

WHO bides his time, and day by day
  Faces defeat full patiently,
And lifts a mirthful roundelay,
  However poor his fortunes be,—
He will not fail in any qualm
  Of poverty—the paltry dime
It will grow golden in his palm,
    Who bides his time.

Who bides his time—he tastes the sweet
  Of honey in the saltest tear;
And though he fares with slowest feet,
  Joy runs to meet him, drawing near:
The birds are heralds of his cause;
  And, like a never-ending rhyme,
The roadsides bloom in his applause,
    Who bides his time.

Who bides his time, and fevers not
  In the hot race that none achieves,
Shall wear cool-wreathen laurel, wrought
  With crimson berries in the leaves;

235

And he shall reign a goodly king,
   And sway his hand o'er every clime,
With peace writ on his signet-ring,
   Who bides his time.

AS WE READ BURNS

WHO is speaking? Who has spoken?
  Whose voice ceasing thus has broken
The sweet pathos of our dreams?
Sweetest bard of sweetest themes,
    Pouring in each poet-heart
    Some rare essence of your art
    Till it seems your singing lip
    Kisses every pencil tip!
Far across the unknown lands—
    Reach of heavenly isle and sea—
How we long to touch the hands
    You outhold so lovingly!

WHEN JUNE IS HERE

WHEN June is here—what art have we to sing
    The whiteness of the lilies 'midst the green
Of noon-tranced lawns? or flash of roses seen
Like redbirds' wings? or earliest ripening
Prince-harvest apples, where the cloyed bees cling
    Round winy juices oozing down between
    The peckings of the robin, while we lean
In under-grasses, lost in marveling;
    Or the cool term of morning, and the stir
Of odorous breaths from wood and meadow walks;
    The Bob-white's liquid yodel, and the whir
Of sudden flight; and, where the milkmaid talks
Across the bars, on tilted barley-stalks
    The dewdrops' glint in webs of gossamer.

AT NOON—AND MIDNIGHT

FAR in the night, and yet no rest for him! The
    pillow next his own
The wife's sweet face in slumber pressed—yet he
    awake—alone! alone!
In vain he courted sleep ;—one thought would ever
    in his heart arise,—
The harsh words that at noon had brought the tear-
    drops to her eyes.

Slowly on lifted arm he raised and listened. All was
    still as death ;
He touched her forehead as he gazed, and listened
    yet, with bated breath :
Still silently, as though he prayed, his lips moved
    lightly as she slept—
For God was with him, and he laid his face with
    hers and wept.

TO JAMES NEWTON MATTHEWS

IN ANSWER TO A LETTER ON THE ANATOMY OF THE
SONNET

OHO! ye sunny, sonnet-singin' vagrant,
    Flauntin' your simmer sangs in sic a
      weather!
Ane maist can straik the bluebells and the heather
Keekin' aboon the snaw, and bloomin' fragrant!
Whiles you, ye whustlin' brither, sic a lay grant
    O' a' these janglin', wranglin' sweets thegither,
    I weel maun perk my ain doon-drappin' feather
And pipe a wee: Tho' boisterous and flagrant
The winds blow whuzzle-whazzle rhymes that trickle
    Fra' aff my tongue less limpid that I'd ha'e them,
I in their little music hap a mickle
    O' canty praises, a' askent to weigh them
Agen your pride, and smile to see them tickle
    The warm nest o' the heart wherein I lay them.

SPIRITS AT HOME

THE FAMILY

THERE was Father, and Mother, and Emmy,
     and Jane,
  And Lou, and Ellen, and John and me—
And Father was killed in the war, and Lou
She died of consumption, and John did too,
  And Emmy she went with the pleurisy.

THE SPIRITS

Father believed in 'em all his life—
  But Mother, at first, she'd shake her head—
Till after the battle of Champion Hill,
When many a flag in the winder-sill
  Had crape mixed in with the white and red!

I used to doubt 'em myself till then—
  But me and Mother was satisfied
When Ellen she set, and Father came
And rapped "God Bless You!" and Mother's name,
  And "The Flag's up here!" . . . And we all just
     cried.

Used to come often, after that,
    And talk to us—just as he used to do,
Pleasantest kind! And once, for John,
He said he was "lonesome, but wouldn't let on—
    Fear Mother would worry, and Emmy and Lou."

But Lou was the bravest girl on earth—
    For all she never was hale and strong,
She'd have her fun!—With her voice clean lost
She'd laugh and joke us that "when *she* crossed
    To Father, *we'd* all come taggin' along!"

Died—just that way! And the raps was thick
    That night, as they often since occur,
Extry loud! And when *Lou* got back
She said it was Father and her—and *"whack!"*
    She tuk the table—and we knowed *her!*

John and Emmy, in five years more,
    Both had went.—And it seemed like fate,—
For the old home *it* burnt down.—But Jane
And me and Ellen we built again
    The new house, here, on the old estate.

And a happier family I don't know
    *Of any*wheres—unless it's *them,*—
Father, with all his love for Lou,
And her there with him, and healthy, too,
    And laughin', with John and little Em.

And, first we moved in the *new* house here,
   They all dropped in for a long powwow:—
"We like your buildin', of course," Lou said,—
"But wouldn't swap with you to save your head—
   For *we* live in the ghost of the old house now!"

ART AND LOVE

H E faced his canvas (as a seer whose ken
 Pierces the crust of this existence through)
 And smiled beyond on that his genius knew
Ere mated with his being. Conscious then
Of his high theme alone, he smiled again
 Straight back upon himself in many a hue
 And tint, and light and shade, which slowly grew
Enfeatured of a fair girl's face, as when
 First time she smiles for love's sake with no fear.
So wrought he, witless that behind him leant
 A woman, with old features, dim and sear,
 And glamoured eyes that felt the brimming tear,
And with a voice, like some sad instrument,
  That sighing said, "I'm dead there; love me
   here!"

SONG

O I would I had a lover!
  A lover! a lover!
O I would I had a lover
  With a twinkering guitar,
    To come beneath my casement
Singing "There is none above her,"
While I, leaning, seemed to hover
  In the scent of his cigar!

Then at morn I'd want to meet him—
  To meet him! to meet him!
O at morn I'd want to meet him,
  When the mist was in the sky,
    And the dew along the path I went
To casually greet him,
And to cavalierly treat him,
  And regret it by and by.

And I'd want to meet his brother—
  His brother! his brother!
O I'd want to meet his brother
  At the german or the play,

To pin a rose on his lapel
And lightly press the other,
And love him like a mother
　　While he thought the other way.

O I'd pitilessly test him!
　　And test him! and test him!
O I'd pitilessly test him
　　Far beyond his own control;
　　　And every tantalizing lure
With which I could arrest him,
I'd loosen to molest him,
　　Till I tried his very soul.

But ah, when I relented!
　　Relented, relented!
But ah, when I relented—
　　When the stars were blurred and dim,
　　　And the moon above, with crescent grace,
Looked off as I repented,
And with rapture half demented,
　　All my heart went out to him!

PAP'S OLD SAYIN'

PAP had one old-fashioned sayin'
    That I'll never quite fergit—
And they's seven growed-up childern
    Of us rickollects it yit!—
Settin' round the dinner-table,
    Talkin' 'bout our friends, perhaps,
Er abusin' of our neghbors,
    I kin hear them words o' Pap's—
        "Shet up, and eat yer vittels!"

Pap he'd never argy with us,
    Ner cut any subject short
Whilse we all kep' clear o' gossip,
    And wuz actin' as we ort:
But ef we'd git out o' order—
    Like sometimes a fambly is,—
Faultin' folks, er one another,
    Then we'd hear that voice o' his—
        "Shet up, and eat yer vittels!"

Wuz no hand hisse'f at talkin'—
    Never hadn't *much* to say,—
Only, as I said, pervidin'
    When we'd rile him thataway:

247

Then he'd allus lose his temper
  Spite o' fate, and jerk his head
And slam down his case-knife vicious'
  Whilse he glared around and said—
    "Shet up, and eat yer vittels!"

Mind last time 'at Pap was ailin'
  With a misery in his side,
And had hobbled in the kitchen—
  Jes' the day before he died,—
Laury Jane she ups and tells him,
  "Pap, you're pale as pale kin be—
Hain't ye 'feard them-air cowcumbers
  Hain't good fer ye?" And says he,
    "Shet up, and eat yer vittels!"

Well! I've saw a-many a sorrow,—
  Forty year', through thick and thin;
I've got best,—and I've got *worsted*,
  Time and time and time ag'in!—
But I've met a-many a trouble
  That I hain't run on to twice,
Haltin'-like and thinkin' over
  Them-air words o' Pap's advice:
    "Shet up, and eat yer vittels!"

GRANNY

GRANNY'S come to our house,
  And ho! my lawzy-daisy!
All the childern round the place
  Is ist a-runnin' crazy!
Fetched a cake fer little Jake,
  And fetched a pie fer Nanny,
And fetched a pear fer all the pack
  That runs to kiss their Granny!

Lucy Ellen's in her lap,
  And Wade and Silas Walker
Both's a-ridin' on her foot,
  And 'Pollos on the rocker;
And Marthy's twins, from Aunt Marinn's,
  And little Orphant Annie,
All's a-eatin' gingerbread
  And giggle-un at Granny!

Tells us all the fairy tales
  Ever thought er wundered—
And 'bundance o' other stories—
  Bet she knows a hunderd!—

Bob's the one fer "Whittington,"
  And "Golden Locks" fer Fanny!
Hear 'em laugh and clap their hands,
  Listenin' at Granny!

"Jack the Giant-Killer" 's good;
  And "Bean-Stalk" 's another!—
So's the one of "Cinderell' "
  And her old godmother;—
That-un's best of all the rest—
  Bestest one of any,—
Where the mices scampers home
  Like we runs to Granny!

Granny's come to our house,
  Ho! my lawzy-daisy!
All the childern round the place
  Is ist a-runnin' crazy!
Fetched a cake fer little Jake,
  And fetched a pie fer Nanny,
And fetched a pear fer all the pack
  That runs to kiss their Granny!

OLD "BEE" FESSLER.

Sketched by James Whitcomb Riley

FESSLER'S BEES.

"Talkin' 'bout yer bees," says Ike,
Speakin' slow and serious like,—
"Devver tell you 'bout old "Bee"—
Old "Bee" Fessler?" Ike says he:—
"Might call him a bee expert,
Whenn it come to handlin' bees,—
Role the sleeves ups of his shirt,
And wade in amongst the trees
Whenn a swarm'ud settle, and—
Blamurdest man on top o' dirt!—
Rake 'em with his naked hand
Right back in the hive agin—
Jes' as easy as you please!
Nary ber 'at split the breeze
Ever jabbed a stinger in
Old "Bee" Fessler—jes' in fun,
Er in airnist I nary one!—
Couldn't agg our ole to, nuther,
Ary one way er the other!

"Old "Bee" Fessler," Ike says he,
"Made a sprishyality
Jes' o' bees, and buitt a shed,
Leettle about a half a mild!—

Had about a thousan' head
O' hives, I reckon — tame and wild! —
Durndest buzzin' ever wuz!
Wuss'n telegraf poles does
When they're sockin' home the news
Tight as they kin let 'er loose!
Visitors rag out and come
Clean from town to hear 'em hum,
And stop at the kivered bridge;
But wuz some 'ud cross the ridge,
Allus, and go closter — so's
They could see 'em hum, I s'pose!
'Peared like stangers down that track
Allus met folks comin' back
Lookin' extry fat and hearty
Fer a city picnic party!

"'Fore he went to Floridy
On his prodjec," Ike says he,
"Old 'Bee' Fessler couldn't 'bide
Childern on his place," says Ike, —
"Yit, fer all, they'd climb inside
And tromp round there, keerless like,
In their bare feet! 'Bee' could tell
Ev'ry townboy by his yell —

BECALMED

I

WOULD that the winds might only blow
  As they blew in the golden long ago!—
Laden with odors of Orient isles
Where ever and ever the sunshine smiles,
And the bright sands blend with the shady trees,
And the lotus blooms in the midst of these.

II

Warm winds won from the midland vales
To where the tress of the Siren trails
O'er the flossy tip of the mountain phlox
And the bare limbs twined in the crested rocks,
High above as the sea-gulls flap
Their lopping wings at the thunderclap.

III

Ah! that the winds might rise and blow
The great surge up from the port below,
Bloating the sad, lank, silken sails
Of the Argo out with the swift, sweet gales

That blew from Colchis when Jason had
His love's full will and his heart was glad—
When Medea's voice was soft and low.
Ah! that the winds might rise and blow!

GRIGGSBY'S STATION

PAP'S got his pattent-right, and rich as all crea-
        tion;
    But where's the peace and comfort that we all had
        before?
Le's go a-visitin' back to Griggsby's Station—
    Back where we ust to be so happy and so pore!

The likes of us a-livin' here! It's jes' a mortal pity
    To see us in this great big house, with cyarpets on
        the stairs,
And the pump right in the kitchen! And the city!
    city! city!—
    And nothin' but the city all around us ever'-
        wheres!

Climb clean above the roof and look from the
        steeple,
    And never see a robin, nor a beech or ellum tree!
And right here in ear-shot of at least a thousan'
        people,
    And none that neighbors with us or we want to
        go and see!

Le's go a-visitin' back to Griggsby's Station—
　　Back where the latch-string's a-hangin' from the
　　　door,
And ever' neighbor round the place is dear as a re-
　　lation—
　　Back where we ust to be so happy and so pore!

I want to see the Wiggenses, the whole kit-and-
　　bilin',
　　A-driven' up from Shallor Ford to stay the Sun-
　　　day through;
And I want to see 'em hitchin' at their son-in-law's
　　and pilin'
　　Out there at 'Lizy Ellen's like they ust to do!

I want to see the piece-quilts the Jones girls is
　　makin';
　　And I want to pester Laury 'bout their freckled
　　　hired hand,
And joke her 'bout the widower she come purt' nigh
　　a-takin',
　　Till her Pap got his pension 'lowed in time to save
　　　his land.

Le's go a-visitin' back to Griggsby's Station—
　　Back where they's nothin' aggervatin' any more,
Shet away safe in the woods around the old
　　location—
　　Back where we ust to be so happy and so pore!

I want to see Marindy and he'p her with her sewin',
    And hear her talk so lovin' of her man that's dead
      and gone,
And stand up with Emanuel to show me how he's
    growin',
    And smile as I have saw her 'fore she putt her
      mournin' on.

And I want to see the Samples, on the old lower
    eighty,
    Where John, our oldest boy, he was tuk and
      burried—for
His own sake and Katy's,—and I want to cry with
    Katy
    As she reads all his letters over, writ from The
      War.

What's in all this grand life and high situation,
    And nary pink nor hollyhawk a-bloomin' at the
      door?—
Le's go a-visitin' back to Griggsby's Station—
    Back where we ust to be so happy and so pore!

FESSLER'S BEES

"TALKIN' 'bout yer bees," says Ike,
   Speakin' slow and ser'ous-like,
"D' ever tell you 'bout old 'Bee'—
Old 'Bee' Fessler?" Ike says-he!
"Might call him a *bee-expert,*
When it come to handlin' bees,—
Roll the sleeves up of his shirt
And wade in amongst the trees
Where a swarm 'u'd settle, and—
Blam'dest man on top of dirt!—
Rake 'em with his naked hand
Right back in the hive ag'in,
Jes' as easy as you please!
Nary bee 'at split the breeze
Ever jabbed a stinger in
Old 'Bee' Fessler—jes' in fun,
Er in *airnest*—nary one!—
Couldn't agg one *on* to, nuther,
Ary one way er the other!

"Old 'Bee' Fessler," Ike says-he,
"Made a speshyality
Jes' o' bees; and built a shed—
Len'th about a half a mild!
Had about a *thousan'* head

256

O' hives, I reckon—tame and wild!
Durndest buzzin' ever wuz—
Wuss'n telegraph-poles does
When they're sockin' home the news
Tight as they kin let 'er loose!
Visitors rag out and come
Clean from town to hear 'em hum,
And stop at the kivered bridge;
But wuz some 'u'd cross the ridge
Allus, and go clos'ter—so 's
They could *see* 'em hum, I s'pose!
'Peared-like strangers down that track
Allus met folks comin' back
Lookin' extry fat and hearty
Fer a city picnic party!

"'Fore he went to Floridy,
Old 'Bee' Fessler," Ike says-he—
"Old 'Bee' Fessler couldn't bide
Childern on his place," says Ike.
"Yit, fer all, they'd climb inside
And tromp round there, keerless-like,
In their bare feet. 'Bee' could tell
Ev'ry town-boy by his yell—
So 's 'at when they bounced the fence,
Didn't make no difference!
He'd jes' git down on one knee
In the grass and pat the bee!—
And, ef 't 'adn't stayed stuck in,
Fess' 'u'd set the sting ag'in,
'N' potter off, and wait around

Fer the old famillyer sound.
Allus boys there, more or less,
Scootin' round the premises!
When the buckwheat wuz in bloom,
Lawzy! how them bees 'u'd boom
Round the boys 'at crossed that way
Fer the crick on Saturday!
Never seemed to me su'prisin'
'At the sting o' bees 'uz p'izin!

"'Fore he went to Floridy,"
Ike says, "nothin' 'bout a bee
'At old Fessler didn't know,—
W'y, it jes' 'peared-like 'at he
Knowed their language, high and low:
Claimed he told jes' by their buzz
What their wants and wishes wuz!
Peek in them-air little holes
Round the porches o' the hive—
Drat their pesky little souls!—
Could 'a' skinned the man alive!
Bore right in there with his thumb,
And squat down and scrape the gum
Outen ev'ry hole, and blow
'N' bresh the crumbs off, don't you know!
Take the roof off, and slide back
Them-air glass concerns they pack
Full o' honey, and jes' lean
'N' grabble 'mongst 'em fer the queen!
Fetch her out and *show* you to her—
Jes', you might say, *interview* her!

"Year er two," says Ike, says-he,
"'Fore he went to Floridy,
Fessler struck the theory,
Honey was the same as *love*—
You could make it day and night:
Said them bees o' his could be
Got jes' twic't the work out of
Ef a feller managed right.
He contended ef bees found
Blossoms all the year around,
He could git 'em down at once
To work all the *winter* months
Same as *summer*. So, one fall,
When their summer's work wuz done,
'Bee' turns in and robs 'em all;
Loads the hives then, one by one,
On the cyars, and 'lowed he'd see
Ef bees loafed in *Floridy!*
Said he bet he'd know the reason
Ef *his* didn't work that season!

"And," says Ike, "it's jes'," says-he,
"Like old Fessler says to me:
'Any man kin fool a *bee*,
Git him down in Floridy!'
'Peared at fust, as old 'Bee' said,
Fer to kind o' turn their head
Fer a spell; but, bless you! they
Didn't lose a half a day
Altogether!—Jes' lit in
Them-air tropics, and them-air

Cacktusses a-ripen-nin',
'N' magnolyers, and sweet peas,
'N' 'simmon and pineapple trees,
'N' ripe bananers, here and there,
'N' dates a-danglin' in the breeze,
'N' figs and reezins ev'rywhere,
All waitin' jes' fer Fessler's bees!
'N' Fessler's bees, with gaumy wings,
A-gittin' down and *whoopin'* things!—
Fessler kind o' overseein'
'Em, and sort o' *'hee-o-heein' !'*

"'Fore he went to *Floridy,*
Old 'Bee' Fessler," Ike says-he,
"Wuzn't counted, jes' to say,
Mean er or'n'ry anyway;
On'y ev'ry 'tarnel dime
'At 'u'd pass him on the road
He'd ketch up with, ev'ry time;
And no mortal ever knowed
Him to spend a copper cent—
'Less on some fool-*'speriment*
With them *bees*—like that-un he
Played on 'em in Floridy.
Fess', of course, *he* tuck his ease,
But 'twus *bilious* on the bees!
Sweat, you know, 'u'd jes' stand out
On their *forreds*—pant and groan,
And grunt round and limp about!—
And old 'Bee,' o' course, a-knowin'
'Twuzn't no fair shake to play

On them pore dumb insecks, ner
To abuse 'em thataway.
Bees has rights, I'm here to say,
And that's all they ast him fer!
Man as mean as *that,* jes' 'pears,
Could 'a' worked bees on the sheers!
Cleared big money—well, I guess,
'Bee' shipped honey, more er less,
Into ev'ry state, perhaps,
Ever putt down in the maps!

"But by time he fetched 'em back
In the spring ag'in," says Ike,
"They wuz actin' s'picious-like:
Though they 'peared to lost the track
O' ev'rything they saw er heard,
They'd lay round the porch, and gap'
At their shadders in the sun,
Do-less like, ontel some bird
Suddenly 'u'd maybe drap
In a bloomin' churry tree,
Twitterin' a tune 'at run
In their minds familiously!
They'd revive up, kind o', then,
Like they argied: 'Well, it's be'n
The most longest summer we
Ever saw er want to see!
Must be *right,* though, er old *'Bee'*
'U'd notify us!' they says-ee;
And they'd sort o' square their chin
And git down to work ag'in—

Moanin' round their honey-makin',
Kind o' like their head was achin'.
Tetchin' fer to see how they
Trusted Fessler thataway—
Him a-lazin' round, and smirkin'
To hisse'f to see 'em workin'!

"But old 'Bee,'" says Ike, says-he,—
"*Now* where is he? *Where's* he gone?
Where's the head he helt so free?
Where's his pride and vanity?
What's his hopes a-restin' on?—
Never knowed a man," says Ike,
"Take advantage of a bee,
'At affliction didn't strike
Round in that vicinity!
Sinners allus suffers some,
And *old Fessler's* reck'nin' come!
That-air man to-day is jes'
Like the grass 'at Scriptur' says
Cometh up, and then turns in
And jes' gits cut down ag'in!
Old 'Bee' Fessler," Ike says-he,
"Says, last fall, says he to me—
'Ike,' says he, 'them bees has jes'
Ciphered out my or'n'riness!
Nary bee in ary swarm
On the whole endurin' farm
Won't have nothin' more to do
With a man as mean as I've
Be'n to them, last year er two!

Nary bee in ary hive
But'll turn his face away,
Like they ort, whenever they
Hear my footprints drawin' nigh!'
And old 'Bee,' he'd sort o' shy
Round oneasy in his cheer,
Wipe his eyes, and yit the sap,
Spite o' all, 'u'd haf' to drap,
As he wound up: 'Wouldn't keer
Quite so much ef they'd jes' light
In and settle things up right,
Like they ort; but—blame the thing!—
'Pears-like they won't even *sting!*
Pepper me, the way I felt,
And I'd thank 'em, ev'ry welt!'
And as miz'able and mean
As 'Bee' looked, ef you'd 'a' seen
Them-air hungry eyes," says Ike,
"You'd fergive him, more'n like.

"Wisht you had 'a' knowed old 'Bee'
'Fore he went to Floridy!"

JONEY

HAD a harelip—Joney had:
 Spiled his looks, and Joney knowed it:
Fellers tried to bore him, bad—
But ef ever he got mad,
 He kep' still and never showed it.
'Druther have his mouth, all pouted
 And split up, and like it wuz,
Than the ones 'at laughed about it.—
 Purty is as purty does!

Had to listen ruther clos't
 'Fore you knowed what he wuz givin'
You; and yet, without no boast,
Joney he wuz jes' the most
 Entertainin' talker livin'!
Take the Scriptur's and run through 'em,
 Might say, like a' auctioneer,
And 'ud argy and review 'em
 'At wuz beautiful to hear!

Harelip and inpediment,
 Both wuz bad, and both ag'in' him—
But the *old folks* where he went,
'Peared like, knowin' his intent,
 'Scused his mouth fer what wuz in him.

And *the childern* all loved Joney—
  And he loved 'em back, you bet!—
Putt their arms around him——on'y
  None had ever kissed him yet!

In young company, someway,
  Boys 'ud grin at one another
On the sly; and girls 'ud lay
Low, with nothin' much to say,
  Er leave Joney with their mother.
Many and many a time he's fetched 'em
  Candy by the paper-sack,
And turned right around and ketched 'em
  Makin' mouths behind his back!

S'prised, sometimes, the slurs he took.—
  Chap said onc't his mouth looked sorter
Like a fish's mouth 'ud look
When he'd be'n jerked off the hook
  And plunked back into the worter.—
Same durn feller—it's su'prisin',
  But it's facts—'at stood and cherred
From the bank that big babtizin'
  'Pike-bridge accident occurred!—

Cherred fer Joney while he give
  Life to little childern drowndin'!
Which wuz fittenest to live—
Him 'at cherred, er him 'at div'
  And saved thirteen lives? . . . They found one

Body, three days later, floated
    Down the by-o, eight mile' south,
All so colored-up and bloated—
    On'y knowed him by his mouth!

Had a harelip—Joney had—
    Folks 'at filed apast all knowed it.—
Them 'at ust to smile looked sad,
But ef *he* thought good er bad,
    He kep' still and never showed it.
'Druther have that mouth, all pouted
    And split up, and like it wuz,
Than the ones 'at laughed about it.—
    Purty is as purty does!

'LONG ABOUT KNEE-DEEP IN JUNE.

Tell you what I like the best;—
  'Long about knee-deep in June,
    'Bout the time strawberries melts
  On the vine,— some afternoon,—
Is to jes' git out and rest,
    And not work at nothin' else!

Jes' the clear sky overhead—
  Sprawl out, someres on the grass
    Where the shadder's thick and soft
As the kivvers on the bed
    Mother fixes in the loft
    ~~While we got~~ Allus when ther's company;
    Through the leaves of some old tree
Watch the swift barn-swallers pass;
  Er the bob-white raise and whiz
  Whare some other's whistle is;
Er old Bluejay, full o' sass,
  In them baseball clothes o' his,
    Sportin' round the orchard, jes'
    Like he owned the premises!
    That's jes' what I'd like to do
    Stiddy fer a year er two!

Aprile's jes' a leetle too
  Brash fer me; and May — I jes'
  'Bominate its promises! — Little hints and o'sunshine,
A few blossoms, and a few Grew around the timbe land —
Chipbirds, and a sprout er two! —
Drap asleep, and it turns in
'Fore daylight and snows agin!
  But when June comes — Clean my throat
    With wild honey! — rench my hair
In the dew! and hold my coat!
    Whoop out loud, and throw my hat! —
June wants me, and I'm to spare! —
Spread them shadders anywheres! —
I'll git down and waller there,
  And obleeged to you at that!
        — James Whitcomb Riley

KNEE-DEEP IN JUNE

I

TELL you what I like the best—
        'Long about knee-deep in June,
    'Bout the time strawberries melts
    On the vine,—some afternoon
Like to jes' git out and rest,
        And not work at nothin' else!

II

Orchard's where I'd ruther be—
Needn't fence it in fer me!—
    Jes' the whole sky overhead,
And the whole airth underneath—
Sort o' so's a man kin breathe
    Like he ort, and kind o' has
Elbow-room to keerlessly
    Sprawl out len'thways on the grass
        Where the shadders thick and soft
    As the kivvers on the bed
        Mother fixes in the loft
Allus, when they's company!

III

Jes' a-sort o' lazin' there—
　S'lazy, 'at you peek and peer
　　Through the wavin' leaves above,
　　Like a feller 'ats in love
And don't know it, ner don't keer!
Ever'thing you hear and see
　Got some sort o' interest—
　　Maybe find a bluebird's nest
Tucked up there conveenently
Fer the boy 'at's ap' to be
Up some other apple tree!
Watch the swallers skootin' past
　Bout as peert as you could ast;
　　Er the Bob-white raise and whiz
　　Where some other's whistle is.

IV

Ketch a shadder down below,
And look up to find the crow—
Er a hawk,—away up there,
'Pearantly *froze* in the air!—
　Hear the old hen squawk, and squat
　Over ever' chick she's got,
Suddent-like!—and she knows where
　That-air hawk is, well as you!—
　You jes' bet yer life she do!—
　　Eyes a-glitterin' like glass,
　　Waitin' till he makes a pass!

V

Pee-wees' singin', to express
  My opinion, 's second-class,
Yit you'll hear 'em more er less;
    Sapsucks gittin' down to biz,
Weedin' out the lonesomeness;
    Mr. Bluejay, full o' sass,
      In them baseball clothes o' his,
Sportin' round the orchard jes'
Like he owned the premises!
    Sun out in the fields kin sizz,
But flat on yer back, I guess,
    In the shade's where glory is!
That's jes' what I'd like to do
Stiddy fer a year er two!

VI

Plague! ef they ain't somepin' in
Work 'at kind o' goes ag'in'
  My convictions!—'long about
    Here in June especially!—
    Under some old apple tree,
      Jes' a-restin' through and through,
  I could git along without
      Nothin' else at all to do
      Only jes' a-wishin' you
Wuz a-gittin' there like me,
And June wuz eternity!

VII

Lay out there and try to see
Jes' how lazy you kin be!—
    Tumble round and souse 'yer head
In the clover-bloom, er pull
      Yer straw hat acrost yer eyes
      And peek through it at the skies,
    Thinkin' of old chums 'at's dead,
        Maybe, smilin' back at you
In betwixt the beautiful
      Clouds o' gold and white and blue!—
Month a man kin railly love—
June, you know, I'm talkin' of!

VIII

March ain't never nothin' new!—
Aprile's altogether too
   Brash fer me! and May—I jes'
   'Bominate its promises,—
Little hints o' sunshine and
Green around the timber-land—
   A few blossoms, and a few
   Chip-birds, and a sprout er two,—
   Drap asleep, and it turns in
   'Fore daylight and *snows* ag'in!—
But when *June* comes—Clear my th'oat
   With wild honey!—Rench my hair

In the dew! and hold my coat!
   Whoop out loud! and th'ow my hat!—
June wants me, and I'm to spare!
Spread them shadders anywhere,
I'll git down and waller there,
   And obleeged to you at that!

THE LAW OF THE PERVERSE

WHERE did the custom come from, any-
        way—
  Sending the boys to "play," at dinner-time,
When we have company? What is there, pray,
    About the starched, unmalleable *guest*
    That, in the host's most genial interest,
Finds *him* first favor on Thanksgiving Day
  Beside the steaming turkey, with its wings
  Akimbo over all the savory things
  It has been stuffed with, yet may never thus
  Make one poor boy's face glad and glorious!

Fancy the exiled boy in the back yard,
  Ahungered so, that any kind of grub
Were welcome, yet with face set stern and hard,
  Hearing the feasters' mirth and mild hubbub,
  And wanting to kill something with a club!—
  Intuitively arguing the unjust
  Distinction, as he naturally must,—
  The guest with all the opportunity—
  The boy with all the appetite! Ah, me!

So is it that, when I, a luckless guest,
   Am thus arraigned at banquet, I sit grim
And sullen, eating nothing with a zest,—
With smirking features, yet a soul distressed,
   Missing the banished boy and envying him—
Ay, longing for a spatter on my vest
     From his deflecting spoon, and yearning for
     The wild swoop of his lips insatiate, or
     His ever-ravenous, marauding eye
     Fore-eating everything, from soup to pie!

OUT OF NAZARETH

"HE shall sleep unscathed of thieves
   Who loves Allah and believes."
Thus heard one who shared the tent,
In the far-off Orient,
Of the Bedouin ben Ahrzz—
Nobler never loved the stars
Through the palm-leaves nigh the dim
Dawn his courser neighed to him!

He said: "Let the sands be swarmed
   With such thieves as I, and thou
Shalt at morning rise, unharmed,
   Light as eyelash to the brow
Of thy camel, amber-eyed,
Ever munching either side,
Striding still, with nestled knees,
Through the midnight's oases.

"Who can rob thee an thou hast
More than this that thou hast cast
At my feet—this dust of gold?
Simply this and that, all told!
Hast thou not a treasure of
Such a thing as men call love?

"Can the dusky band I lead
Rob thee of thy daily need
Of a whiter soul, or steal
What thy lordly prayers reveal?
Who could be enriched of thee
By such hoard of poverty
As thy niggard hand pretends
To dole me—thy worst of friends?
   Therefore shouldst thou pause to bless
One indeed who blesses thee:
   Robbing thee, I dispossess
But myself.—Pray thou for me!"

"He shall sleep unscathed of thieves
Who loves Allah and believes."

TIME

I

THE ticking—ticking—ticking of the clock!—
    That vexed me so last night!—"For though
        Time keeps
    Such drowsy watch," I moaned, "he never sleeps,
But only nods above the world to mock
Its restless occupant, then rudely rock
    It as the cradle of a babe that weeps!"
    I seemed to see the seconds piled in heaps
Like sand about me; and at every shock
    O' the bell, the pilèd sands were swirled away
As by a desert-storm that swept the earth
    Stark as a granary floor, whereon the gray
And mist-bedrizzled moon amidst the dearth
    Came crawling, like a sickly child, to lay
    Its pale face next mine own and weep for day.

II

Wait for the morning! Ah! we wait indeed
    For daylight, we who toss about through stress
    Of vacant-armed desires and emptiness
Of all the warm, warm touches that we need,

And the warm kisses upon which we feed
  Our famished lips in fancy! May God bless
  The starved lips of us with but one caress
Warm as the yearning blood our poor hearts bleed!
. . . A wild prayer!—bite thy pillow, praying so—
  Toss this side, and whirl that, and moan for
      dawn;
Let the clock's seconds dribble out their woe
And Time be drained of sorrow! Long ago
  We heard the crowing cock, with answer drawn
  As hoarsely sad at throat as sobs. . . . Pray on!

IKE WALTON'S PRAYER

I CRAVE, dear Lord,
  No boundless hoard
Of gold and gear,
  Nor jewels fine,
  Nor lands, nor kine,
Nor treasure-heaps of anything.—
  Let but a little hut be mine
  Where at the hearthstone I may hear
    The cricket sing,
    And have the shine
Of one glad woman's eyes to make,
For my poor sake,
  Our simple home a place divine ;—
Just the wee cot—the cricket's chirr—
Love, and the smiling face of her.

  I pray not for
  Great riches, nor
For vast estates and castle halls,—
Give me to hear the bare footfalls
  Of children o'er
  An oaken floor
New-rinsed with sunshine, or bespread

With but the tiny coverlet
And pillow for the baby's head;
And, pray Thou, may
The door stand open and the day
　　Send ever in a gentle breeze,
　　　With fragrance from the locust trees,
　　　　And drowsy moan of doves, and blur
Of robin-chirps, and drone of bees,
　　　With after-hushes of the stir
Of intermingling sounds, and then
　　　The goodwife and the smile of her
Filling the silences again—
　　　　The cricket's call
　　　　　And the wee cot,
　　　　Dear Lord of all,
　　　　　Deny me not!

　　I pray not that
　　Men tremble at
　My power of place
　　And lordly sway,—
I only pray for simple grace
To look my neighbor in the face
　Full honestly from day to day—
Yield me his horny palm to hold,
　　　And I'll not pray
　　　　For gold;—
The tanned face, garlanded with mirth,
It hath the kingliest smile on earth;
The swart brow, diamonded with sweat,

Hath never need of coronet.
And so I reach,
Dear Lord, to Thee,
And do beseech
Thou givest me
The wee cot, and the cricket's chirr,
Love, and the glad sweet face of her!

THE WAY IT WUZ

LAS' July—and, I persume,
    'Bout as hot
As the old Gran'-jury room
    Whare they sot!—
Fight 'twixt Mike and Dock McGreff. . . .
'Pears to me jes' like as ef
    I'd a-dremp' the whole blame thing—
        Allus ha'nts me roun' the gizzard
    When they's nightmares on the wing
        And a feller's blood's jes' friz!
      Seed the row from A to Izzard—
    'Cause I wuz a-standin' as clos't to 'em
        As me and you is!

Tell you the way it wuz—
    And I don't *want* to see,
Like *some* fellers does,
    When they's goern to be
Any kind o' fuss—
On'y makes a rumpus wuss
    Fer to *interfere*
        When theyr dander's riz—
    Might as lif to *cheer!*
But I wuz a-standin' as clos't to 'em
        As me and you is!

I wuz kind o' strayin'
　Past the blame saloon—
Heerd some fiddler playin'
　That old "Hee-cup tune!"
I'd *stopped*-like, you know,
Fer a minit er so,
　And wuz jes' about
Settin' down, when—*Jeemses-whizz!*—
　Whole durn winder-sash fell out!
And thare laid Dock McGreff, and Mike
A-straddlin' him, all bloody-like,
　And both a-gittin' down to biz!—
And I wuz a-standin' as clos't to 'em
　As me and you is!

I wuz the on'y man aroun'—
(Durn old-fogey town!
　'Peared more like, to me,
　Sund'y than *Saturd'y!*)
　Dog come 'crost the road
　　And tuk a smell
　　　And putt right back:
　Mishler driv by 'ith a load
　　O' cantalo'pes he couldn't sell—
　　　Too mad, 'i jack!
　To even ast
　What wuz up, as he went past!
Weather most outrageous hot!—
　　Fairly hear it sizz

Roun' Dock and Mike—tel Dock he shot,—
   And Mike he slacked that grip o' his
   And fell, all spraddled out. Dock riz
'Bout half up, a-spittin' red,
   And shuck his head. . . .
And I wuz a-standin' as clos't to 'em
   As me and you is!

And Dock he says,
   A-whisperin'-like,—
      "It hain't no use
   A-tryin'!—Mike
      He's jes' ripped my daylights loose!—
Git that blame-don fiddler to
Let up, and come out here—You
Got some burryin' to do,—
   Mike makes *one,* and, I expects,
'Bout ten seconds, I'll make *two!*"
   And he drapped back, whare he'd riz,
'Crost Mike's body, black and blue,
   Like a great big letter X !—
And I wuz a-standin' as clos't to 'em
   As me and you is!

CURLY LOCKS

CURLY Locks! Curly Locks! wilt thou be mine?
  Thou shalt not wash the dishes, nor yet feed
    the swine,—
But sit on a cushion and sew a fine seam,
And feast upon strawberries, sugar and cream.

Curly Locks! Curly Locks! wilt thou be mine?
The throb of my heart is in every line,
And the pulse of a passion as airy and glad
In its musical beat as the little Prince had!

Thou shalt not wash the dishes, nor yet feed the
    swine!—
O I'll dapple thy hands with these kisses of mine
Till the pink of the nail of each finger shall be
As a little pet blush in full blossom for me.

But sit on a cushion and sew a fine seam,
And thou shalt have fabric as fair as a dream,—
The red of my veins, and the white of my love,
And the gold of my joy for the braiding thereof.

And feast upon strawberries, sugar and cream
From a service of silver, with jewels agleam,—
At thy feet will I bide, at thy beck will I rise,
And twinkle my soul in the night of thine eyes!

Curly Locks! Curly Locks! wilt thou be mine?
Thou shalt not wash the dishes, nor yet feed the
swine,—
But sit on a cushion and sew a fine seam,
And feast upon strawberries, sugar and cream.

GRANT

Sir Launcelot rode overthwart and endlong in a wide forest, and held no path but as wild adventure led him. . . . And he returned and came again to his horse, and took off his saddle and his bridle, and let him pasture; and unlaced his helm, and ungirdled his sword, and laid him down to sleep upon his shield before the cross.—AGE OF CHIVALRY.

WHAT shall we say of the soldier, Grant,
　　His sword put by and his great soul free
How shall we cheer him now or chant
　　His requiem befittingly?
The fields of his conquest now are seen
　　Ranged no more with his armèd men—
But the rank and file of the gold and green
　　Of the waving grain is there again.

286

Though his valiant life is a nation's pride,
　And his death heroic and half divine,
And our grief as great as the world is wide,
　There breaks in speech but a single line :—
We loved him living, revere him dead !—
　A silence then on our lips is laid :
We can say no thing that has not been said,
　　Nor pray one prayer that has not been
　　　prayed.

But a spirit within us speaks : and lo,
　We lean and listen to wondrous words
That have a sound as of winds that blow,
　And the voice of waters and low of herds ;
And we hear, as the song flows on serene,
　The neigh of horses, and then the beat
Of hooves that scurry o'er pastures green,
　And the patter and pad of a boy's bare feet.

A brave lad, wearing a manly brow,
　Knit as with problems of grave dispute,
And a face, like the bloom of the orchard
　　bough,
　Pink and pallid, but resolute ;
And flushed it grows as the clover-bloom,
　And fresh it gleams as the morning dew,
As he reins his steed where the quick quails
　　boom
　　Up from the grasses he races through.

And ho! as he rides what dreams are his?
  And what have the breezes to suggest?—
Do they whisper to him of shells that whiz
    O'er fields made ruddy with wrongs re-
      dressed?
Does the hawk above him an Eagle float?
  Does he thrill and his boyish heart beat high,
Hearing the ribbon about his throat
    Flap as a Flag as the winds go by?

And does he dream of the Warrior's fame—
  This western boy in his rustic dress?
For, in miniature, this is the man that came
    Riding out of the Wilderness!—
The selfsame figure—the knitted brow—
  The eyes full steady—the lips full mute—
And the face, like the bloom of the orchard
    bough,
    Pink and pallid, but resolute.

Ay, this is the man, with features grim
  And stoical as the Sphinx's own,
That heard the harsh guns calling him,
  As musical as the bugle blown,
When the sweet spring heavens were clouded
    o'er
    With a tempest, glowering and wild,
And our country's flag bowed down before
    Its bursting wrath as a stricken child.

Thus, ready mounted and booted and spurred,
  He loosed his bridle and dashed away!—
Like a roll of drums were his hoof-beats heard,
  Like the shriek of the fife his charger's
      neigh!
And over his shoulder and backward blown,
  We heard his voice, and we saw the sod
Reel, as our wild steeds chased his own
  As though hurled on by the hand of God!

And still, in fancy, we see him ride
  In the blood-red front of a hundred frays,
His face set stolid, but glorified
  As a knight's of the old Arthurian days:
And victor ever as courtly, too,
  Gently lifting the vanquished foe,
And staying him with a hand as true
  As dealt the deadly avenging blow.

So, brighter than all of the cluster of stars
  Of the flag enshrouding his form to-day,
His face shines forth from the grime of wars
  With a glory that shall not pass away:
He rests at last: he has borne his part
  Of salutes and salvos and cheers on cheers—
But O the sobs of his country's heart,
  And the driving rain of a nation's tears!

ON THE BANKS O' DEER CRICK

ON the banks o' Deer Crick! There's the place
    fer me!—
Worter slidin' past ye jes' as clair as it kin be:—
See yer shadder in it, and the shadder o' the sky,
And the shadder o' the buzzard as he goes a-lazin'
    by;
Shadder o' the pizen-vines, and shadder o' the
    trees—
And I purt' nigh said the shadder o' the sunshine
    and the breeze!
Well!—I never seen the ocean ner I never seen the
    sea.—
On the banks o' Deer Crick's grand enough fer me!

On the banks o' Deer Crick—mil'd er two from
    town—
'Long up where the mill-race comes a-loafin'
    down,—
Like to git up in there—'mongst the sycamores—
And watch the worter at the dam, a-frothin' as she
    pours:
Crawl out on some old log, with my hook and line,
Where the fish is jes' so thick you kin see 'em shine
As they flicker round yer bait, *coaxin'* you to jerk,
Tel yer tired ketchin' of 'em, mighty nigh, as *work!*

ON THE BANKS O' DEER CRICK.

On the banks o' Deer Crick — thur's the place fer me! —
Worter slidin' past you jes as clair as it kin be —
See yer shadder in it, and the shadder o' the sky,
And the shadder o' the buzzard as he goes a-lazin' by;
Shadder o' the pizin-vines, and shadder o' the trees —
And I purt' nigh said the shadder of the sunshine and the breeze! —
Well, I never seed the ocean, ner I never seed the sea, —
But on the banks o' Deer Crick's grand enough fer me!

On the Banks o' Deer Crick, mild er two fum town —
'Long up whur the mill-race comes a-loafin' down, —
Like to git up in there 'mongst the sycamores,
And watch the worter at the dam a-frothin' as she pours;
Crawl out on some old log, with my hook-and-line,
Whur the fish is jest so thick you kin see 'em shine
As they flicker round yer bait, coaxin' you to jerk,
Till you're tired ketchin' of 'em, mightly nigh as work!

On the banks o' Deer Crick — allus my delight
Jest to be around there — take it day er night!
Watch the snipes and killdees foolin' all the day —
And these-here little worter-bugs a-skootin' ever' way! —

Greenfields & Running Brooks p29.

Snakefeeders glancin' round and dartin' out o' sight;
And dew=fall, and bullfrogs, and lightnin=bugs at night;
Stars up through the treetops; and in the crick below,
And smell o' mint, through the dark, clean frum the old by=o!

Er go up, say, some Saturdy—'way up at "Irvin's Hole"
And find whur he's had a fire, and hid his fishin'=pole:
Have yer "dog=leg" with ye, and yer pipe and "cut=and=dry"
And pockit full o' cornbread, and sting er two o' rye;
Soak yer hide with sunshine, and waller in the shade,
Like the Good Book tells us, "whur they're none to make afraid,"
Well—I never seed the ocean, ner I never seed the sea,
But on the banks o' Deer Crick's grand enough fer me!

James Whitcomb Riley.

On the banks o' Deer Crick!—Allus my delight
Jes' to be around there—take it day er night!—
Watch the snipes and killdees foolin' half the day—
Er these-'ere little worter-bugs skootin' ever'
    way!—
Snake-feeders glancin' round, er dartin' out o'
    sight;
And dewfall, and bullfrogs, and lightnin'-bugs at
    night—
Stars up through the tree-tops—er in the crick
    below,—
And smell o' mussrat through the dark clean from
    the old by-o!

Er take a tromp, some Sund'y, say, 'way up to
    "Johnson's Hole,"
And find where he's had a fire, and hid his fishin'-
    pole:
Have yer "dog-leg" with ye, and yer pipe and "cut-
    and-dry"—
Pocketful o' corn-bread, and slug er two o'
    rye. . . .
Soak yer hide in sunshine and waller in the shade—
Like the Good Book tells us—"where there're none
    to make afraid!"
Well!—I never seen the ocean ner I never seen the
    sea.—
On the banks o' Deer Crick's grand enough fer me!

BILLY COULD RIDE

I

O THE way that Billy could ride!
   You should hear Grandfather tell of the
      lad—
For Grandfather was a horseman too,
Though he couldn't ride now as he used to do,
It yet was his glory and boast and pride,
That he'd "back" Billy for all he had—
And that's a cool million, I'll say to you!—
And you should hear him, with all his praise
Of this boy Billy, and his wild ways;—
The way that he handled a horse, and the way
He rode in town on election day—
The way he bantered, and gaffed, and guyed,
And the ways he swapped, and the ways he
      lied,
And the way he'd laugh at his victims grim,
Till half of the time they would laugh with
      him,
Forgetting their anger, and pacified—
Seeing the way that Billy could ride!

II

Billy was born for a horse's back!—
That's what Grandfather used to say:—
He'd seen him in dresses, a-many a day,
On a two-year-old, in the old barn-lot,
Prancing around, with the bridle slack,
And his two little sunburnt legs outshot
So straight from the saddle-seat you'd swear
A spirit-level had plumbed him there!
And all the neighbors that passed the place
Would just haul up in the road and stare
To see the little chap's father boost
The boy up there on his favorite roost,
To canter off, with a laughing face.—
Put him up there, he was satisfied—
And O the way that Billy could ride!

III

At celebration or barbecue—
And Billy, a boy of fifteen years—
Couldn't he cut his didoes there?—
What else would you expect him to,
On his little mettlesome chestnut mare,
With her slender neck, and her pointed ears,
And the four little devilish hooves of hers?
The "delegation" moved too slow
For the time that Billy wanted to go!
And to see him dashing out of the line
At the edge of the road and down the side

Of the long procession, all laws defied,
And the fife and drums, was a sight divine,
To the girls, in their white-and-spangled pride,
Wearily waving their scarfs about
In the great "Big Wagon," all gilt without
And jolt within, as they lumbered on
Into the town where Billy had gone
An hour ahead, like a knightly guide—
O but the way that Billy could ride!

IV

"Billy can ride! Oh, Billy can ride!
But what on earth can he do beside?"
That's what the farmers used to say,
As time went by a year at a stride,
And Billy was twenty if he was a day!
And many a wise old father's foot
Was put right down where it should be put,
While many a dutiful daughter sighed
In vain for one more glorious ride
With the gallant Billy, who none the less
Smiled at the old man's selfishness
And kissed his daughter, and rode away,—
Till one especially rich old chap—
Noted for driving a famous bay—
Gave poor Billy so sharp a rap
Regarding HIS daughter, that Billy replied
By noising it over the country wide,
That the old curmudgeon was simply mad
Because he (Billy) undoubtedly had

A faster horse than the famous bay,
And that was all that he had to say!—
Touched his horse in the flank—and *zipp!*—
Talk about horses and horsemanship!—
Folks stared after him just wild-eyed. . . .
Oomh! the way that Billy could ride!

V

Bang the cymbals! and thump the drum!
Stun the guineas! and pound the gong!
Mr. Bull, git up and come!
And beller and paw for five days long!
Whoop and howl till you drown the band
That hoots and toots in the "Judges' Stand!"
For this is the term of the county fair,
And you bet Billy will be there!—
And watch him there, old horsemen, all!
And judges, you, in your lifted stall!
And gamblers, you, as you clap and clack,
As the order is heard to clear the track!
And watch him, you, by the "Floral Hall,"
With sweet face, pink as the parasol
You wave as you stand on the buggy-seat!—
And you, young man, as you feel her hand
Tremble in yours, as there you stand!
And watch him, too, you old man gray,
With your houses, lands, and your wealth com-
    plete—
Not forgetting the famous bay
You ride with him in the race to-day!—

And lash, as you start there side by side!
Lash! for the sake of your bay defied!
Lash! for the proof of your boasted pride!
Lash! as you'd lash a cur that lied!
Lash! but watch him with both eyes wide—
For O the way that Billy can ride.

VI

Side by side in the open track
The horses stood—such a glossy pair!—
Trim as sparrows about to fly—
Plumage of mane and song of eye!
Ho! They were beautiful!—bay and black—
The sunshine glittered along each back—
Glanced at the shoulders, and flickered and run
In dapples of light that would daze the sun!—
The veins of their limbs like tremulous vines
The breeze blows through, and the vibrant lines
Of their nostrils like to the lips of the cups
Of the gods, brimmed over with roseate sups—
From swish of tail to the toss of mane,
Pharaoh's favorites lived again!—
Lived, and served, and as nobly, too,
As they sprang to the race, and onward flew!
Ho! but the sight of them side by side!—
Their masters' faces seemed glorified
As they flashed from view—in an instant gone,
And you saw but their shoulders, as they
        rode on,
Narrowing—narrowing—less and less—
As you gazed after in breathlessness.

VII

Shoulder to shoulder, and neck to neck—
And the hearts of the crowd spun round with
    them
As they dwindled away to the selfsame speck—
When sudden—a flash—like the flash of a gem
That had dropped in the dust, while onward
    came
But one wild rider, who homeward led,
So mad with delight that he shrieked his
    name—
And it was not "Billy"—but all the same,
Though far behind, he was far ahead!—
As the one rode in on "his famous bay,"
His gray hair streaming beneath his hat,
And the wind-blown, upturned brim of that
Flat on his forehead—was no acclaim,—
The crowd was looking the other way!
Where, far in the distance, and through the
    mist
Of the dust, you saw where a hand was kissed
As in hasty adieu—nor was that all,
But, fairly and clearly and sharply defined,
You saw the black horse, with Billy astride,
With a sweet little witch of a woman behind,
Gaily waving a pink parasol,
And the crowd answered roundly with cheer
    upon cheer,

As the horse lightly wheeled with their mani-
    fold weight,
And dashed from your gaze through the big
    lower gate,
While back down the track, midst a tumult of
    jeers,
Was seen to rack out, on a "winded" bay,
An aged parent—amazed—irate—
On a race that might not end for years.—
But end it did. . . . " 'Who won the race!' "
Grandfather paused, with a graver face,—
"Well, Billy won—but the reason why,
Was the bay was 'blowed'—and so was I!

"Fizzles in everything else he's tried—
But O the way that Billy can ride!"

DAVE FIELD

LET me write you a rune of a rhyme, Dave
   Field,
  For the sake of the past we knew,
When we were vagrants along the road,
   Yet glad as the skies were blue;
When we struck hands, as in alien lands
   Old friend to old friend is revealed,
And each hears a tongue that he understands,
   And a laugh that he loves, Dave Field.

Ho! let me chant you a stave, Dave Field,
   Of those indolent days of ours,
With our chairs atilt at the wayside inn
   Or our backs in the woodland flowers;
With your pipe alit, and the breath of it
   Like a nimbus about your head,
While I sipped, like a monk, of your winy wit,
   With my matins all unsaid.

Let me drone you a dream of the world, Dave
   Field,
  And the glory it held for us—
You with your pencil-and-canvas dreams,
   And I with my pencil thus;

Yet with never a thought of the prize we sought,
   Being at best but a pain,
As we looked from the heights and our blurred
    eyes caught
   The scenes of our youth again.

Oh, let me sing you a song, Dave Field,
   Jolly and hale, but yet
With a quaver of pathos along the lines,
   And the throb of a vain regret;—
A sigh for the dawn long dead and gone,
   But a laugh for the dawn concealed,
As bravely a while we still toil on
   Toward the topmost heights, Dave Field.

WHEN WE THREE MEET

WHEN we three meet? Ah! friend of
   mine
Whose verses well and flow as wine,—
 My thirsting fancy thou dost fill
 With draughts delicious, sweeter still
Since tasted by those lips of thine.

I pledge thee, through the chill sunshine
Of autmun, with a warmth divine,
 Thrilled through as only I shall thrill
  When we three meet.

I pledge thee, if we fast or dine,
We yet shall loosen, line by line,
 Old ballads, and the blither trill
 Of our-time singers—for there will
Be with us all the Muses nine
  When we three meet.

JOSH BILLINGS

DEAD IN CALIFORNIA, OCTOBER 15, 1885

JOLLY-HEARTED old Josh Billings,
  With his wisdom and his wit,
And his gravity of presence,
  And the drollery of it!—
Has he left us, and forever?—
  When so many merry years
He has only left us laughing—
  And he leaves us now in tears?

Has he turned from his "Deer Publik,"
  With his slyly twinkling eyes
Now grown dim and heavy-lidded
  In despite of sunny skies?—
Yet with rugged brow uplifted,
  And the long hair tossed away,
Like an old heroic lion,
  With a mane of iron-gray.

Though we lose him, still we find him
  In the mirth of every lip,
And we fare through all his pages,
  In his glad companionship:

302

His voice is wed with Nature's,
  Laughing in each woody nook
With the chirrup of the robin
  And the chuckle of the brook.

But the children—O the children!—
  They who leaped to his caress,
And felt his arms about them,
  And his love and tenderness,—
Where—where will they find comfort
  As their tears fall like the rain,
And they swarm his face with kisses
  That he answers not again?

THE LAND OF THUS-AND-SO

"HOW would Willie like to go
⠀⠀⠀To the Land of Thus-and-So?
Everything is proper there—
All the children comb their hair
Smoother than the fur of cats,
Or the nap of high silk hats;
Every face is clean and white
As a lily washed in light;
Never vaguest soil or speck
Found on forehead, throat or neck;
Every little crimpled ear,
In and out, as pure and clear
As the cherry-blossom's blow
In the Land of Thus-and-So.

"Little boys that never fall
Down the stairs, or cry at all—
Doing nothing to repent,
Watchful and obedient;
Never hungry, nor in haste—
Tidy shoe-strings always laced,
Never button rudely torn

304

From its fellows all unworn;
Knickerbockers always new—
Ribbon, tie, and collar, too;
Little watches, worn like men,
Always promptly half past ten—
Just precisely right, you know,
For the Land of Thus-and-So!

"And the little babies there
Give no one the slightest care—
Nurse has not a thing to do
But be happy and sigh 'Boo!'
While Mamma just nods, and knows
Nothing but to doze and doze:
Never litter round the grate;
Never lunch or dinner late;
Never any household din
Peals without or rings within—
Baby coos nor laughing calls
On the stairs or through the halls—
Just Great Hushes to and fro
Pace the Land of Thus-and-So!

"Oh! the Land of Thus-and-So!
Isn't it delightful, though?"
"Yes," lisped Willie, answering me
Somewhat slow and doubtfully—
"Must be awful nice, but I
Ruther wait till by and by
'Fore I go there—maybe when
I be dead I'll go there *then*.—

But"—the troubled little face
Closer pressed in my embrace—
"Le's don't never *ever* go
To the Land of Thus-and-So!"

THE HOSS

THE hoss he is a splendud beast;
  He is man's friend, as heaven desined,
And, search the world from west to east,
  No honester you'll ever find!

Some calls the hoss "a pore dumb brute,"
  And yit, like Him who died fer you,
I say, as I theyr charge refute,
  " 'Fergive; they know not what they do!' "

No wiser animal makes tracks
  Upon these earthly shores, and hence
Arose the axium, true as facts,
  Extoled by all, as "Good hoss-sense!"

The hoss is strong, and knows his stren'th,—
  You hitch him up a time er two
And lash him, and he'll go his len'th
  And kick the dashboard out fer you!

But, treat him allus good and kind,
  And never strike him with a stick,
Ner aggervate him, and you'll find
  He'll never do a hostile trick.

A hoss whose master tends him right
    And worters him with daily care,
Will do your biddin' with delight,
    And act as docile as *you* air.

He'll paw and prance to hear your praise,
    Because he's learnt to love you well;
And, though you can't tell what he says,
    He'll nicker all he wants to tell.

He knows you when you slam the gate
    At early dawn, upon your way
Unto the barn, and snorts elate,
    To git his corn, er oats, er hay.

He knows you, as the orphant knows
    The folks that loves her like theyr own,
And raises her and "finds" her clothes,
    And "schools" her tel a womern-grown!

I claim no hoss will harm a man,
    Ner kick, ner run away, cavort,
Stump-suck, er balk, er "catamaran,"
    Ef you'll jes' treat him as you ort.

But when I see the beast abused,
    And clubbed around as I've saw some,
I want to see his owner noosed,
    And jes' yanked up like Absolum!

Of course they's differunce in stock,—
  A hoss that has a little yeer,
And slender build, and shaller hock,
  Can beat his shadder, mighty near!

Whilse one that's thick in neck and chist
  And big in leg and full in flank,
That tries to race, I still insist
  He'll have to take the second rank.

And I have jes' laid back and laughed,
  And rolled and wallered in the grass
At fairs, to see some heavy-draft
  Lead out at *first,* yit come in *last!*

Each hoss has his appinted place,—
  The heavy hoss should plow the soil;—
The blooded racer, he must race,
  And win big wages fer his toil.

I never bet—ner never wrought
  Upon my feller man to bet—
And yit, at times, I've often thought
  Of my convictions with regret.

I bless the hoss from hoof to head—
  From head to hoof, and tale to mane!—
I bless the hoss, as I have said,
  From head to hoof, and back again!

I love my God the first of all,
   Then Him that perished on the cross,
And next, my wife,—and then I fall
   Down on my knees and love the hoss.

A OLD PLAYED-OUT SONG

IT'S the curiousest thing in creation,
   Whenever I hear that old song
"Do They Miss Me at Home," I'm so bothered,
   My life seems as short as it's long!—
Fer ev'rything 'pears like adzackly
   It 'peared in the years past and gone,—
When I started out sparkin', at twenty,
   And had my first neckercher on!

Though I'm wrinkelder, older and grayer
   Right now than my parents was then,
You strike up that song "Do They Miss Me,"
   And I'm jes' a youngster again!—
I'm a-standin' back thare in the furries
   A-wishin' fer evening to come,
And a-whisperin' over and over
   Them words "Do They Miss Me at Home?"

You see, *Marthy Ellen she* sung it
   The first time I heerd it; and so,
As she was my very first sweethart,
   It reminds me of her, don't you know;—

How her face ust to look, in the twilight,
  As I tuck her to Spellin'; and she
Kep' a-hummin' that song tel I ast her,
  Pine-blank, ef she ever missed *me!*

I can shet my eyes now, as you sing it,
  And hear her low answerin' words;
And then the glad chirp of the crickets,
  As clear as the twitter of birds;
And the dust in the road is like velvet,
  And the ragweed and fennel and grass
Is as sweet as the scene of the lilies
  Of Eden of old, as we pass.

"Do They Miss Me at Home?" Sing it lower—
  And softer—and sweet as the breeze
That powdered our path with the snowy
  White bloom of the old locus' trees!
Let the whipperwills he'p you to sing it,
  And the echoes 'way over the hill,
Tel the moon boolges out, in a chorus
  Of stars, and our voices is still.

But, oh! "They's a chord in the music
  That's missed when *her* voice is away!"
Though I listen from midnight tel morning,
  And dawn tel the dusk of the day!
And I grope through the dark, lookin' up'ards
  And on through the heavenly dome,
With my longin' soul singin' and sobbin'
  The words "Do They Miss Me at Home?"

LITTLE ORPHANT ANNIE

INSCRIBED

WITH ALL FAITH AND AFFECTION

To all the little children:—The happy ones; and sad
   ones;
The sober and the silent ones; the boisterous and
   glad ones;
The good ones—Yes, the good ones, too; and all the
   lovely bad ones.

LITTLE Orphant Annie's come to our house
   to stay,
An' wash the cups an' saucers up, an' brush the
   crumbs away,
An' shoo the chickens off the porch, an' dust the
   hearth, an' sweep,
An' make the fire, an' bake the bread, an' earn her
   board-an'-keep;

An' all us other childern, when the supper-things is
> done,
We set around the kitchen fire an' has the mostest
> fun
A-list'nin' to the witch-tales 'at Annie tells about,
An' the Gobble-uns 'at gits you
> Ef you
>> Don't
>>> Watch
>>>> Out!

Wunst they wuz a little boy wouldn't say his
> prayers,—
An' when he went to bed at night, away up-stairs,
His Mammy heerd him holler, an' his Daddy heerd
> him bawl,
An' when they turn't the kivvers down, he wuzn't
> there at all!
An' they seeked him in the rafter-room, an' cubby-
> hole, an' press,
An' seeked him up the chimbly-flue, an' ever'-
> wheres, I guess;
But all they ever found wuz thist his pants an'
> roundabout :—
An' the Gobble-uns 'll git you
> Ef you
>> Don't
>>> Watch
>>>> Out!

An' one time a little girl 'ud allus laugh an' grin,
An' make fun of ever' one, an' all her blood-an'-kin;
An' wunst, when they was "company," an' ole folks
    wuz there,
She mocked 'em an' shocked 'em, an' said she didn't
    care!
An' thist as she kicked her heels, an' turn't to run
    an' hide,
They wuz two great big Black Things a-standin' by
    her side,
An' they snatched her through the ceilin' 'fore she
    knowed what she's about!
An' the Gobble-uns 'll git you
        Ef you
          Don't
            Watch
              Out!

An' little Orphant Annie says, when the blaze is
    blue,
An' the lamp-wick sputters, an' the wind goes
    woo-oo!
An' you hear the crickets quit, an' the moon is gray,
An' the lightnin'-bugs in dew is all squenched
    away,—
You better mind yer parunts, an' yer teachurs fond
    an' dear,
An' churish them 'at loves you, an' dry the orphant's
    tear,

An' he'p the pore an' needy ones 'at clusters all
    about,
Er the Gobble-uns 'll git you
       Ef you
          Don't
             Watch
               Out!

A DOS'T O' BLUES

I GOT no patience with blues at all!
  And I ust to kind o' talk
Ag'inst 'em, and claim, tel along last Fall,
  They wuz none in the fambly stock;
But a nephew of mine, from Eelinoy,
  That visitud us last year,
He kind o' convinct me differunt
  Whilse he wuz a-stayin' here.

From ev'ry-which-way that blues is from,
  They'd pester him *ev'ry*-ways;
They'd come to him in the night, and come
  On Sund'ys, and rainy days;
They'd tackle him in corn-plantin' time,
  And in harvest, and airly Fall,—
But a dos't o' blues in the *Winter*-time,
  He 'lowed, wuz the worst of all!

Said "All diseases that ever *he* had—
  The mumps, er the rhumatiz—
Er ev'ry-other-day-aigger—bad
  As ever the blame thing is!—

Er a cyarbuncle, say, on the back of his neck,
  Er a felon on his thumb,—
But you keep *the blues* away from him,
  And all o' the rest could come !"

And he'd moan, "They's nary a leaf below !
  Ner a spear o' grass in sight !
And the whole wood-pile's clean under snow !
  And the days is dark as night !
You can't go out—ner you can't stay in—
  Lay down—stand up—ner set !"
And a tetch o' regular tyfoid-blues
  Would double him jes' clean shet !

I writ his parunts a postal-kyard
  He could stay tel Spring-time come ;
And Aprile—*first,* as I rickollect—
  Wuz the day we shipped him home !
Most o' his *relatives,* sence then,
  Has eether give up, er quit,
Er jes' died off ; but I understand
  He's the same old color yit !

THE TRAIN-MISSER

At Union Station

'LL where in the world my eyes has bin—
   Ef I hain't missed that train ag'in!
Chuff! and whistle! and toot! and ring!
But blast and blister the dasted train!—
How it does it I can't explain!
Git here thirty-five minutes before
The durn thing's due!—and, drat the thing!
It'll manage to git past—shore!

The more I travel around, the more
I got no sense!—To stand right here
And let it beat me! 'Ll ding my melts!
I got no gumption, ner nothin' else!
Ticket Agent's a dad-burned bore!
Sell you a ticket's all they keer!—
Ticket Agents ort to all be
Prosecuted—and that's jes' what!—
How'd I know which train's fer me?
And how'd I know which train was not?
Goern and comin' and gone astray,
And backin' and switchin' ever'-which-way!

Ef I could jes' sneak round behind
Myse'f, where I could git full swing,
I'd lift my coat, and kick, by jing!
Till I jes' got jerked up and fined!—
Fer here I stood, as a durn fool's apt
To, and let that train jes' chuff and choo
Right apast me—and mouth jes' gapped
Like a blamed old sandwitch warped in two!

THE PLAINT HUMAN

SEASON of snows, and season of flowers,
  Seasons of loss and gain !—
Since grief and joy must alike be ours,
  Why do we still complain?

Ever our failing, from sun to sun,
  O my intolerant brother :—
We want just a little too little of one,
  And much too much of the other.

WHICH ANE

WHICH ane, an' which ane,
  An' which ane for thee?—
Here thou hast thy vera choice
  An' which sall it be?—
Ye hae the Holy Brither,
  An' ye hae the Scholarly;
An', last, ye hae the butt o' baith—
  Which sall it be?

Ane's oot o' Edinborough,
  Wi' the Beuk an' Gown;
An' ane's cam frae Cambridge;
  An' ane frae scaur an' down:
An' Deil tak the hindmaist!
  Sae the test gaes roun':
An' here ye hae the lairdly twa,
  An' ane frae scaur an' down.

Yon's Melancholy—
  An' the pipes a-skirlin'—
Gangs limp an' droopet,
  Like a coof at hirlin',—

Droopet aye his lang skirts
I' the wins unfurlin';
Yon's Melancholy—
An' the pipes a-skirlin'!

Which ane, an' which ane,
An' which ane for thee?
Here thou hast thy vera choice:
An' which sall it be?—
Ye hae the Holy Brither,
An' ye hae the Scholarly;
An', last, ye hae the butt o' baith—
Which sall it be?

Elbuck ye'r bag, mon!
An' pipe as ye'd burst!
Can ye gie's a waur, mon
E'en than the first?—
Be it Meister Wisemon,
I' the classics versed,
An' a slawer gait yet
E'en than the first?

Then gie us Merriment:
Loose him like a linnet
Teeterin' on a bloomin' spray—
We ken him i' the minute,—
Twinklin' is ane ee asklent,
Wi' auld Clootie in it—
Auld Swaney Lintwhite,
We ken him i' the minute!

An' which ane, an' which ane,
  An' which ane for thee?—
For thou shalt hae thy vera choice,
  An' which sall it be?
Ye hae the Holy Brither,
  An' ye hae the Scholarly;
A' last, ye hae the butt o' baith—
  Which sall it be?

REGARDIN' TERRY HUT

SENCE I tuk holt o' Gibbses' Churn
   And be'n a-handlin' the concern,
I've traveled round the grand old State
Of Indiany, lots, o' late!—
I've canvassed Crawferdsville and sweat
Around the town o' Layfayette;
I've saw a many a County-seat
I *ust* to think was hard to beat:
At constant dreenage and expense
I've worked Greencastle and Vincennes—
Drapped out o' Putnam into Clay,
Owen, and on down thataway
Plum into Knox, on the back-track
Fer home ag'in—and glad I'm back!—
I've saw these towns, as I say—but
They's none 'at beats old Terry Hut!

It's more'n likely you'll insist
I claim this 'cause I'm predjudist,
Bein' born'd here in ole Vygo
In sight o' Terry Hut;—but no,
Yer clean dead wrong!—and I maintain
They's nary drap in ary vein

O' mine but what's as free as air
To jes' take issue with you there!—
'Cause, boy and man, fer forty year,
I've argied *ag'inst* livin' here,
And jawed around and traded lies
About our lack o' enterprise,
And tuk and turned in and agreed
All other towns was in the lead,
When—drat my melts!—they couldn't cut
No shine a-tall with Terry Hut!

Take, even, statesmanship, and wit,
And ginerel git-up-and-git,
Old Terry Hut is sound clean through!—
Turn old Dick Thompson loose, er Dan
*Vore*hees—and where's they any man
Kin even hold a candle to
Their eloquence?—And where's as clean
A fi-nan-seer as Rile' McKeen—
Er puorer, in his daily walk,
In railroad er in racin' stock!
And there's 'Gene Debs—a man 'at stands
And jes' holds out in his two hands
As warm a heart as ever beat
Betwixt here and the Jedgment Seat!—
All these is reasons why I putt
Sich bulk o' faith in Terry Hut.

So I've come back, with eyes 'at sees
My faults, at last,—to make my peace
With this old place, and truthful' swear—

Like Gineral Tom Nelson does,—
"They hain't no city anywhere
On God's green earth lays over us!"
Our city govament is *grand*—
"Ner is they better farmin'-land
Sun-kissed"—as Tom goes on and says—
"Er dower'd with sich advantages!"
And I've come back, with welcome tread,
From journeyin's vain, as I have said,
To settle down in ca'm content,
And cuss the towns where I have went,
And brag on ourn, and boast and strut
Around the streets o' Terry Hut!

A TALE OF THE AIRLY DAYS

OH! tell me a tale of the airly days—
    Of the times as they ust to be;
"Piller of Fi-er" and "Shakespeare's Plays"
    Is a'most too deep fer me!
I want plane facts, and I want plane words,
    Of the good old-fashioned ways,
When speech run free as the songs of birds
    'Way back in the airly days.

Tell me a tale of the timber-lands—
    Of the old-time pioneers;
Somepin' a pore man understands
    With his feelin's 's well as ears.
Tell of the old log house,—about
    The loft, and the puncheon flore—
The old fi-er-place, with the crane swung out,
    And the latch-string thrugh the door.

Tell of the things jest as they was—
    They don't need no excuse!—
Don't tetch 'em up like the poets does,
    Tel theyr all too fine fer use!—

Say they was 'leven in the fambily—
    Two beds, and the chist, below,
And the trundle-beds that each helt three,
    And the clock and the old bureau.

Then blow the horn at the old back-door
    Tel the echoes all halloo,
And the childern gethers home onc't more,
    Jest as they ust to do:
Blow fer Pap tel he hears and comes,
    With Tomps and Elias, too,
A-marchin' home, with the fife and drums
    And the old Red White and Blue!

Blow and blow tel the sound draps low
    As the moan of the whipperwill,
And wake up Mother, and Ruth and Jo,
    All sleepin' at Bethel Hill:
Blow and call tel the faces all
    Shine out in the back-log's blaze,
And the shadders dance on the old hewed wall
    As they did in the airly days.

THE ROSSVILLE LECTUR' COURSE

[*Set down from the real facts of the case that come under notice of the author whilse visitun far distunt relatives who wuz then residin' at Rossville, Mich.*]

FOLKS up here at Rossville got up a Lectur'
Course:—
All the leadin' citizens they wuz out in force;
Met and talked at Williamses', and 'greed to meet
ag'in;
And helt another corkus when the next reports wuz
in:
Met ag'in at Samuelses'; and met ag'in at Moore's
And Johnts putt the shutters up and jest barr'd the
doors!—
And yit, I'll jest be dagg-don'd! ef't didn't take a
week
'Fore we'd settled whare to write to git a man to
speak!

Found out whare the *"Bureau"* wuz; and then and
thare agreed
To strike whilse the iron's hot and foller up the
lead.—

Simp wuz Secatary; so he tuk his pen in hand,
And ast 'em what they'd tax us fer the one on
    "Holy Land"—
"One of Colonel J. De-Koombs's Abelust and Best
Lectur's," the circ'lar stated, "Give East er West!"
Wanted fifty dollars and his kyar-fare to and from,
And Simp wuz hence instructed fer to write him not
    to come.

Then we talked and jawed around another week er
    so,
And writ the *"Bureau"* 'bout the town a-bein' sorto'
    slow—
Old-fogey-like, and pore as dirt, and lackin' inter-
    prise,
And ignornter'n any other, 'cordin' to its size:
Tel finully the *"Bureau"* said they'd send a cheaper
    man
Fer forty dollars, who would give "A Talk About
    Japan"—
"A reg'lar Japanee hise'f," the pamphlet claimed;
    and so,
Nobody knowed his languige, and of course we let
    him go!

Kindo' then let up a spell—but rallied onc't ag'in,
And writ to price a feller on what's called the
    "violin"—
A Swede, er Pole, er somepin'—but no matter what
    he wuz,
Doc Cooper said he'd heerd him, and he wuzn't
    wuth a kuss!

And then we ast fer *Swingse's* terms; and *Cook,*
    and *Ingersoll*—
And blame! ef forty dollars looked like anything at
    all!
And then *Burdette,* we tried fer *him;* and Bob he
    writ to say
He wuz busy writin' ortographts and couldn't git
    away.

At last—along in Aprile—we signed to take this-
    here
Bill Nye of Californy, 'at wuz posted to appear
"The Comicalest Funny Man 'at Ever Jammed a
    Hall!"
So we made big preperations, and swep' out the
    church and all!
And night he wuz to lectur', and the neghbors all
    wuz thare,
And strangers packed along the aisles 'at come from
    ev'rywhare,
Committee got a telegrapht the preacher read, 'at
    run—
"Got off at Rossville, *Indiany,* 'stid of Michigun."

HER BEAUTIFUL EYES

O HER beautiful eyes! they are as blue as the
  dew
On the violet's bloom when the morning is new,
And the light of their love is the gleam of the sun
O'er the meadows of Spring where the quick
  shadows run:
As the morn shifts the mists and the clouds from
  the skies—
So I stand in the dawn of her beautiful eyes.

And her beautiful eyes are as midday to me,
When the lily-bell bends with the weight of the bee,
And the throat of the thrush is apulse in the heat,
And the senses are drugged with the subtle and
  sweet
And delirious breaths of the air's lullabies—
So I swoon in the noon of her beautiful eyes.

O her beautiful eyes! they have smitten mine own
As a glory glanced down from the glare of The
  Throne;
And I reel, and I falter and fall, as afar
Fell the shepherds that looked on the mystical Star,
And yet dazed in the tidings that bade them arise—
So I grope through the night of her beautiful eyes.

WANT TO BE WHUR MOTHER IS

"WANT to be whur mother is! Want to be
            whur mother is!"
Jeemses Rivers! won't some one ever shet that howl
            o' his?
        That-air yellin' drives me wild!
        Cain't none of ye stop the child?
        Want yer Daddy? "Naw." Gee whizz!
        "Want to be whur mother is!"

"Want to be whur mother is! Want to be whur
            mother is!"
Coax him, Sairy! Mary, sing somepin' fer him!
            Lift him, Liz—
        Bang the clock-bell with the key—
        E. the *meat-ax!* Gee-mun-nee!
        Listen to them lungs o' his!
        "Want to be whur mother is!"

334

"Want to be whur mother is! Want to be whur
      mother is!"
Preacher guess 'll pound all night on that old pulpit
      o' his;
      'Pears to me some wimmin jest
      Shows religious interest
      Mostly 'fore their fambly's riz!
      "Want to be whur mother is!"

.   .   .   .

"Want to be whur mother is! Want to be whur
      mother is!"
Nights like these and whipperwills allus brings that
      voice of his!
      Sairy; Mary; 'Lizabeth;
      Don't set there and ketch yer death
      In the dew—er rheumatiz—
      Want to be whur mother is?

BABE HERRICK

AS a rosebud might, in dreams,
  'Mid some lilies lie, meseems
Thou, pink youngling, on the breast
Of thy mother slumberest.

TO A JILTED SWAIN

GET thee back neglected friends;
  And repay, as each one lends,
Tithes of shallow-sounding glee
Or keen-ringing raillery:
Get thee from lone vigils; be
But in jocund company,
Where is laughter and acclaim
Boisterous above the name.—
Get where sulking husbands sip
Ale-house cheer, with pipe at lip;
And where Mol the barmaid saith
Curst is she that marrieth.

KNEELING WITH HERRICK

DEAR Lord, to Thee my knee is bent.—
　　Give me content—
Full-pleasured with what comes to me,
　　Whate'er it be:
An humble roof—a frugal board,
　　And simple hoard;
The wintry fagot piled beside
　　The chimney wide,
While the enwreathing flames up-sprout
　　And twine about
The brazen dogs that guard my hearth
　　And household worth:
Tinge with the embers' ruddy glow
　　The rafters low;
And let the sparks snap with delight,
　　As fingers might
That mark deft measures of some tune
　　The children croon:
Then, with good friends, the rarest few
　　Thou holdest true,

Ranged round about the blaze, to share
    My comfort there,—
Give me to claim the service meet
    That makes each seat
A place of honor, and each guest
    Loved as the rest.

IN THE SOUTH

THERE is a princess in the South
  About whose beauty rumors hum
Like honey-bees about the mouth
  Of roses dewdrops falter from;
    And O her hair is like the fine
    Clear amber of a jostled wine
    In tropic revels; and her eyes
    Are blue as rifts of Paradise.

Such beauty as may none before
  Kneel daringly, to kiss the tips
Of fingers such as knights of yore
  Had died to lift against their lips:
    Such eyes as might the eyes of gold
    Of all the stars of night behold
    With glittering envy, and so glare
    In dazzling splendor of despair.

So, were I but a minstrel, deft
  At weaving, with the trembling strings
Of my glad harp, the warp and weft
  Of rondels such as rapture sings,—

I'd loop my lyre across my breast,
Nor stay me till my knee found rest
In midnight banks of bud and flower
Beneath my lady's lattice-bower.

And there, drenched with the teary dews,
  I'd woo her with such wondrous art
As well might stanch the songs that ooze
  Out of the mockbird's breaking heart;
    So light, so tender, and so sweet
    Should be the words I would repeat,
    Her casement, on my gradual sight,
    Would blossom as a lily might.

THE HAPPY LITTLE CRIPPLE

I'M thist a little crippled boy, an' never goin' to
    grow
An' git a great big man at all!—'cause Aunty told
    me so.
When I was thist a baby onc't I falled out of the
    bed
An' got "The Curv'ture of the Spine"—'at's what
    the Doctor said.
I never had no Mother nen—fer my Pa runned away
An' dassn't come back here no more—'cause he was
    drunk one day
An' stobbed a man in thish-ere town, an' couldn't
    pay his fine!
An' nen my Ma she died—an' I got "Curv'ture of
    the Spine"!

I'm nine years old! An' you can't guess how much
    I weigh, I bet!—
Last birthday I weighed thirty-three!—An' I weigh
    thirty yet!
I'm awful little fer my size—I'm purt' nigh littler
    nan
Some babies is!—an' neighbers all calls me "The
    Little Man"!

An' Doc one time he laughed an' said: "I s'pect,
    first think you know,
You'll have a little spike-tail coat an' travel with a
    show!"
An' nen I laughed—till I looked round an' Aunty
    was a-cryin'—
Sometimes she acts like that, 'cause I got "Curv'ture
    of the Spine"!

I set—while Aunty's washin'—on my little long-leg
    stool,
An' watch the little boys an' girls a-skippin' by to
    school;
An' I peck on the winder, an' holler out an' say:
"Who wants to fight The Little Man 'at dares you
    all to-day?"
An' nen the boys climbs on the fence, an' little girls
    peeks through,
An' they all says: " 'Cause you're so big, you think
    we're 'feard o' you!"
An' nen they yell, an' shake their fist at me, like I
    shake mine—
They're thist in fun, you know, 'cause I got "Curv'-
    ture of the Spine"!

At evening, when the ironin' 's done, an' Aunty's
    fixed the fire,
An' filled an' lit the lamp, an' trimmed the wick an'
    turned it higher,
An' fetched the wood all in fer night, an' locked the
    kitchen door,
An' stuffed the old crack where the wind blows in
    up through the floor—

She sets the kittle on the coals, an' biles an' makes
the tea,
An' fries the liver an' the mush, an' cooks a egg fer
me;
An' sometimes—when I cough so hard—her elder-
berry wine
Don't go so bad fer little boys with "Curv'ture of
the Spine"!

An' nen when she putts me to bed—an' 'fore she
does she's got
My blanket-nighty, 'at she maked, all good an' warm
an' hot,
Hunged on the rocker by the fire—she sings me
hymns, an' tells
Me 'bout The Good Man—yes, an' Elves, an' Old
Enchanter spells;
An' tells me more—an' more—an' more!—tel I'm
asleep, purt' nigh—
Only I thist set up ag'in an' kiss her when she cry,
A-tellin' on 'bout *some* boy's Angel-mother—an' it's
mine! . . .
My *Ma's a Angel*—but *I'm* got "The Curv'ture of
the Spine"!

But Aunty's all so childish-like on my account, you
see,
I'm most afeard she'll be took down—an' 'at's what
bothers *me!*—

'Cause ef my good old Aunty ever would git sick
    an' die,
I don't know what she'd do in Heaven—till *I* come,
    by an' by :—
Fer she's so ust to all my ways, an' ever'thing, you
    know,
An' no one there like me, to nurse an' worry over
    so !—
'Cause all the little childerns there's so straight an'
    strong an' fine,
They's nary angel 'bout the place with "Curv'ture of
    the Spine" !

HAS SHE FORGOTTEN

I

HAS she forgotten? On this very May
  We were to meet here, with the birds and
      bees,
As on that Sabbath, underneath the trees
We strayed among the tombs, and stripped away
The vines from these old granites, cold and gray—
And yet, indeed, not grim enough were they
To stay our kisses, smiles and ecstasies,
Or closer voice-lost vows and rhapsodies.
Has she forgotten—that the May has won
Its promise?—that the bird-songs from the tree
Are sprayed above the grasses as the sun
Might jar the dazzling dew down showeringly?
Has she forgotten life—love—every one—
Has she forgotten me—forgotten me?

II

Low, low down in the violets I press
My lips and whisper to her. Does she hear,
And yet hold silence, though I call her dear,
Just as of old, save for the tearfulness
Of the clenched eyes, and the soul's vast distress?

Has she forgotten thus the old caress
That made our breath a quickened atmosphere
That failed nigh unto swooning with the sheer
Delight? Mine arms clutch now this earthen heap
Sodden with tears that flow on ceaselessly
As autumn rains the long, long, long nights weep
In memory of days that used to be,—
Has she forgotten these? And, in her sleep,
Has she forgotten me—forgotten me?

III

To-night, against my pillow, with shut eyes,
I mean to weld our faces—through the dense
Incalculable darkness make pretense
That she has risen from her reveries
To mate her dreams with mine in marriages
Of mellow palms, smooth faces, and tense ease
Of every longing nerve of indolence,—
Lift from the grave her quiet lips, and stun
My senses with her kisses—draw the glee
Of her glad mouth, full blithe and tenderly,
Across mine own, forgetful if is done
The old love's awful dawn-time when said we,
"To-day is ours!" . . . Ah, Heaven! can it be
She has forgotten me—forgotten me!

ILLILEO

ILLILEO, the moonlight seemed lost across the
  vales—
The stars but strewed the azure as an armor's scat-
    tered scales;
The airs of night were quiet as the breath of silken
    sails,
And all your words were sweeter than the notes of
    nightingales.

Illileo Legardi, in the garden there alone,
With your figure carved of fervor, as the Psyche
    carved of stone,
There came to me no murmur of the fountain's
    undertone
So mystically, musically mellow as your own.

You whispered low, Illileo—so low the leaves were
    mute,
And the echoes faltered breathless in your voice's
    vain pursuit;
And there died the distant dalliance of the sere-
    nader's lute:
And I held you in my bosom as the husk may hold
    the fruit.

Illileo, I listened. I believed you. In my bliss,
What were all the worlds above me since I found
 you thus in this?—
Let them reeling reach to win me—even Heaven I
 would miss,
Grasping earthward!—I would cling here, though I
 clung by just a kiss.

And blossoms should grow odorless—and lilies all
 aghast—
And I said the stars should slacken in their paces
 through the vast,
Ere yet my loyalty should fail enduring to the last.—
So vowed I. It is written. It is changeless as the
 past.

Illileo Legardi, in the shade your palace throws
Like a cowl about the singer at your gilded porti-
 coes,
A moan goes with the music that may vex the high
 repose
Of a heart that fades and crumbles as the crimson
 of a rose.

THE JOLLY MILLER

IT was a Jolly Miller lived on the River Dee;
   He looked upon his piller, and there he found
      a flea:
"O Mr. Flea! you have bit me,
   And you shall shorely die!"
So he scrunched his bones ag'inst the stones—
   And there he let him lie!

'Twas then the Jolly Miller he laughed and told his
      wife,
And *she* laughed fit to kill her, and dropped her
      carving knife!—
"O Mr. Flea!" "Ho-ho!" "Tee-hee!"
   They *both* laughed fit to kill,
Until the sound did almost drown
   The rumble of the mill!

"Laugh on, my Jolly Miller! and Missus Miller,
      too!—
But there's a weeping-willer will soon wave over
      you!"

The voice was all so awful small—
    So very small and slim!—
He durst' infer that it was her,
    Ner her infer 'twas him!

That night the Jolly Miller, says he, "It's, Wifey
    dear,
That cat o' yourn, I'd kill her!—her actions is so
    queer,—
She's rubbin' 'g'inst the grindstone-legs,
    And yowlin' at the sky—
And I 'low the moon hain't greener
    Than the yaller of her eye!"

And as the Jolly Miller went chuckle-un to bed,
Was *Somepin'* jerked his piller from underneath his
    head!
"O Wife," says he, on-easi-lee,
    "Fetch here that lantern there!"
But *Somepin'* moans in thunder-tones,
    "You tetch it ef you dare!"

'Twas then the Jolly Miller he trimbled and he
    quailed—
And his wife choked until her breath come back, 'n'
    she *wailed!*
And *"Oh!"* cried she, "it is *the Flea,*
    All white and pale and wann—
He's got you in his clutches, and
    He's bigger than a man!"

"Ho! ho! my Jolly Miller" (*fer 'twas the Flea,
    fer shore!*),
*"I reckon you'll not rack my bones ner scrunch 'em
    any more!"*
Then *the Flea-Ghost* he grabbed him clos't,
    With many a ghastly smile,
And from the door-step stooped and hopped
    About four hunderd mile!

HE COMETH IN SWEET SENSE

H E cometh in sweet sense to thee,
   Be it or dawn, or noon, or night,—
No deepest pain, nor halest glee,
   But He discerneth it aright.

If there be tears bedim thine eyes,
   His sympathy thou findest plain,—
The darkest midnight of the skies
   He weepeth with the tears of rain.

If thou art joyful, He hath had
   His gracious will, and lo, 'tis well,—
As thou art glad, so He is glad,
   Nor mercy strained one syllable.

Wild vows are words, as prayers are words.—
   God's mercy is not measured by
Our poor deservings: He affords
   To listen, if we laugh or cry.

KINGRY'S MILL

ON old Brandywine—about
    Where White's Lots is now laid out,
And the old crick narries down
To the ditch that splits the town,—
Kingry's Mill stood. Hardly see
Where the old dam ust to be;
Shallor, long, dry trought o' grass
Where the old race ust to pass!

That's be'n forty years ago—
Forty years o' frost and snow—
Forty years o' shade and shine
Sence them boyhood-days o' mine!—
All the old landmarks o' town
Changed about, er rotted down!
Where's the Tanyard? Where's the Still?
Tell me where's old Kingry's Mill?

Don't seem furder back, to me,
I'll be dogg'd! than yisterd'y,
Sence us fellers, in bare feet
And straw hats, went through the wheat,

Cuttin' 'crost the shortest shoot
Fer that-air old ellum-root
Jest above the mill-dam—where
The blame' cars now crosses there!

Through the willers down the crick
We could see the old mill stick
Its red gable up, as if
It jest knowed we'd stol'd the skiff!
See the winders in the sun
Blink like they wuz wunderun'
What the miller ort to do
With sich boys as me and you!

But old Kingry!—who could fear
That old chap, with all his cheer?—
Leanin' at the winder-sill,
Er the half-door o' the mill,
Swappin' lies, and pokin' fun,
'N' jigglin' like his hoppers done—
Laughin' grists o' gold and red
Right out o' the wagon-bed!

What did *he* keer where we went?—
"Jest keep out o' devilment,
And don't fool around the belts,
Bolts, ner burrs, ner nothin' else
'Bout the blame *machinery,*
And that's all I ast!" says-ee.
Then we'd climb the stairs, and play
In the bran-bins half the day!

Rickollect the dusty wall,
And the spider-webs, and all!
Rickollect the trimblin' spout
Where the meal come josslin' out—
Stand and comb yer fingers through
The fool-truck an hour er two—
Felt so sort o' warm-like and
Soothin' to a feller's hand!

Climb, high up above the stream,
And "coon" out the wobbly beam
And peek down from out the lof'
Where the weather-boards was off—
Gee-mun-*nee!* w'y, it takes grit
Even jest to think of it!—
Lookin' way down there below
On the worter roarin' so!

Rickollect the flume, and wheel,
And the worter slosh and reel
And jest ravel out in froth
Flossier'n satin cloth!
Rickollect them paddles jest
Knock the bubbles galley-west,
And plunge under, and come up,
Drippin' like a worter-pup!

And, to see them old things gone
That I onc't was bettin' on,
In rale p'int o' fact, I feel
Kind o' like that worter-wheel,—

Sort o' drippy-like and wet
Round the eyes—but paddlin' yet,
And, in mem'ry, loafin' still
Down around old Kingry's Mill!

THE EARTHQUAKE

CHARLESTON, SEPTEMBER 1, 1886

AN hour ago the lulling twilight leant
    Above us like a gentle nurse who slips
  A slow palm o'er our eyes, in soft eclipse
Of feigned slumber of most sweet content.
The fragrant zephyrs of the tropic went
    And came across the senses, like to sips
    Of lovers' kisses, when upon her lips
Silence sets finger in grave merriment.
Then—sudden—did the earth moan as it slept,
    And start as one in evil dreams, and toss
Its peopled arms up, as the horror crept,
    And with vast breast upheaved and rent across,
Fling down the storied citadel where wept,
    And still shall weep, a world above its loss.

Dr. Wyckliffe Smith, Jo Sneathen and Mr. Riley, taken at
Delphi, Indiana

A FALL-CRICK VIEW OF THE EARTH-QUAKE

I KIN hump my back and take the rain,
    And I don't keer how she pours;
I kin keep kind o' ca'm in a thunder-storm,
    No matter how loud she roars;
I hain't much skeered o' the lightnin',
    Ner I hain't sich awful shakes
Afeard o' *cyclones*—but I don't want none
    O' yer dad-burned old earthquakes!

As long as my legs keeps stiddy,
    And long as my head keeps plum',
And the buildin' stays in the front lot,
    I still kin whistle, *some!*
But about the time the old clock
    Flops off'n the mantel-shelf,
And the bureau skoots fer the kitchen,
    I'm a-goin' to skoot, myself!

Plague-take! ef you keep me stabled
    While any earthquakes is around!—
I'm jes' like the stock,—I'll beller
    And break fer the open ground!

And I 'low you'd be as nervous
  And in jes' about my fix,
When yer whole farm slides from inunder
    you,
  And on'y the mor'gage sticks!

Now cars hain't a-goin' to kill you
  Ef you don't drive 'crost the track;
Crediters never'll jerk you up
  Ef you go and pay 'em back;
You kin stand all moral and mundane storms
  Ef you'll on'y jes' behave—
But a' EARTHQUAKE:—Well, ef it wanted you
  It 'ud husk you out o' yer grave!

WHEN THE WORLD BU'STS THROUGH

Casually Suggested by an Earthquake

WHERE'S a boy a-goin',
   An' what's he goin' to do,
An' how's he goin' to do it,
   When the world bu'sts through?
Ma she says "she can't tell
   What we're comin' to!"
An' Pop says "he's ist skeered
   Clean—plum—through!"

S'pose we'd be a-playin'
   Out in the street,
An' the ground 'ud split up
   'Bout forty feet!—
Ma says "she ist knows
   We 'ud tumble in";
An' Pop says "he bets you
   Nen we wouldn't grin!"

S'pose we'd ist be 'tendin'
   Like we had a show,
Down in the stable
   Where we mustn't go,—

Ma says, "The earthquake
   Might make it fall";
An' Pop says, "More'n like
   Swaller barn an' all!"

Landy! ef we both wuz
   Runnin' 'way from school,
Out in the shady woods
   Where it's all so cool!—
Ma says "a big tree
   Might sqush our head";
An' Pop says, "Chop 'em out
   Both—killed—dead!"

But where's a boy goin',
   An' what's he goin' to do,
An' how's he goin' to do it,
   Ef the world bu'sts through?
Ma she says "she can't tell
   What we're comin' to!"
An' Pop says "he's ist skeered
   Clean—plum—through!"

THE OLD RETIRED SEA-CAPTAIN

THE old sea-captain has sailed the seas
   So long, that the waves at mirth,
Or the waves gone wild, and the crests of these,
   Were as near playmates from birth:
He has loved both the storm and the calm, because
   They seemed as his brothers twain,—
The flapping sail was his soul's applause,
   And his rapture, the roaring main.

But now—like a battered hulk seems he,
   Cast high on a foreign strand,
Though he feels "in port," as it need must be,
   And the stay of a daughter's hand—
Yet ever the round of the listless hours,—
   His pipe, in the languid air—
The grass, the trees, and the garden flowers,
   And the strange earth everywhere!

And so betimes he is restless here
   In this little inland town,
With never a wing in the atmosphere
   But the windmill's, up and down;

His daughter's home in this peaceful vale,
  And his grandchild 'twixt his knees—
But never the hail of a passing sail,
  Nor the surge of the angry seas!

He quits his pipe, and he snaps its neck—
  Would speak, though he coughs instead,
Then paces the porch like a quarter-deck
  With a reeling mast o'erhead!
Ho! the old sea-captain's cheeks glow warm,
  And his eyes gleam grim and weird,
As he mutters about, like a thunder-storm,
  In the cloud of his beetling beard.

JIM

HE was jes' a plain, ever'-day, all-round kind of
     a jour.,
     Consumpted-lookin'—but la!
The jokeiest, wittiest, story-tellin', song-singin',
     laughin'est, jolliest
     Feller you ever saw!
Worked at jes' coarse work, but you kin bet he was
     fine enough in his talk,
     And his feelin's too!
Lordy! ef he was on'y back on his bench ag'in
     to-day, a-carryin' on
     Like he ust to do!

Any shopmate'll tell you there never was, on top o'
     dirt,
     A better feller'n Jim!
You want a favor, and couldn't git it anywheres
     else—
     You could git it o' him!
Most free-heartedest man thataway in the world,
     I guess!
     Give up ever' nickel he's worth—
And, ef you'd a-wanted it, and named it to him, and
     it was his,
     He'd 'a' give you the earth!

Allus a-reachin' out, Jim was, and a-he'ppin' some
      Pore feller on to his feet—
He'd 'a' never 'a' keered how hungry he was hisse'f,
      So's *the feller* got somepin' to eat!
Didn't make no differ'nce at all to him how *he* was
      dressed,
      He ust to say to me,—
"You togg out a tramp purty comfortable in winter-
      time, a-huntin' a job,
      And he'll git along!" says he.

Jim didn't have, ner never could git ahead, so overly
      much
      O' this world's goods at a time.—
'Fore now I've saw him, more'n onc't, lend a dollar,
      and haf to, more'n likely,
      Turn round and borry a dime!
Mebby laugh and joke about it hisse'f fer a while—
      then jerk his coat,
      And kind o' square his chin,
Tie on his apern, and squat hisse'f on his old shoe-
      bench,
      And go to peggin' ag'in!

Patientest feller, too, I reckon, 'at ever jes' natch-
      urly
      Coughed hisse'f to death!
Long enough after his voice was lost he'd laugh in
      a whisper and say
      He could git ever'thing but his breath—

"*You* fellers," he'd sort o' twinkle his eyes and say,
    "Is a-pilin' on to me
A mighty big debt fer that-air little weak-chested
    ghost o' mine to pack
    Through all Eternity!"

Now there was a man 'at jes' 'peared-like, to me,
    'At ortn't *'a' never* 'a' died!
"But death hain't a-showin' no favors," the old boss
    said—
    "On'y to *Jim!*" and cried:
And Wigger, who puts up the best sewed-work in
    the shop—
    Er the whole blame neighberhood,—
He says, "When God made Jim, I bet you He didn't
    do anything else that day
    But jes' set around and feel good!"

OLD OCTOBER

OLD October's purt' nigh gone,
And the frosts is comin' on
Little *heavier* every day—
Like our hearts is thataway!
Leaves is changin' overhead
Back from green to gray and red,
Brown and yeller, with their stems
Loosenin' on the oaks and e'ms;
And the balance of the trees
Gittin' balder every breeze—
Like the heads we're scratchin' on!
Old October's purt' nigh gone.

I love Old October so,
I can't bear to see her go—
Seems to me like losin' some
Old-home relative er chum—
'Pears like sort o' settin' by
Some old friend 'at sigh by sigh
Was a-passin' out o' sight
Into everlastin' night!
Hickernuts a feller hears
Rattlin' down is more like tears
Drappin' on the leaves below—
I love Old October so!

Can't tell what it is about
Old October knocks me out!—
I sleep well enough at night—
And the blamedest appetite
Ever mortal man possessed,—
Last thing et, it tastes the best!—
Warnuts, butternuts, pawpaws,
'Iles and limbers up my jaws
Fer raal service, sich as new
Pork, spareribs, and sausage, too.—
Yit, fer all, they's somepin' 'bout
Old October knocks me out!

JUDITH

OHER eyes are amber-fine—
Dark and deep as wells of wine,
While her smile is like the noon
Splendor of a dày of June.
If she sorrow—lo! her face
It is like a flowery space
In bright meadows, overlaid
With light clouds and lulled with shade.
If she laugh—it is the trill
Of the wayward whippoorwill
Over upland pastures, heard
Echoed by the mocking-bird
In dim thickets dense with bloom
And blurred cloyings of perfume.
If she sigh—a zephyr swells
Over odorous asphodels
And wan lilies in lush plots
Of moon-drown'd forget-me-nots.
Then, the soft touch of her hand—
Takes all breath to understand
What to liken it thereto!—
Never rose-leaf rinsed with dew
Might slip soother-suave than slips
Her slow palm, the while her lips
Swoon through mine, with kiss on kiss
Sweet as heated honey is.

THE LEGEND GLORIFIED

"I DEEM that God is not disquieted"—
   This in a mighty poet's rhymes I read;
And blazoned so forever doth abide
Within my soul the legend glorified.

Though awful tempests thunder overhead,
I deem that God is not disquieted,—
The faith that trembles somewhat yet is sure
Through storm and darkness of a way secure.

Bleak winters, when the naked spirit hears
The break of hearts, through stinging sleet of tears,
I deem that God is not disquieted;
Against all stresses am I clothed and fed.

Nay, even with fixed eyes and broken breath,
My feet dip down into the tides of death,
Nor any friend be left, nor prayer be said,
I deem that God is not disquieted.

ON A FLY-LEAF

IN JOHN BOYLE O'REILLY'S POEMS

SINGERS there are of courtly themes—
  Drapers in verse—who would dress their
    rhymes
In robes of ermine; and singers of dreams
  Of gods high-throned in the classic times;
Singers of nymphs, in their dim retreats,
  Satyrs, with scepter and diadem;
But the singer who sings as a man's heart beats
  Well may blush for the rest of them.

I like the thrill of such poems as these,—
  All spirit and fervor of splendid fact—
Pulse, and muscle, and arteries
  Of living, heroic thought and act!—
Where every line is a vein of red
  And rapturous blood all unconfined
As it leaps from a heart that has joyed and bled
  With the rights and the wrongs of all mankind.

OLD MAN'S NURSERY RHYME

IN the jolly winters
  Of the long-ago,
It was not so cold as now—
  Oh! No! No!
Then, as I remember,
  Snowballs to eat
Were as good as apples now,
  And every bit as sweet!

In the jolly winters
  Of the dead-and-gone,
Bub was warm as summer,
  With his red mitts on,—
Just in his little waist-
  And-pants all together,
Who ever heard him growl
  About cold weather?

In the jolly winters
  Of the long-ago—
Was it *half* so cold as now?
  Oh! No! No!

Who caught his death o' cold,
  Making prints of men
Flat-backed in snow that now's
  Twice as cold again?

In the jolly winters
  Of the dead-and-gone,
Startin' out rabbit-huntin'
  Early as the dawn,—
Who ever froze his fingers,
  Ears, heels, or toes,—
Or'd 'a' cared if he had?
  Nobody knows!

Nights by the kitchen stove,
  Shellin' white and red
Corn in the skillet, and
  Sleepin' four abed!
Ah! the jolly winters
  Of the long-ago!
We were not as old as now—
  Oh! No! No!

LEWIS D. HAYES

OBIT DECEMBER 28, 1886

IN the midmost glee of the Christmas
  And the mirth of the glad New Year,
A guest has turned from the revel,
  And we sit in silence here.

The band chimes on, yet we listen
  Not to the air's refrain,
But over it ever we strive to catch
  The sound of his voice again;—

For the sound of his voice was music,
  Dearer than any note
Shook from the strands of harp-strings,
  Or poured from the bugle's throat.—

A voice of such various ranges,
  His utterance rang from the height
Of every rapture, down to the sobs
  Of every lost delight.

Though he knew Man's force and his purpose,
   As strong as his strongest peers,
He knew, as well, the kindly heart,
   And the tenderness of tears.

So is it the face we remember
   Shall be always as a child's
That, grieved some way to the very soul,
   Looks bravely up and smiles.

O brave it shall look, as it looked its last
   On the little daughter's face—
Pictured only—against the wall,
   In its old accustomed place—

Where the last gleam of the lamplight
   Out of the midnight dim
Yielded its grace, and the earliest dawn
   Gave it again to him.

A LOCAL POLITICIAN FROM AWAY BACK

JEDGE is good at argyin'—
    No mistake in that!
Most folks 'at tackles *him*
    He'll skin 'em like a cat!
You see, the Jedge is read up,
    And b'en in politics,
Hand-in-glove, you might say,
    Sence back in '56.

Elected to the Shurrif, first,
    Then elected Clerk;
Went into lawin' then,
    And buckled down to work;
Practised three or four terms,
    Then he run for jedge—
Speechified a little 'round,
    And went in like a wedge!

Run fer Legislatur' twic't—
    Made her, ever' pop!
Keeps on the way he's doin',
    Don't know where he'll stop!

Some thinks he's got his eye
    On the gov'nership;—
Well, ef he tuk the track,
    Guess he'd make the trip.

But I started out to tell ye—
    (Now I allus liked *the man*—
Not fer his politics,
    But *social'*, understan'!—
Fer, 's regards to *my* views,
    Political and sich,—
When we come together there
    We're purty ap' to hitch)—

Ketched him in at Knox's shop
    On'y t'other day—
Gittin' shaved, the Jedge was,
    Er somepin' thataway.—
Well, I tetched him up some
    On the silver bill:—
Jedge says, "I won't discuss it;"
    I says, "You *will!*"

I-says-ee, "I reckon
    You'll concede with me,
Coin's the on'y ginuine
    Money," I-says-ee;
Says I, "What's a dollar-bill?"
    Says I, "What's a ten—
Er forty-'leven hunderd of 'em?—
    Give us *specie*, then!"

I seed I was a-gittin'
  The Jedge kind o' red
Around the gills. He hawked some
  And cle'red his throat and said—
"Facts is too complicated
  'Bout the bill in view,"
Squirmed and told the barber then
  He wisht he'd hurry through.

'Ll, then, I knowed I had him,—
  And the crowd around the fire
Was all a-winkin' at me,
  As the barber raised him higher—
Says I, "Jedge, what's a dollar?—
  Er a half-un," I-says-ee—
"What's a *quarter?*—What's a *dime?*"
  "What's *cents?*" says he.

W'y, I had him fairly b'ilin'!
  "You needn't comb my hair,"
He says to the barber—
  "I want fresh air;"
And you'd 'a' died a-laughin'
  To 'a' seed him grab his hat,
As I-says-ee, says I, "Judge,
  Where you goin' at!"

Jedge is good at argyin',
  By-and-large; and yit
Beat him at his own game
  And he's goin' to git!

And yit the Jedge is read up,
    And b'en in politics,
Hand-in-glove, you might say,
    Sence back in '56.

THE MUTE SINGER

I

THE morning sun seemed fair as though
It were a great red rose ablow
In lavish bloom,
With all the air for its perfume,—
Yet he who had been wont to sing,
Could trill no thing.

II

Supine, at noon, as he looked up
Into the vast inverted cup
Of heavenly gold,
Brimmed with its marvels manifold,
And his eye kindled, and his cheek—
Song could not speak.

III

Night fell forebodingly; he knew
Soon must the rain be falling, too,—
And, home, heartsore,
A missive met him at the door—
—Then Song lit on his lips, and he
Sang gloriously.

381

THE CYCLONE

SO lone I stood, the very trees seemed drawn
   In conference with themselves.—Intense—in-
      tense
Seemed everything;—the summer splendor on
   The sight,—magnificence!

A babe's life might not lighter fail and die
   Than failed the sunlight.—Though the hour was
      noon,
The palm of midnight might not lighter lie
   Upon the brow of June.

With eyes upraised, I saw the underwings
   Of swallows—gone the instant afterward—
While from the elms there came strange twitterings,
   Stilled scarce ere they were heard.

The river seemed to shiver; and, far down
   Its darkened length, I saw the sycamores
Lean inward closer, under the vast frown
   That weighed above the shores.

Then was a roar, born of some awful burst! . . .
  And one lay, shrieking, chattering, in my path—
Flung—he or I—out of some space accurst
  As of Jehovah's wrath:

Nor barely had he wreaked his latest prayer,
  Ere back the noon flashed o'er the ruin done,
And, o'er uprooted forests tousled there,
  The birds sang in the sun.

IN DAYS TO COME

I N days to come—whatever ache
  Of age shall rack our bones, or quake
  Our slackened thews—whate'er grip
  Rheumatic catch us i' the hip,—
We, each one, for the other's sake,
Will of our very wailings make
  Such quips of song as well may shake
The spasm'd corners from the lip—
    In days to come.

Ho! ho! how our old hearts shall rake
The past up!—how our dry eyes slake
  Their sight upon the dewy drip
  Of juicy-ripe companionship,
And blink stars from the blind opaque—
    In days to come.

THE STEPMOTHER

FIRST she come to our house,
  Tommy run and hid;
And Emily and Bob and me
  We cried jus' like we did
When Mother died,—and we all said
'At we all wisht 'at we was dead!

And Nurse she couldn't stop us;
  And Pa he tried and tried,—
We sobbed and shook and wouldn't look,
  But only cried and cried;
And nen some one—we couldn't jus'
Tell who—was cryin' same as us!

Our Stepmother! Yes, it was her,
  Her arms around us all—
'Cause Tom slid down the banister
  And peeked in from the hall.—
And we all love her, too, because
She's purt' nigh good as Mother was!

WHEN MY DREAMS COME TRUE

I

WHEN my dreams come true—when my dreams
come true—
Shall I lean from out my casement, in the starlight
and the dew,
To listen—smile and listen to the tinkle of the
strings
Of the sweet guitar my lover's fingers fondle, as
he sings?
And as the nude moon slowly, slowly shoulders into
view,
Shall I vanish from his vision—when my dreams
come true?

When my dreams come true—shall the simple gown
I wear
Be changed to softest satin, and my maiden-braided
hair
Be raveled into flossy mists of rarest, fairest gold,
To be minted into kisses, more than any heart can
hold?—
Or "the summer of my tresses" shall my lover
liken to
"The fervor of his passion"—when my dreams
come true?

II

When my dreams come true—I shall bide among
    the sheaves
Of happy harvest meadows; and the grasses and the
    leaves
Shall lift and lean between me and the splendor of
    the sun,
Till the noon swoons into twilight, and the gleaners'
    work is done—
Save that yet an arm shall bind me, even as the
    reapers do
The meanest sheaf of harvest—when my dreams
    come true.

When my dreams come true! when my dreams
    come true!
True love in all simplicity is fresh and pure as
    dew;—
The blossom in the blackest mold is kindlier to the
    eye
Than any lily born of pride that looms against the
    sky:
And so it is I know my heart will gladly welcome
    you,
My lowliest of lovers, when my dreams come true.

THE CHANT OF THE CROSS-BEARING CHILD

I BEAR dis cross dis many a mile.
  O de cross-bearin' chile—
    De cross-bearin' chile!

I bear dis cross 'long many a road
Wha' de pink ain't bloom' an' de grass done mowed.
  O de cross-bearin' chile—
    De cross-bearin' chile!

Hit's on my conscience all dese days
Fo' ter bear de cross 'ut de good Lord **lays**
On my po' soul, an' ter lif my praise
  O de cross-bearin' chile—
    De cross-bearin' chile!

I's nigh 'bout weak ez I mos' kin be,
Yit de Marstah call an' He say,—"You's **free**
Fo' ter 'cept dis cross, an' ter cringe yo' **knee**
To no n'er man in de worl' but Me!"
  O de cross-bearin' chile—
    De cross-bearin' chile!

388

Says you guess wrong, ef I let you guess—
Says you 'spec' mo', an'-a you git less:—
Says you go eas', says you go wes',
An' whense you fine de road 'ut you like bes'
You betteh take chice er any er de res'!
  O de cross-bearin' chile—
   De cross-bearin' chile!

He build my feet, an' He fix de signs
Dat de shoe hit pinch an' de shoe hit bines
Ef I on'y w'ah eights an'-a wanter w'ah nines;
I hone fo' de rain, an' de sun hit shines,
An' whilse I hunt de sun, hit's de rain I fines.—
O-a trim my lamp, an'-a gyrd my lines!
  O de cross-bearin' chile—
   De cross-bearin' chile!

I wade de wet, an' I walk de dry:
I done tromp long, an' I done clim' high;
An' I pilgrim on ter de jasper sky,
An' I taken de resk fo' ter cas' my eye
Wha' de Gate swing wide an' de Lord draw nigh,
An' de Trump hit blow, an' I hear de cry,—
"You lay dat cross down by an' by!—
  O de Cross-bearin' Chile—
   De Cross-bearin' Chile!"

THREE DEAD FRIENDS

ALWAYS suddenly they are gone—
 The friends we trusted and held secure—
Suddenly we are gazing on,
 Not a *smiling* face, but the marble-pure
Dead mask of a face that nevermore
 To a smile of ours will make reply—
  The lips close-locked as the eyelids are,—
Gone—swift as the flash of the molten ore
 A meteor pours through a midnight sky,
  Leaving it blind of a single star.

Tell us, O Death, Remorseless Might!
 What is this old, unescapable ire
You wreak on us?—from the birth of light
 Till the world be charred to a core of fire!
We do no evil thing to you—
 We seek to evade you—that is all—
  That is your will—you will not be known
Of men. What, then, would you have us do?—
 Cringe, and wait till your vengeance fall,
  And your graves be fed, and the trumpet
   blown?

You desire no friends; but *we*—O we
  Need them so, as we falter here,
Fumbling through each new vacancy,
  As each is stricken that we hold dear.
One you struck but a year ago;
  And one not a month ago; and one—
    (God's vast pity!)—and one lies now
Where the widow wails, in her nameless woe,
  And the soldiers pace, with the sword and gun,
    Where the comrade sleeps, with the laureled
      brow.

And what did the first?—that wayward soul,
  Clothed of sorrow, yet nude of sin,
And with all hearts bowed in the strange control
  Of the heavenly voice of his violin.
Why, it was music the way he *stood,*
  So grand was the poise of the head and so
    Full was the figure of majesty!—
One heard with the eyes, as a deaf man would,
  And with all sense brimmed to the overflow
    With tears of anguish and ecstasy.

And what did the girl, with the great warm light
  Of genius sunning her eyes of blue,
With her heart so pure, and her soul so white—
  What, O Death, did she do to you?
Through field and wood as a child she strayed,
  As Nature, the dear sweet mother led;
    While from her canvas, mirrored back,

Glimmered the stream through the everglade
  Where the grape-vine trailed from the trees to
      wed
    Its likeness of emerald, blue and black.

And what did he, who, the last of these,
  Faced you, with never a fear, O Death?
Did you hate *him* that he loved the breeze,
  And the morning dews, and the rose's breath?
Did you hate him that he answered not
  Your hate again—but turned, instead,
    His only hate on his country's wrongs?
Well—you possess him, dead!—but what
  Of the good he wrought? With laureled head
    He bides with us in his deeds and songs.

Laureled, first, that he bravely fought,
  And forged a way to our flag's release;
Laureled, next, for the harp he taught
  To wake glad songs in the days of peace—
Songs of the woodland haunts he held
  As close in his love as they held their bloom
    In their inmost bosoms of leaf and vine—
Songs that echoed and pulsed and welled
  Through the town's pent streets, and the sick
      child's room,
    Pure as a shower in soft sunshine.

Claim them, Death; yet their fame endures.
  What friend next will you rend from us
In that cold, pitiless way of yours,
  And leave us a grief more dolorous?

Speak to us!—tell us, O Dreadful Power!—
  Are we to have not a lone friend left?—
    Since, frozen, sodden, or green the sod,
In every second of every hour,
    Some one, Death, you have thus bereft,
      Half inaudibly shrieks to God.

WHEN SHE COMES HOME

WHEN she comes home again! A thousand
  ways
 I fashion, to myself, the tenderness
 Of my glad welcome: I shall tremble—yes;
And touch her, as when first in the old days
I touched her girlish hand, nor dared upraise
  Mine eyes, such was my faint heart's sweet dis-
   tress
  Then silence: and the perfume of her dress:
The room will sway a little, and a haze
  Cloy eyesight—soul-sight, even—for a space;
And tears—yes; and the ache here in the throat,
  To know that I so ill deserve the place
Her arms make for me; and the sobbing note
  I stay with kisses, ere the tearful face
  Again is hidden in the old embrace.

LUTHER A. TODD

OBIT JULY 27, 1887, KANSAS CITY, MISSOURI

GIFTED, and loved and praised
  By every friend;
Never a murmur raised
  Against him, to the end!
With tireless interest
He wrought as he thought best,—
  And—lo, we bend
Where now he takes his rest!

His heart was loyal, to
  Its latest thrill,
To the home-loves he knew—
  And now forever will,—
Mother and brother—they
The first to pass away,—
  And, lingering still,
The sisters bowed to-day.

Pure as a rose might be,
  And sweet, and white,
His father's memory
  Was with him day and night:—

395

He spoke of him, as one
May now speak of the son,—
  Sadly and tenderly,
Yet as a trump had done.

Say, then, of him: He knew
  Full depths of care
And stress of pain, and you
  Do him scant justice there,—
Yet in the lifted face
Grief left not any trace,
  Nor mark unfair,
To mar its manly grace.

It was as if each day
  Some new hope dawned—
Each blessing in delay,
  To him, was just beyond;
Between whiles, waiting, he
Drew pictures cunningly—
  Fantastic—fond—
Things that we laughed to see.

Sometimes, as we looked on
  His crayon's work,
Some angel-face would dawn
  Out radiant, from the mirk
Of features old and thin,
Or jowled with double-chin,
  And eyes asmirk,
And gaping mouths agrin.

That humor in his art,
  Of genius born,
Welled warmly from a heart
  That could not but adorn
All things it touched with love—
The eagle, as the dove—
  The burst of morn—
The night—the stars above.

Sometimes, amid the wild
  Of faces queer,
A mother, with her child
  Pressed warm and close to her;
This, I have thought, somehow,
The wife, with head abow,
  Unreconciled,
In the great shadow now.

.   .   .   .

O ye of sobbing breath,
  Put by all sighs
Of anguish at his death—
  Turn—as he turned his eyes,
In that last hour, unknown
In strange lands, all alone—
  Turn toward the skies,
And, smiling, cease thy moan.

WHEN OLD JACK DIED

WHEN Old Jack died, we stayed from school
    (they said,
At home, we needn't go that day), and none
Of us ate any breakfast—only one,
And that was Papa—and his eyes were red
When he came round where we were, by the shed
Where Jack was lying, half-way in the sun
And half-way in the shade. When we begun
To cry out loud, Pa turned and dropped his head
And went away; and Mamma, she went back
Into the kitchen. Then, for a long while,
All to ourselves, like, we stood there and cried.
We thought so many good things of Old Jack,
And funny things—although we didn't smile—
We couldn't only cry when Old Jack died.

When Old Jack died, it seemed a human friend
Had suddenly gone from us; that some face
That we had loved to fondle and embrace
From babyhood, no more would condescend
To smile on us forever. We might bend
With tearful eyes above him, interlace

Our chubby fingers o'er him, romp and race,
Plead with him, call and coax—aye, we might send
The old halloo up for him, whistle, hist,
(If sobs had let us) or, as wildly vain,
Snapped thumbs, called "Speak," and he had not
    replied;
We might have gone down on our knees and kissed
The tousled ears, and yet they must remain
Deaf, motionless, we knew—when Old Jack died.

When Old Jack died, it seemed to us, some way,
That all the other dogs in town were pained
With our bereavement, and some that were chained,
Even, unslipped their collars on that day
To visit Jack in state, as though to pay
A last, sad tribute there, while neighbors craned
Their heads above the high board fence, and
    deigned
To sigh "Poor Dog!" remembering how they
Had cuffed him, when alive, perchance, because,
For love of them he leaped to lick their hands—
Now, that he could not, were they satisfied?
We children thought that, as we crossed his paws,
And o'er his grave, 'way down the bottom-lands,
Wrote "Our First Love Lies Here," when Old
    Jack died.

WHEN THE HEARSE COMES BACK

A THING 'at's 'bout as tryin' as a healthy man kin
      meet
Is some poor feller's funeral a-joggin' 'long the
    street:
The slow hearse and the hosses—slow enough, to
    say the least,
Fer to even tax the patience of the gentleman de-
    ceased!
The low scrunch of the gravel—and the slow grind
    of the wheels,—
The slow, slow go of ev'ry woe 'at ev'rybody feels!
So I ruther like the contrast when I hear the whip-
    lash crack
A quickstep fer the hosses,
           When the
               Hearse
                  Comes
                     Back!

Meet it goin' to'rds the cimet'ry, you'll want to drap
    yer eyes—
But ef the plumes don't fetch you, it'll ketch you
    otherwise—
You'll haf to see the caskit, though you'd ort to look
    away
And 'conomize and save yer sighs fer any other
    day!

Yer sympathizin' won't wake up the sleeper from
    his rest—
Yer tears won't thaw them hands o' his 'at's froze
    acrost his breast!
And this is why—when airth and sky's a-gittin'
    blurred and black—
I like the flash and hurry
         When the
           Hearse
              Comes
                 Back!

It's not 'cause I don't 'preciate it ain't no time fer
    jokes,
Ner 'cause I' got no common human feelin' fer the
    folks;—
I've went to funerals myse'f, and tuk on some,
    perhaps—
Fer my heart's 'bout as mal'able as any other
    chap's,—
I've buried father, mother—but I'll haf to jes' git
    you
To "excuse *me*," as the feller says.—The p'int I'm
    drivin' to
Is, simply, when we're plum broke down and all
    knocked out o' whack,
It he'ps to shape us up, like,
         When the
           Hearse
              Comes
                 Back!

The idy! wadin' round here over shoe-mouth deep
    in woe,
When they's a graded 'pike o' joy and sunshine,
    don't you know!
When evening strikes the pastur', cows'll pull out
    fer the bars,
And skittish-like from out the night'll prance the
    happy stars.
And so when *my* time comes to die, and I've got
    ary friend
'At wants expressed my last request—I'll, mebby,
    rickommend
To drive slow, ef they haf to, goin' 'long the
    out'ard track,
But I'll smile and say, "You speed 'em
            When the
               Hearse
                  Comes
                     Back!"

NESSMUK

I HAIL thee, Nessmuk, for the lofty tone
  Yet simple grace that marks thy poetry!
 True forester thou art, and still to be,
Even in happier fields than thou hast known.
Thus, in glad visions, glimpses am I shown
  Of groves delectable—"preserves" for thee—
  Ranged but by friends of thine—I name thee
      three:—
First, Chaucer, with his bald old pate new-grown
  With changeless laurel; next, in Lincoln-green,
    Gold belted, bowed and bugled, Robin Hood;
  And next, Ike Walton, patient and serene:
These three, O Nessmuk, gathered hunter-wise,
Are camped on hither slopes of Paradise,
    To hail thee first and greet thee, as they should.

BACK FROM A TWO-YEARS' SENTENCE

BACK from a two-years' sentence!
  And though it had been ten,
You think, I were scarred no deeper
  In the eyes of my fellow men.
"My fellow men"?—sounds like a satire,
  You think—and I so allow,
Here in my home since childhood,
  Yet more than a stranger now!

Pardon!—Not wholly a stranger,—
  For I have a wife and child:
That woman has wept for two long years,
  And yet last night she smiled!—
Smiled, as I leapt from the platform
  Of the midnight train, and then—
All that I knew was that smile of hers,
  And our babe in my arms again!

Back from a two-years' sentence—
  But I've thought the whole thing through,—
A hint of it came when the bars swung back
  And I looked straight up in the blue

Of the blessed skies with my hat off!
   Oho! I've a wife and child:
That woman has wept for two long years,
   And yet last night she smiled!

TO ROBERT LOUIS STEVENSON

ON HIS FIRST VISIT TO AMERICA

ROBERT LOUIS STEVENSON!
Blue the lift and braw the dawn
O' yer comin' here amang
Strangers wha hae luved ye lang!
Strangers tae ye we maun be,
Yet tae us ye're kenned a wee
By the writin's ye hae done,
Robert Louis Stevenson.

Syne ye've pit yer pen tae sic'
Tales it stabbt us tae the quick—
Whiles o' tropic isles an' seas
An' o' gowden treesuries—
Tales o' deid men's banes; an' tales
Swete as sangs o' nightingales
When the nune o' mirk's begun—
Robert Louis Stevenson.

Sae we hail thee! nane the less
For the "burr" that ye caress
Wi' yer denty tongue o' Scots,
Makin' words forget-me-nots

406

O' yer bonnie braes that were
Sung o' Burns the Poemer—
And that later lavrock, one
Robert Louis Stevenson.

THEM FLOWERS

TAKE a feller 'at's sick and laid up on the shelf,
   All shaky, and ga'nted, and pore—
Jes' all so knocked out he can't handle hisself
   With a stiff upper-lip any more;
Shet him up all alone in the gloom of a room
   As dark as the tomb, and as grim,
And then take and send him some roses in bloom,
   And you can have fun out o' him!

You've ketched him 'fore now—when his liver
     was sound
   And his appetite notched like a saw—
A-mockin' you, maybe, fer romancin' round
   With a big posy-bunch in yer paw;
But you ketch him, say, when his health is away,
   And he's flat on his back in distress,
And *then* you kin trot out yer little bokay
   And not be insulted, I guess!

You see, it's like this, what his weaknesses is,—
   Them flowers makes him think of the days
Of his innocent youth, and that mother o' his,
   And the roses that *she* us't to raise:—

So here, all alone with the roses you send—
  Bein' sick and all trimbly and faint,—
My eyes is—my eyes is—my eyes is—old friend—
  Is a-leakin'—I'm blamed ef they ain't!

THE ROBINS' OTHER NAME

IN the Orchard-Days, when you
  Children look like blossoms, too;
Bessie, with her jaunty ways
And trim poise of head and face,
Must have looked superior
Even to the blossoms,—for
Little Winnie once averred
Bessie looked just like the bird
Tilted on the topmost spray
Of the apple boughs in May,
With the redbreast, and the strong,
Clear, sweet warble of his song.—
"I don't know their *name*," Win said—
"I ist *maked* a name instead."—
So forever afterwards
We called robins "Bessie-birds."

THE RAIN

I

THE rain! the rain! the rain!
  It gushed from the skies and streamed
Like awful tears; and the sick man thought
  How pitiful it seemed!
And he turned his face away
  And stared at the wall again,
His hopes nigh dead and his heart worn out.
  O the rain! the rain! the rain!

II

The rain! the rain! the rain!
  And the broad stream brimmed the shores;
And ever the river crept over the reeds
  And the roots of the sycamores:
A corpse swirled by in a drift
  Where the boat had snapt its chain—
And a hoarse-voiced mother shrieked and raved.
  O the rain! the rain! the rain!

III

The rain! the rain! the rain!—
  Pouring, with never a pause,
Over the fields and the green byways—
  How beautiful it was!
And the new-made man and wife
  Stood at the window-pane
Like two glad children kept from school.
  O the rain! the rain! the rain!

TO EDGAR WILSON NYE

O "WILLIAM," in thy blithe companionship
   What liberty is mine—what sweet release
From clamorous strife, and yet what boisterous
      peace!
Ho! ho! it is thy fancy's finger-tip
That dints the dimple now, and kinks the lip
   That scarce may sing, in all this glad increase
   Of merriment! So, pray-thee, do not cease
To cheer me thus;—for, underneath the quip
Of thy droll sorcery, the wrangling fret
   Of all distress is stilled—no syllable
Of sorrow vexeth me—no tear-drops wet
   My teeming lids save those that leap to tell
Thee thou'st a guest that overweepeth, yet
   Only because thou jokest overwell.

A DISCOURAGING MODEL

JUST the airiest, fairiest slip of a thing,
　　With a Gainsborough hat, like a butterfly's wing,
Tilted up at one side with the jauntiest air,
And a knot of red roses sewn in under there
　　　　Where the shadows are lost in her hair.

Then a cameo face, carven in on a ground
Of that shadowy hair where the roses are wound;
And the gleam of a smile, O as fair and as faint
And as sweet as the masters of old used to paint
　　　　Round the lips of their favorite saint!

And that lace at her throat—and the fluttering hands
Snowing there, with a grace that no art understands,
The flakes of their touches—first fluttering at
The bow—then the roses—the hair—and then that
　　　　Little tilt of the Gainsborough hat.

Ah, what artist on earth with a model like this,
Holding not on his palette the tint of a kiss,
Nor a pigment to hint of the hue of her hair
Nor the gold of her smile—O what artist could dare
　　　　To expect a result half so fair?

THE SERENADE

THE midnight is not more bewildering
   To her drowsed eyes, than, to her ears, the
      sound
Of dim, sweet singing voices, interwound
With purl of flute and subtle twang of string,
Strained through the lattice, where the roses cling
   And, with their fragrance, waft the notes around
   Her haunted senses. Thirsting beyond bound
Of her slow-yielding dreams, the lilt and swing
   Of the mysterious, delirious tune,
She drains like some strange opiate, with awed eyes
   Upraised against her casement, where, aswoon,
The stars fail from her sight, and up the skies
   Of alien azure rolls the full round moon
   Like some vast bubble blown of summer noon.

DOC SIFERS

OF all the doctors I could cite you to in this-'ere
town
Doc Sifers is my favorite, jes' take him up and
down!
Count in the Bethel Neighberhood, and Rollins,
and Big Bear,
And Sifers' standin' jes' as good as ary doctor's
there!

There's old Doc Wick, and Glenn, and Hall, and
Wurgler, and McVeigh,
But I'll buck Sifers 'g'inst 'em all and down 'em
any day!
Most old Wick ever knowed, I s'pose, was *whisky!*
Wurgler—well,
He et morphine—ef actions shows, and facts' re-
liable!

But Sifers—though he ain't no sot, he's got his
faults; and yit
When you *git* Sifers onc't, you've got *a doctor,*
don't fergit!

He ain't much at his office, er his house, er any-
    where
You'd natchurly think certain fer to ketch the
    feller there.—

But don't blame Doc: he's got all sorts o' cur'ous
    notions—as
The feller says, his odd-come-shorts, like smart
    men mostly has.
He'll more'n like be potter'n' 'round the Blacksmith
    Shop; er in
Some back lot, spadin' up the ground, er gradin' it
    ag'in.

Er at the work bench, planin' things; er buildin' lit-
    tle traps
To ketch birds; galvenizin' rings; er graftin' plums,
    perhaps.
Make anything! good as the best!—a gun-stock—er
    a flute;
He whittled out a set o' chesstmen onc't o' laurel
    root.

Durin' the Army—got his trade o' surgeon there—
    I own
To-day a finger-ring Doc made out of a Sesesh
    bone!
An' glued a fiddle onc't fer me—jes' all so busted
    you
'D 'a' throwed the thing away, but he fixed her as
    good as new!

And take Doc, now, in *ager,* say, er *biles,* er *rheu-
    matiz,*
And all afflictions thataway, and he's the best
    they is!
Er janders—milksick—I don't keer—k-yore any-
    thing he tries—
A abscess; getherin' in yer yeer; er granilated eyes!

There was the Widder Daubenspeck they all give
    up fer dead;
A blame cowbuncle on her neck, and clean out of
    her head!
First had this doctor, what's-his-name, from "Pud-
    blesburg," and then
This little red-head, "Burnin' Shame" they call him
    —Dr. Glenn.

And they "consulted" on the case, and claimed she'd
    haf to die,—
I jes' was joggin' by the place, and heerd her dorter
    cry,
And stops and calls her to the fence; and I-says-I,
    "Let me
Send Sifers—bet you fifteen cents he'll k-yore her!"
    "Well," says she,

"Light out!" she says: And, lipp-tee-cut, I loped in
    town, and rid
'Bout two hours more to find him, but I kussed him
    when I did!

He was down at the Gunsmith Shop a-stuffin' birds!
    Says he,
"My sulky's broke." Says I, "You hop right on and
    ride with me!"

I got him there.—"Well, Aunty, ten days k'yores
    you," Sifers said,
"But what's yer idy livin' when yer jes' as good as
    dead?"
And there's Dave Banks—jes' back from war with-
    out a scratch—one day
Got ketched up in a sickle-bar, a reaper runaway.—

His shoulders, arms, and hands and legs jes' sawed
    in strips! And Jake
Dunn starts fer Sifers—feller begs to shoot him fer
    God-sake.
Doc, 'course, was gone, but he had penned the no-
    tice, "At Big Bear—
Be back to-morry; Gone to 'tend the Bee Conven-
    tion there."

But Jake, he tracked him—rid and rode the whole
    endurin' night!
And 'bout the time the roosters crowed they both
    hove into sight.
Doc had to ampitate, but 'greed to save Dave's arms,
    and swore
He could 'a' saved his legs ef he'd b'en there the day
    before.

Like when his wife's own mother died 'fore Sifers
    could be found,
And all the neighbors fer and wide a' all jes' chasin'
    round;
Tel finally—I had to laugh—it's jes' like Doc, you
    know,—
Was learnin' fer to telegraph, down at the old deepo.

But all they're faultin' Sifers fer, there's none of
    'em kin say
He's biggoty, er keerless, er not posted any way;
He ain't built on the common plan of doctors now-
    adays,
He's jes' a great, big, brainy man—that's where
    the trouble lays!

AFTERWHILES

WHERE are they—the Afterwhiles—
　　Luring us the lengthening miles
Of our lives? Where is the dawn
With the dew across the lawn
Stroked with eager feet the far
Way the hills and valleys are?
Where the sun that smites the frown
Of the eastward-gazer down?
Where the rifted wreaths of mist
O'er us, tinged with amethyst,
Round the mountain's steep defiles?
Where are all the afterwhiles?

Afterwhile—and we will go
Thither, yon, and to and fro—
From the stifling city streets
To the country's cool retreats—
From the riot to the rest
Where hearts beat the placidest:
Afterwhile, and we will fall
Under breezy trees, and loll
In the shade, with thirsty sight
Drinking deep the blue delight
Of the skies that will beguile
Us as children—afterwhile.

Afterwhile—and one intends
To be gentler to his friends,—
To walk with them, in the hush
Of still evenings, o'er the plush
Of home-leading fields, and stand
Long at parting, hand in hand:
One, in time, will joy to take
New resolves for some one's sake,
And wear then the look that lies
Clear and pure in other eyes—
He will soothe and reconcile
His own conscience—afterwhile.

Afterwhile—we have in view
A far scene to journey to,—
Where the old home is, and where
The old mother waits us there,
Peering, as the time grows late,
Down the old path to the gate.—
How we'll click the latch that locks
In the pinks and hollyhocks,
And leap up the path once more
Where she waits us at the door!—
How we'll greet the dear old smile,
And the warm tears—afterwhile!

Ah, the endless afterwhiles!—
Leagues on leagues, and miles on miles,
In the distance far withdrawn,
Stretching on, and on, and on,
Till the fancy is footsore

And faints in the dust before
The last milestone's granite face,
Hacked with: Here Beginneth Space.
O far glimmering worlds and wings,
Mystic smiles and beckonings,
Lead us through the shadowy aisles,
Out into the afterwhiles.

A HOME-MADE FAIRY TALE

BUD, come here to your uncle a spell,
   And I'll tell you something you mustn't tell—
For it's a secret and shore-'nuf true,
And maybe I oughtn't to tell it to you!—
But out in the garden, under the shade
Of the apple trees, where we romped and played
Till the moon was up, and you thought I'd gone
Fast asleep,—That was all put on!
For I was a-watchin' something queer
Goin' on there in the grass, my dear!—
'Way down deep in it, there I see
A little dude-Fairy who winked at me,
And snapped his fingers, and laughed as low
And fine as the whine of a mus-kee-to!
I kept still—watchin' him closer—and
I noticed a little guitar in his hand,
Which he leant 'g'inst a little dead bee—and laid
His cigarette down on a clean grass-blade,
And then climbed up on the shell of a snail—
Carefully dusting his swallowtail—
And pulling up, by a waxed web-thread,
This little guitar, you remember, I said!
And there he trinkled and trilled a tune,—

"My Love, so Fair, Tans in the Moon!"
Till, presently, out of the clover-top
He seemed to be singing to, came, k'pop!
The purtiest, daintiest Fairy face
In all this world, or any place!
Then the little ser'nader waved his hand,
As much as to say, "We'll excuse *you!*" and
I heard, as I squinted my eyelids to,
A kiss like the drip of a drop of dew!

A VOICE FROM THE FARM

IT is my dream to have you here with me,
  Out of the heated city's dust and din—
  Here where the colts have room to gambol in,
And kine to graze, in clover to the knee.
I want to see your wan face happily
  Lit with the wholesome smiles that have not been
  In use since the old games you used to win
When we pitched horseshoes: And I want to be
At utter loaf with you in this dim land
  Of grove and meadow, while the crickets make
  Our own talk tedious, and the bat wields
His bulky flight, as we cease converse and
  In a dusk like velvet smoothly take
  Our way toward home across the dewy fields.

From a photograph taken when thirty-five years old

THE OLD HOME BY THE MILL

THIS is "The old Home by the Mill"—fer we
    still call it so,
Although the *old mill,* roof and sill, is all gone long
    ago.
The old home, though, and the old folks—the old
    spring, and a few
Old cattails, weeds and hartychokes, is left to wel-
    come you!

Here, Marg'et!—fetch the man a *tin* to drink out
    of! Our spring
Keeps kindo'-sorto' cavin' in, but don't *"taste"*
    anything!
She's kindo' *agin',* Marg'et is—"the *old* process"—
    like me,
All ham-stringed up with rhumatiz, and on in
    seventy-three.

Jest me and Marg'et lives alone here—like in long
    ago;
The childern all putt off and gone, and married,
    don't you know?

One's millin' 'way out West somewhare; two other
    miller-boys
In Minnyopolis they air; and one's in Illinoise.

The *oldest* gyrl—the first that went—married and
    died right here;
The next lives in Winn's Settlement—fer purt' nigh
    thirty year!
And youngest one—was allus fer the old home
    here—but no!—
Her man turns in and he packs *her* 'way off to
    Idyho!

I don't miss them like *Marg'et* does—'cause I got
    her, you see;
And when she pines for them—that's 'cause *she's*
    only jest got *me!*
I laugh, and joke her 'bout it all.—But talkin' sense,
    I'll say,
When she was tuk so bad last Fall, I laughed then
    t'other way!

I hain't so favor'ble impressed 'bout *dyin';* but ef I
Found I was only second-best when *us two* come to
    die,
I'd 'dopt the "new process," in full, ef *Marg'et*
    died, you see,—
I'd jest crawl in my grave and pull the green grass
    over me!

THE OLD MAN AND JIM

OLD man never had much to say—
   'Ceptin' to Jim,—
And Jim was the wildest boy he had—
   And the old man jes' wrapped up in him!
Never heerd him speak but once
Er twice in my life,—and first time was
When the army broke out, and Jim he went,
The old man backin' him, fer three months;
And all 'at I heerd the old man say
Was, jes' as we turned to start away,—
   "Well, good-by, Jim:
      Take keer of yourse'f!"

'Peared-like, he was more satisfied
   Jes' *lookin'* at Jim
And likin' him all to hisse'f-like, see?—
   'Cause he was jes' wrapped up in him!
And over and over I mind the day
The old man come and stood round in the way
While we was drillin', a-watchin' Jim—
And down at the deepot a-heerin' him say,
   "Well, good-by, Jim:
      Take keer of yourse'f!"

Never was nothin' about the *farm*
    Disting'ished Jim;
Neighbors all ust to wonder why
    The old man 'peared wrapped up in him:
But when Cap. Biggler he writ back
'At Jim was the bravest boy we had
In the whole dern rigiment, white er black,
And his fightin' good as his farmin' bad—
'At he had led, with a bullet clean
Bored through his thigh, and carried the flag
Through the bloodiest battle you ever seen,—
The old man wound up a letter to him
'At Cap. read to us, 'at said: "Tell Jim
    Good-by,
        And take keer of hisse'f!"

Jim come home jes' long enough
    To take the whim
'At he'd like to go back in the calvery—
    And the old man jes' wrapped up in him!
Jim 'lowed 'at he'd had sich luck afore,
Guessed he'd tackle her three years more.
And the old man give him a colt he'd raised,
And follered him over to Camp Ben Wade,
And laid around fer a week er so,
Watchin' Jim on dress-parade—
Tel finally he rid away,
And last he heerd was the old man say,—
    "Well, good-by, Jim:
        Take keer of yourse'f!"

Tuk the papers, the old man did,
   A-watchin' fer Jim—
Fully believin' he'd make his mark
   Some way—jes' wrapped up in him!—
And many a time the word 'u'd come
'At stirred him up like the tap of a drum—
At Petersburg, fer instunce, where
Jim rid right into their cannons there,
And *tuk* 'em, and p'inted 'em t'other way,
And socked it home to the boys in gray,
As they scooted fer timber, and on and on—
Jim a lieutenant and one arm gone,
And the old man's words in his mind all day,—
    "Well, good-by, Jim:
      Take keer of yourse'f!"

Think of a private, now, perhaps,
   We'll say like Jim,
'At's clumb clean up to the shoulder-straps—
   And the old man jes' wrapped up in him!
Think of him—with the war plum' through,
And the glorious old Red-White-and-Blue
A-laughin' the news down over Jim,
And the old man, bendin' over him—
The surgeon turnin' away with tears
'At hadn't leaked fer years and years,
As the hand of the dyin' boy clung to
His father's, the old voice in his ears,—
    "Well, good-by, Jim:
      Take keer of yourse'f!"

OUR OLD FRIEND NEVERFAIL

O IT'S good to ketch a relative 'at's richer and
      don't run
When you holler out to hold up, and'll joke and
      have his fun;
It's good to hear a man called bad and then find out
      he's not,
Er strike some chap they call lukewarm 'at's really
      red-hot;
It's good to know the Devil's painted jes' a leetle
      black,
And it's good to have most anybody pat you on the
      back;—
But jes' the best thing in the world's our old friend
      Neverfail,
When he wags yer hand as honest as an old dog
      wags his tail!

I like to strike the man I owe the same time I can
      pay,
And take back things I've borried, and su'prise folks
      thataway;
I like to find out that the man I voted fer last fall,
That didn't git elected, was a scoundrel after all;

I like the man that likes the pore and he'ps 'em when
    he can;
I like to meet a ragged tramp 'at's still a gentleman;
But most I like—with you, my boy—our old friend
    Neverfail,
When he wags yer hand as honest as an old dog
    wags his tail!

DAN O'SULLIVAN

DAN O'SULLIVAN: It's your
        Lips have kissed "The Blarney," sure!—
To be trillin' praise av me,
Dhrippin' swhate wid poethry!—
Not that I'd not have ye sing—
Don't lave off for anything—
Jusht be aisy whilst the fit
Av me head shwells up to it!

Dade and thrue, I'm not the man,
Whilst yer singin', loike ye can,
To cry shtop because ye've blesht
My songs more than all the resht:—
I'll not be the b'y to ax
Any shtar to wane or wax,
Or ax any clock that's woun'
To run up inshtid av down!

Whist yez! Dan O'Sullivan!—
Him that made the Irishman
Mixt the birds in wid the dough,
And the dew and mistletoe

434

Wid the whusky in the quare
Muggs av us—and here we air,
Three parts right, and three parts wrong,
Shpiked with beauty, wit and song!

AT "THE LITERARY"

FOLKS in town, I reckon, thinks
  They git all the fun they air
Runnin' loose 'round!—but, 'y jinks!
We' got fun, and fun to spare,
Right out here amongst the ash
And oak timber ever'where!
Some folks else kin cut a dash
'Sides town-people, don't fergit!—
'Specially in *winter*-time,
When they's snow, and roads is fit.
In them circumstances I'm
Resig-nated to my lot—
Which putts me in mind o' what
    'S called "The Literary."

Us folks in the country sees
Lots o' fun!—Take spellin'-school;
Er ole hoe-down jamborees;
Er revivals; er ef you'll
Tackle taffy-pullin's you
Kin git fun, and quite a few!—
Same with huskin's. But all these
Kind o' frolics they hain't new

436

By a hunderd year' er two
Cipher on it as you please!
But I'll tell you what I jest
Think walks over all the rest—
Anyway it suits *me* best,—
　　That's "The Literary."

First they started it—" 'y gee !"
Thinks-says-I, "this settle-ment
'S gittin' too high-toned fer me!"
But when all begin to jine,
And I heerd *Izory* went,
I jest kind o' drapped in line,
Like you've seen some sandy, thin,
Scrawny shoat putt fer the crick
Down some pig-trail through the thick
Spice-bresh, where the whole drove's been
'Bout six weeks 'fore he gits in !—
"Can't tell nothin'," I-says-ee,
" 'Bout it tel you go and see
　　Their blame 'Literary' !"

Very first night I was there
I was 'p'inted to be what
They call "Critic"—so's a fair
And square jedgment could be got
On the pieces 'at was read,
And on the debate,—"Which air
Most destructive element,
Fire er worter?" Then they hed
Compositions on "Content,"

"Death," and "Botany"; and Tomps
He read one on "Dreenin' Swamps"
I p'nounced the boss, and said,
"So fur, 'at's the best thing read
　　In yer 'Literary'!"

Then they *sung* some—tel I called
Order, and got back ag'in
In the critic's cheer, and hauled
All o' the p'formers in:—
Mandy Brizendine read one
I fergit; and Doc's was "Thought";
And Sarepty's, hern was "None
Air Denied 'at Knocks"; and Daut—
Fayette Strawnse's little niece—
She got up and spoke a piece:
Then Izory she read hern—
"Best thing in the whole concern,"
I-says-ee; "now le' 's adjourn
　　This-here 'Literary'!"

They was some contendin'—yit
We broke up in harmony.
Road outside as white as grit,
And as slick as slick could be!—
I'd fetched 'Zory in my sleigh,—
And I had a heap to say,
Drivin' back—in fact, I driv
'Way around the old north way,
Where the Daubenspeckses live.
'Zory allus—'fore that night—

Never 'peared to feel jest right
In my company.—You see,
On'y thing on earth saved me
    Was that "Literary"!

SHE "DISPLAINS" IT

"HAD, too!"
    "Hadn't, neither!"
So contended Bess and May—
    Neighbor children, who were boasting
Of their grandmammas, one day.

    "Had, too!"
        "Hadn't, neither!"
All the difference begun
    By May's saying she'd *two* grandmas—
While poor Bess had only one.

    "Had, too!"
        "Hadn't, neither!"
Tossing curls, and kinks of friz!—
    "How could you have *two* gran'muvvers
When ist *one* is all they is?"

    "Had, too!"
        "Hadn't, neither!—
'Cause ef you had *two*," said Bess,
    "You'd *displain* it!" Then May answered,
"My gran'mas wuz *twins*, I guess!"

DEAD, MY LORDS

DEAD, my lords and gentlemen!—
Stilled the tongue, and stayed the pen;
Cheek unflushed and eye unlit—
Done with life, and glad of it.

Curb your praises now as then:
Dead, my lords and gentlemen.—
What he wrought found its reward
In the tolerance of the Lord.

Ye who fain had barred his path,
Dread ye now this look he hath?—
Dead, my lords and gentlemen—
Dare ye not smile back again?

Low he lies, yet high and great
Looms he, lying thus in state.—
How exalted o'er ye when
Dead, my lords and gentlemen!

A MAN BY THE NAME OF BOLUS

A MAN by the name of Bolus—(all 'at we'll ever
know
Of the stranger's name, I reckon—and I'm kind o'
glad it's so!)—
Got off here, Christmas morning, looked 'round the
town, and then
Kind o' sized up the folks, I guess, and—went away
again!

The fac's is, this man Bolus got "run in," Christ-
mas-day;
The town turned out to see it, and cheered, and
blocked the way;
And they dragged him 'fore the Mayor—fer he
couldn't er *wouldn't* walk—
And socked him down fer trial—though he couldn't
er *wouldn't* talk!

Drunk? They was no doubt of it!—W'y, the marshal
of the town
Laughed and testified 'at he fell *up*-stairs 'stid o'
down!

This man by the name of Bolus?—W'y, he even
    drapped his jaw
And snored on through his "hearin' "—drunk as
    you ever saw!

One feller spit in his boot-leg, and another 'n'
    drapped a small
Little chunk o' ice down his collar,—but he didn't
    wake at all!
And they all nearly split when his Honor said, in
    one of his witty ways,
To "chalk it down fer him, 'Called away—be back
    in thirty days!' "

That's where this man named Bolus slid, kind o'
    like in a fit,
Flat on the floor; and—drat my ears! I hear 'em
    a-laughin' yit!
Somebody fetched Doc Sifers from jes' acrost the
    hall—
And all Doc said was, "Morphine! We're too late!"
    and that's all!

That's how they found his name out—piece of a
    letter 'at read:
"Your wife has lost her reason, and little Nathan's
    dead—
Come ef you kin,—fergive *her*—but, Bolus, as fer
    me,
This hour I send a bullet through where my heart
    ort to be!"

Man by the name of Bolus!—As his revilers broke
Fer the open air, 'peared-like, to me, I heerd a voice
　　'at spoke—
*Man by the name of Bolus! git up from where you
　　lay—*
*Git up and smile white at 'em, with your hands
　　crossed thataway!*

THE TRAVELING MAN

I

COULD I pour out the nectar the gods only can,
  I would fill up my glass to the brim
And drink the success of the Traveling Man,
  And the house represented by him;
And could I but tincture the glorious draught
  With his smiles, as I drank to him then,
And the jokes he has told and the laughs he has
      laughed,
  I would fill up the goblet again—

And drink to the sweetheart who gave him good-by
  With a tenderness thrilling him this
Very hour, as he thinks of the tear in her eye
  That salted the sweet of her kiss;
To her truest of hearts and her fairest of hands
  I would drink, with all serious prayers,
Since the heart she must trust is a Traveling Man's,
  And as warm as the ulster he wears.

II

I would drink to the wife, with the babe on her
    knee,
  Who awaits his returning in vain—
Who breaks his brave letters so tremulously
  And reads them again and again!
And I'd drink to the feeble old mother who sits
  At the warm fireside of her son
And murmurs and weeps o'er the stocking she
    knits,
  As she thinks of the wandering one.

I would drink a long life and a health to the friends
  Who have met him with smiles and with cheer—
To the generous hand that the landlord extends
  To the wayfarer journeying here:
And I pledge, when he turns from this earthly abode
  And pays the last fare that he can,
Mine Host of the Inn at the End of the Road
  Will welcome the Traveling Man!

THE ABSENCE OF LITTLE WESLEY

SENCE little Wesley went, the place seems all
    so strange and still—
W'y, I miss his yell o' "Gran-pap!" as I'd miss the
    whipperwill!
And to think I ust to *scold* him fer his everlastin'
    noise,
When I on'y rickollect him as the best o' little boys!
I wisht a hunderd times a day 'at he'd come tromp-
    in' in,
And all the noise he ever made was twic't as loud
    ag'in!—
It 'u'd seem like some soft music played on some
    fine insturment,
'Longside o' this loud lonesomeness, sence little
    Wesley went!

Of course the clock don't tick no louder than it ust
    to do—
Yit now they's times it 'pears like it 'u'd bu'st
    itse'f in two!
And let a rooster, suddent-like, crow som'ers clos't
    around,
And seems's ef, mighty nigh it, it 'u'd lift me off the
    ground!

And same with all the cattle when they bawl around
 the bars,
In the red o' airly morning, er the dusk and dew and
 stars,
When the neighbers' boys 'at passes never stop, but
 jes' go on,
A-whistlin' kind o' to theirse'v's—sence little Wesley's gone!

And then, o' nights, when Mother's settin' up on-
 common late,
A-bilin' pears er somepin', and I set and smoke and
 wait,
Tel the moon out through the winder don't look
 bigger'n a dime,
And things keeps gittin' stiller—stiller—stiller all
 the time,—
I've ketched myse'f a-wishin' like—as I clumb on
 the cheer
To wind the clock, as I hev done fer more'n fifty
 year—
A-wishin' 'at the time hed come fer us to go to bed,
With our last prayers, and our last tears, sence little
 Wesley's dead!

WHEN THE GREEN GITS BACK IN THE TREES

IN spring, when the green gits back in the trees,
And the sun comes out and *stays,*
And yer boots pulls on with a good tight squeeze,
And you think of yer barefoot days;
When you *ort* to work and you want to *not,*
And you and yer wife agrees
It's time to spade up the garden-lot,
When the green gits back in the trees—
Well! work is the least o' *my* idees
When the green, you know, gits back in the
trees!

When the green gits back in the trees, and bees
Is a-buzzin' aroun' ag'in
In that kind of a lazy go-as-you-please
Old gait they bum roun' in;
When the groun's all bald whare the hay-rick stood,
And the crick's riz, and the breeze
Coaxes the bloom in the old dogwood,
And the green gits back in the trees,—
I like, as I say, in sich scenes as these,
The time when the green gits back in the trees!

449

When the whole tail-fethers o' Winter-time
   Is all pulled out and gone!
And the sap it thaws and begins to climb,
   And the swet it starts out on
A feller's forred, a-gittin' down
   At the old spring on his knees—
I kindo' like jest a-loaferin' roun'
   When the green gits back in the trees—
     Jest a-potterin' roun' as I—durn—please—
     When the green, you know, gits back in the
      trees!

HOW IT HAPPENED

I GOT to *thinkin'* of her—both her parunts dead
    and gone—
And all her sisters married off, and none but her and
    John
A-livin' all alone thare in that lonesome sorto' way,
And him a blame' old bachelor, confirm'der ev'ry
    day!
I'd knowed 'em all, from childern, and theyr daddy
    from the time
He settled in the neghborhood, and hadn't ary a
    dime
Er dollar, when he married, fer to start housekeepin'
    on!—
So I got to *thinkin'* of her—both her parunts dead
    and gone!

I got to *thinkin'* of her; and a-wundern what *she*
    done
That all *her sisters* kep' a-gittin' married, one by
    one,
And her without *no* chances—and the best girl of
    the pack—
A' old maid, with her hands, you might say, tied
    behind her back!

451

And *Mother,* too, afore she died,—*she* ust to jest
    take on,
When none of 'em wuz left, you know, but Evaline
    and John,
And jest declare to goodness 'at the young men must
    be bline
To not see what a wife they'd git ef they got
    Evaline!

I got to *thinkin'* of her: In my great affliction she
Wuz sich a comfort to us, and so kind and negh-
    borly,—
She'd come, and leave her housework, fer to he'p
    out little Jane,
And talk of *her own* mother 'at she'd never see
    again—
They'd sometimes *cry* together—though, fer the
    most part, she
Would have the child so rickonciled and happy-like
    'at we
Felt lonesomer'n ever when she'd putt her bonnet on
And say she'd railly *haf* to be a-gittin' back to John!

I got to *thinkin'* of her, as I say,—and more and
    more
I'd think of her dependence, and the burdens 'at
    she bore,—
Her parunts both a-bein' dead, and all her sisters
    gone
And married off, and her a-livin' thare alone with
    John—

You might say jest a-toilin' and a-slavin' out her
    life
Fer a man 'at hadn't pride enugh to git hisse'f a
    wife—
'Less some one married *Evaline* and packed her off
    some day!—
So I got to *thinkin'* of her—and—It happened
    thataway.

GLADNESS

MY ole man named Silas: he
    Dead long 'fo' ole Gin'l Lee
S'rendah, whense de wah wuz done.
Yanks dey tuk de plantation—
Mos' high-handed evah you see!—
Das rack round', an' fiah an' bu'n,
An' jab de beds wid deir bay-net-gun,
An' sweah we niggahs all scotch-free,—
An' Massah John C. Pemberton
        Das tuk an' run!

"Gord Armighty, marm," he 'low,
"He'p you an' de chillen now!"
Blaze crack out 'n de roof inside
Tel de big house all das charified!
Smoke roll out 'n de ole haymow
An' de wa'house do'—an' de fiah das roah—
An' all dat 'backer, 'bout half dried,
        Hit smell das fried!

Nelse, my ol'est boy, an' John,—
Atter de baby das wuz bo'n,
Erlongse dem times, an' lak ter 'a' died,
An' Silas he be'n slip an' gone

'Bout eight weeks ter de Union side,—
Dem two boys dey start fo' ter fine
An' jine deir fader acrost de line.
Ovahseeah he wade an' tromp
Eveh-which-way fo' to track 'em down—
Sic de bloodhoun' fro' de swamp—
An' bring de news dat John he drown'—
   But dey save de houn'!

Someway ner Nelse git fru'
An' fight fo' de ole Red, White, an' Blue,
Lak his fader is, ter er heart's delight—
An' nen crope back wid de news, one night—
Sayes, "Fader's killed in a scrimmage-fight,
An' saunt farewell ter ye all, an' sayes
Fo' ter name de baby 'Gladness,' 'caze
Mighty nigh she 'uz be'n borned free!"
An' de boy he smile so strange at me
I sayes, "Yo' 's hurt *yo'se'f!*" an' he
Sayes, "I's killed, too—an' dat's all else!"
   An' dah lay Nelse!

Hope an' Angrish, de twins, be'n sole
'Fo' dey mo' 'n twelve year ole:
An' Mary Magdaline sole too.
An' dah I's lef', wid Knox-Andrew,
An' Lily, an' Maje, an' Margaret,
An' little gal-babe, 'at's borned dat new
She scaisely ole fo' ter be named yet—
Less'n de name 'at Si say to—
   An' co'se hit *do.*

An' I taken dem chillen, evah one
(An' a-oh my Mastah's will be done!),
An' I break fo' de Norf, whah dey all raised free
(An' a-oh good Mastah, come git me!).
Knox-Andrew, on de day he died,
Lef' his fambly er shop an' er lot berside;
An' Maje die ownin' er team—an' he
  Lef' all ter me.

Lily she work at de Gran' Hotel—
(Mastah! Mastah! take me—do!)—
An' Lily she ain' married well:
He stob a man—an' she die too;
An' Margaret she too full er pride
Ter own her kin tel er day she died!
But Gladness!—'t ain' soun' sho'-nuff true,—
But she teached school!—an' er white folks, too,
Ruspec' dat gal 'mos' high ez I do!—
'Caze she 'uz de bes' an' de mos' high bred—
De las' chile bo'n, an' de las chile dead,
  O' all ten head!

  .   .   .   .

Gladness! Gladness! a-oh my chile!
Wa'm my soul in yo' sweet smile!
Daughter o' Silas! o-rise an' sing
Tel er heart-beat pat lak er pigeon-wing!
Sayes, O Gladness! wake dem eyes—
Sayes, a-lif' dem folded han's, an' rise—
Sayes, a-coax me erlong ter Paradise,
    An' a-hail de King,
      O Gladness!

THE WIFE-BLESSÈD

IN youth he wrought, with eyes ablur,
   Lorn-faced and long of hair—
In youth—in youth he painted her
   A sister of the air—
Could clasp her not, but felt the stir
   Of pinions everywhere.

She lured his gaze, in braver days,
   And tranced him siren-wise;
And he did paint her, through a haze
   Of sullen paradise,
With scars of kisses on her face
   And embers in her eyes.

And now—nor dream nor wild conceit—
   Though faltering, as before—
Through tears he paints her, as is meet,
   Tracing the dear face o'er
With lilied patience meek and sweet
   As Mother Mary wore.

ROBERT BURNS WILSON

WHAT intuition named thee?—Through
        what thrill
Of the awed soul came the command divine
Into the mother-heart, foretelling thine
Should palpitate with his whose raptures will
Sing on while daisies bloom and lavrocks trill
    Their undulating ways up through the fine
    Fair mists of heavenly reaches? Thy pure line
Falls as the dew of anthems, quiring still
The sweeter since the Scottish singer raised
  His voice therein, and, quit of every stress
    Of earthly ache and longing and despair,
Knew certainly each simple thing he praised
  Was no less worthy, for its lowliness,
    Than any joy of all the glory There.

'MONGST THE HILLS O' SOMERSET

'MONGST the Hills o' Somerset
    Wisht I was a-roamin' yet!
My feet won't get usen to
These low lands I'm trompin' through.
Wisht I could go back there, and
Stroke the long grass with my hand,
Kind o' like my sweetheart's hair
Smoothed out underneath it there!
Wisht I could set eyes once more
On our shadders, on before,
Climbin', in the airly dawn,
Up the slopes 'at love growed on
Natchurl as the violet
'Mongst the Hills o' Somerset!

How 't 'u'd rest a man like me
Jes' fer 'bout an hour to be
Up there where the morning air
Could reach out and ketch me there!—
Snatch my breath away, and then
Rensh and give it back again
Fresh as dew, and smellin' of
The old pinks I ust to love,

And a-flavor'n' ever' breeze
With mixt hints o' mulberries
And May-apples, from the thick
Bottom-lands along the crick
Where the fish bit, dry er wet,
'Mongst the Hills o' Somerset!

Like a livin' pictur' things
All comes back: the bluebird swings
In the maple, tongue and bill
Trillin' glory fit to kill!
In the orchard, jay and bee
Ripens the first pears fer me,
And the "Prince's Harvest" they
Tumble to me where I lay
In the clover, provin' still
"A boy's will is the wind's will."
Clean fergot is time, and care,
And thick hearin', and gray hair—
But they's nothin' I ferget
'Mongst the Hills o' Somerset!

Middle-aged—to be edzact,
Very middle-aged, in fact,
Yet a-thinkin' back to then,
I'm the same wild boy again!
There's the dear old home once more,
And there's Mother at the door—
Dead, I know, fer thirty year',
Yet she's singin', and I hear;
And there's Jo, and Mary Jane,

And Pap, comin' up the lane!
Dusk's a-fallin'; and the dew,
'Pears like, it's a-fallin' too—
Dreamin' we're all livin' yet
'Mongst the Hills o' Somerset!

A PASSING HAIL

LET us rest ourselves a bit!
    Worry?—Wave your hand to it—
Kiss your finger-tips and smile
It farewell a little while.

Weary of the weary way
We have come from Yesterday,
Let us fret us not, instead,
Of the weary way ahead.

Let us pause and catch our breath
On the hither side of death,
While we see the tender shoots
Of the grasses—not the roots,—

While we yet look down—not up—
To seek out the buttercup
And the daisy where they wave
O'er the green home of the grave.

Let us launch us smoothly on
The soft billows of the lawn,
And drift out across the main
Of our childish dreams again:

462

Voyage off, beneath the trees,
O'er the field's enchanted seas,
Where the lilies are our sails,
And our sea-gulls, nightingales:

Where no wilder storm shall beat
Than the wind that waves the wheat,
And no tempest-burst above
The old laughs we used to love:

Lose all troubles—gain release,
Languor, and exceeding peace,
Cruising idly o'er the vast,
Calm mid-ocean of the Past.

Let us rest ourselves a bit!
Worry?—wave your hand to it—
Kiss your finger-tips, and smile
It farewell a little while.

"LAST CHRISTMAS WAS A YEAR AGO"

The Old Lady Speaks

LAST Christmas was a year ago,
　　Says I to David, I-says-I,
"We're goin' to morning-service, so
You hitch up right away: I'll try
To tell the girls jes' what to do
Fer dinner.—We'll be back by two."
I didn't wait to hear what he
Would more'n like say back to me,
But banged the stable door and flew
Back to the house, jes' plumb chilled through.

Cold! *Wooh!* how cold it was!　My-oh!
Frost flyin', and the air, you know,
"Jes' sharp enough," heerd David swear,
"To shave a man and cut his hair!"
And blow and blow! and snow and snow!—
Where it had drifted 'long the fence
And 'crost the road,—some places, though,
Jes' swep' clean to the gravel, so
The goin' was as bad fer sleighs
As 'twas fer wagons,—and both ways,

'Twixt snow-drifts and the bare ground, I've
Jes' wundered we got through alive;
I hain't saw nothin', 'fore er sence,
'At beat it anywheres, I know—
Last Christmas was a year ago.

And David said, as we set out,
'At Christmas services was 'bout
As cold and wuthless kind o' love
To offer up as he knowed of;
And as fer him, he railly thought
'At the Good Bein' up above
Would think more of us—as He ought—
A-stayin' home on sich a day,
And thankin' of Him thataway!
And jawed on, in a' undertone,
'Bout leavin' Lide and Jane alone
There on the place, and me not there
To oversee 'em, and p'pare
The stuffin' fer the turkey, and
The sass and all, you understand.

I've allus managed David by
Jes' sayin' *nothin'*. That was why
He'd chased Lide's beau away—'cause Lide
She'd allus take up Perry's side
When David tackled him; and so,
Last Christmas was a year ago,—
Er ruther, 'bout *a week afore,*—
David and Perry'd quarr'l'd about

Some tom-fool argyment, you know,
And Pap told him to "Jes' git out
O' there, and not to come no more,
And, when he went, to shet the door!"
And as he passed the winder, we
Saw Perry, white as white could be,
March past, onhitch his hoss, and light
A see-gyar, and lope out o' sight.
Then Lide she come to me and cried!
And I said nothin'—was no need.
And yit, you know, that man jes' got
Right out o' there's ef he'd be'n shot,
P'tendin' he must go and feed
The stock er somepin'. Then I tried
To git the pore girl pacified.

But, gittin' back to—where was we?—
Oh, yes!—where David lectered me
All way to meetin', high and low,
Last Christmas was a year ago:
Fer all the awful cold, they was
A fair attendunce; mostly, though,
The crowd was round the stoves, you see,
Thawin' their heels and scrougin' us.
Ef 't 'adn't be'n fer the old Squire
Givin' *his* seat to us, as in
We stomped, a-fairly perishin',
And David could 'a' got no fire,
He'd jes' 'a' drapped there in his tracks:
And Squire, as I was tryin' to yit
Make room fer him, says, "No; the fac's

Is, *I* got to git up and git
'*Ithout* no preachin'. Jes' got word—
Trial fer life—can't be deferred!"
And out he putt!

. . . . . . And all way through
The sermont—and a long one, too—
I couldn't he'p but think o' Squire
And us changed round so, and admire
His gintle ways,—to give his warm
Bench up, and have to face the storm.
And when I noticed David he
Was needin' jabbin'—I thought best
To kind o' sort o' let him rest:
'Peared-like he slep' so peacefully!
And then I thought o' home, and how
And what the gyrls was doin' now,
And kind o' prayed, 'way in my breast,
And breshed away a tear er two
As David waked, and church was through.

By time we'd "howdyed" round and shuck
Hands with the neighbors, must 'a' tuck
A half-hour longer: ever' one
A-sayin' "Christmas gift!" afore
David er me—so we got none!
But David warmed up, more and more,
And got so jokey-like, and had
His sperits up, and 'peared so glad,
I whispered to him, "S'pose you ast
A passel of 'em come and eat

Their dinners with us. Gyrls's got
A full-and-plenty fer the lot
And all their kin!" So David passed
The invite round: and ever' seat
In ever' wagon-bed and sleigh
Was jes' packed, as we rode away,—
The young folks, mil'd er so along,
A-strikin' up a sleighin'-song,
Tel David laughed and yelled, you know,
And jes' whirped up and sent the snow
And gravel flyin' thick and fast—
Last Christmas was a year ago.
W'y, that-air seven-mil'd ja'nt we come—
Jes' seven mil'd scant from church to home—
It didn't 'pear, *that* day, to be
Much furder railly 'n 'bout *three!*

But I was purty squeamish by
The time home hove in sight and I
See two vehickles standin' there
Already. So says I, *"Prepare!"*
All to myse'f. And presently
David he sobered; and says he,
"Hain't that-air Squire Hanch's old
Buggy," he says, "and claybank mare?"
Says I, "Le' 's git in out the cold—
Your company's nigh 'bout froze!" He says,
"Whose sleigh's that-air, a-standin' there?"
Says I, "It's no odds *whose—you* jes'
Drive to the house and let us out,
'Cause we're jes' *freezin'*, nigh about!"

Well, David swung up to the door,
And out we piled. And first I heerd
Jane's voice, then *Lide's*,—I thought afore
I reached that gyrl I'd jes' die, shore;
And *when* I reached her, wouldn't keered
Much ef I had, I was so glad,
A-kissin' her through my green veil,
And jes' excitin' her so bad,
'At *she* broke down *herse'f*—and Jane,
She cried—and we all hugged again.
And *David?*—David jes' turned pale!—
Looked at the gyrls, and then at me,
Then at the open door—and then—
"Is old Squire Hanch in there?" says he.
The old Squire suddently stood in
The doorway, with a sneakin' grin.
"Is Perry Anders in there, too?"
Says David, limberin' all through,
As Lide and me both grabbed him, and
Perry stepped out and waved his hand
And says, "Yes, Pap." And David jes'
Stooped and kissed Lide, and says, "I guess
Yer *mother's* much to blame as you.
Ef *she* kin resk him, I kin too!"

The dinner we had then hain't no
Bit better'n the one to-day
'At we'll have fer 'em! Hear some sleigh
A-jinglin' now. David, fer *me*,
I wish you'd jes' go out and see
Ef they're in sight yit. It jes' does

Me good to think, in times like these,
Lide's done so well.   And David he's
More tractabler'n what he was,
Last Christmas was a year ago.

LITTLE JOHNTS'S CHRIS'MUS

WE got it up a-purpose, jes' fer little Johnts,
    you know;
His mother was so pore an' all, an' had to manage
    so.—
Jes' bein' a War-widder, an' her pension mighty
    slim,
She'd take in weavin', er work out, er anything
    fer him!

An' little Johnts was puny-like—but law, the *nerve*
    he had!—
You'd want to kind o' pity him, but couldn't, very
    bad,—
His pants o' army-blanket an' his coat o' faded blue
Kep' hintin' of his father like, an' pity wouldn't do!

So we collogued together onc't, one winter-time, 'at
    we—
Jes' me an' Mother an' the girls, and Wilse, John-
    Jack an' Free—
Would jine and git up little Johnts, by time 'at
    Chris'mus come,
Some sort o' doin's, don't you know, 'at would
    su'prise him some.

An' so, all on the quiet, Mother she turns in an'
    gits
Some blue-janes—cuts an' makes a suit; an' then
    sets down and knits
A pair o' little galluses to go 'long with the rest—
An' putts in a red-flannen back an' buckle on the
    vest.—

The little feller'd be'n so much around our house,
    you see,
An' be'n sich he'p to her an' all, an' handy as could
    be,
'At Mother couldn't do too much fer little Johnts—
    No, *sir!*
She ust to jes' declare 'at "he was meat-an'-drink to
    her!"

An' Piney, Lide, an' Madeline they watch their
    chance an' rid
To Fountaintown with Lijey's folks; an' bought a
    book, they did,
O' fairy tales, with pictur's in; an' got a little pair
O' red-top boots 'at John-Jack said he'd be'n
    a-pricin' there.

An' Lide got him a little sword, an' Madeline, a
    drum;
An' shootin'-crackers—Lawzy-day! an' they're so
    danger-some!

An' Piney, ever' time the rest 'ud buy some other
    toy,
She'd take an' turn in then an' buy more candy fer
    the boy!

"Well," thinks-says-I, when they got back, *"your
    pocketbooks is dry!"*—
But little Johnts was there hisse'f that afternoon,
    so I—
Well, *all* of us kep' mighty mum, tel we got him
    away
By tellin' him to be shore an' come to-morry—
    Chris'mus Day—

An' fetch *his mother* 'long with him! An' how he
    scud acrost
The fields—his towhead, in the dusk, jes' like a
    streak o' frost!—
His comfert flutter'n' as he run—an' old Tige, don't
    you know,
A-jumpin' high fer rabbits an' a plowin' up the
    snow!

It must 'a' be'n 'most *ten* that night afore we got
    to bed—
With Wilse an' John-Jack he'ppin' us; an' Freeman
    in the shed,
An' Lide out with the lantern while he trimmed the
    Chris'mus Tree
Out of a little scrub-oak-top 'at suited to a "T"!

All night I dreamp' o' hearin' things a-skulkin'
  round the place—
An' "Old Kriss," with his whiskers off, an' freckles
  on his face—
An' reindeers, shaped like shavin'-hosses at the
  cooper-shop,
A-stickin' down the chimbly, with their heels out at
  the top!

By time 'at Mother got me up 'twas plum daylight
  an' more—
The front yard full o' neighbers all a-crowdin'
  round the door,
With Johnts's mother leadin'; yes—an' little Johnts
  hisse'f,
Set up on Freeman's shoulder, like a jug up on the
  she'f!

Of course I can't describe it when they all got in to
  where
We'd conjered up the Chris'mus Tree an' all the
  fixin's there!—
Fer all the shouts o' laughture—clappin' hands, an'
  crackin' jokes,
Was heap o' kissin' goin' on amongst the women-
  folks:—

Fer, lo-behold-ye! there they had that young-un!—
  An' his chin
A-wobblin'-like;—an', shore enough, at last he
  started in—

An'—sich another bellerin', in all my mortal days,
I never heerd, er 'spect to hear, in woe's app'inted
    ways!

An' Mother grabs him up an' says: "It's more'n he
    can bear—
It's all too *suddent* fer the child, an' too su'prisin'!
    —*There!*"
"Oh, no it ain't"—sobbed little Johnts—"I ain't
    su'prised—but I'm
A-cryin' 'cause I watched you all, an' knowed it all
    the time!"

THAT-AIR YOUNG-UN

THAT-AIR young-un ust to set
By the crick here day by day.—
Watch the swallers dip and wet
Their slim wings and skoot away;
Watch these little snipes along
The low banks tilt up and down
'Mongst the reeds, and hear the song
Of the bullfrogs croakin' roun':
Ust to set here in the sun
Watchin' things, and listenun,
'Peared-like, mostly to the roar
Of the dam below, er to
That-air riffle nigh the shore
Jes' acrost from me and you.
Ust to watch him from the door
Of the mill.—'Ud rigg him out
With a fishin'-pole and line—
Dig worms fer him—nigh about
Jes' spit on his bait!—but he
Never keered much, 'pearantly,
To ketch fish!—He'd ruther fine

Out some sunny place, and set
Watchin' things, with droopy head,
And "a-listenun," he said—
"Kind o' listenun above
The old crick to what the wet
Warter was a-talkin' of!"

Jevver hear sich talk as that?
Bothered *Mother* more'n me
What the child was cipher'n' at.—
Come home onc't and said 'at he
Knowed what the snake-feeders thought
When they grit their wings; and knowed
Turkle-talk, when bubbles riz
Over where the old roots growed
Where he th'owed them pets o' his—
Little turripuns he caught
In the County Ditch and packed
In his pockets days and days!—
Said he knowed what goslin's quacked—
Could tell what the killdees sayes,
And grasshoppers, when they lit
In the crick and "minnies" bit
Off their legs.—"But, *blame!*" sayes he,
Sort o' lookin' clean above
Mother's head and on through me—
(And them eyes!—I see 'em yet!)—
"*Blame!*" he says, "ef I kin see,
Er make *out,* jes' what the wet
Warter is a-talkin' of!"

Made me *nervous!* Mother, though,
Said best not to scold the child—
The Good Bein' knowed.—And so
We was only rickonciled
When he'd be asleep.—And then,
Time, and time, and time again,
We've watched over him, you know—
Her a-sayin' nothin'—jes'
Kind o' smoothin' back his hair,
And, all to herse'f, I guess,
Studyin' up some kind o' prayer
She ain't tried yet.—Onc't she said,
Cotin' Scriptur', " 'He,' " says she,
In a solemn whisper, " 'He
Givuth His beloved sleep!' "
And jes' then I heerd the rain
Strike the shingles, as I turned
Res'less to'rds the wall again.
Pity strong men dast to weep!—
Specially when up above
Thrash! the storm comes down, and you
Feel the midnight plum soaked through
Heart and soul, and wunder, too,
What the warter's talkin' of!

.   .   .   .   .

Found his hat 'way down below
Hinchman's Ford.—'Ves' Anders he
Rid and fetched it. Mother she
Went *wild* over that, you know—
Hugged it! kissed it!—*Turribul!*

My hopes then was all gone too. . . .
Brung him in, with both hands full
O' warter-lilies—'peared-like new-
Bloomed fer him—renched whiter still
In the clear rain, mixin' fine
And finer in the noon sunshine. . . .
Winders of the old mill looked
On him where the hill-road crooked
In on through the open gate. . . .
Laid him on the old settee
On the porch there. Heerd the great
Roarin' dam acrost—and we
Heerd a crane cry in amongst
The sycamores—and then a dove
Cutterin' on the mill-roof—then
Heerd the crick, and thought again,
"*Now* what's it a-talkin' of ?"

THE PIPES OF PAN

THE Pipes of Pan! Not idler now are they
    they
  Than when their cunning fashioner first blew
  The pith of music from them: Yet for you
And me their notes are blown in many a way
Lost in our murmurings for that old day
  That fared so well without us.—Waken to
  The pipings here at hand:—The clear halloo
Of truant voices, and the roundelay
The waters warble in the solitude
Of blooming thickets, where the robin's breast
  Sends up such ecstasy o'er dale and dell
Each tree top answers, till in all the wood
There lingers not one squirrel in his nest
  Whetting his hunger on an empty shell.

DOWN AROUND THE RIVER

NOON-TIME and June-time, down around the
　　river!
Have to furse with Lizey Ann—but lawzy! I
　　fergive her!
Drives me off the place, and says 'at all 'at she's
　　a-wishin',
Land o' gracious! time'll come I'll git enough o'
　　fishin'!
Little Dave, a-choppin' wood, never 'pears to
　　notice;
Don't know where she's hid his hat, er keerin'
　　where his coat is,—
Specalatin', more'n like, he hain't a-goin' to mind
　　me,
And guessin' where, say twelve o'clock, a feller'd
　　likely find me.

Noon-time and June-time, down around the river!
Clean out o' sight o' home, and skulkin' under
　　kivver
Of the sycamores, jack-oaks, and swamp-ash and
　　ellum—

Idies all so jumbled up, you kin hardly tell 'em!—
Tired, you know, but *lovin'* it, and smilin' jes' to
    think 'at
Any sweeter tiredness you'd fairly want to *drink* it.
Tired o' fishin'—tired o' fun—line out slack and
    slacker—
All you want in all the world's a little more
    tobacker!

Hungry, but *a-hidin'* it, er jes' a-not a-keerin':—
Kingfisher gittin' up and skootin' out o' hearin';
Snipes on the t'other side, where the County Ditch
    is,
Wadin' up and down the aidge like they'd rolled
    their britches!
Old turkle on the root kind o' sort o' drappin'
Intoo th' worter like he don't know how it happen!
Worter, shade and all so mixed, don't know which
    you'd orter
Say, th' *worter* in the shadder—*shadder* in the
    worter!

Somebody hollerin'—'way around the bend in
Upper Fork—where yer eye kin jes' ketch the
    endin'
Of the shiney wedge o' wake some muss-rat's a-
    makin'
With that pesky nose o' his! Then a sniff o' bacon,
Corn-bread and 'dock-greens—and little Dave a-
    shinnin'

'Crost the rocks and mussel-shells, a-limpin' and a-
    grinnin',
With yer dinner fer ye, and a blessin' from the
    giver.
Noon-time and June-time down around the river!

HIS MOTHER

DEAD! my wayward boy—*my own*—
　　Not *the Law's!* but *mine*—the good
God's free gift to me alone,
　　Sanctified by motherhood.

"Bad," you say: Well, who is not?
　　"Brutal"—"with a heart of stone"—
And "red-handed."—Ah! the hot
　　Blood upon your own!

I come not, with downward eyes,
　　To plead for him shamedly,—
God did not apologize
　　When he gave the boy to me.

Simply, I make ready now
　　For *His* verdict.—*You* prepare—
You have killed us both—and how
　　Will you face us There?

IN BOHEMIA

HA! My dear! I'm back again—
    Vender of Bohemia's wares!
Lordy! How it pants a man
    Climbing up those awful stairs!
        Well, I've made the dealer say
        Your sketch *might* sell, anyway!
        And I've made a publisher
        Hear my poem, Kate, my dear.

In Bohemia, Kate, my dear—
    Lodgers in a musty flat
On the top floor—living here
    Neighborless, and used to that,—
        Like a nest beneath the eaves,
        So our little home receives
        Only guests of chirping cheer—
        We'll be happy, Kate, my dear!

Under your north light there, you
    At your easel, with a stain
On your nose of Prussian blue,
    Paint your bits of shine and rain;

With my feet thrown up at will
O'er my littered window-sill,
I write rhymes that ring as clear
As your laughter, Kate, my dear.

Puff my pipe, and stroke my hair—
Bite my pencil-tip and gaze
At you, mutely mooning there
O'er your "Aprils" and your "Mays"!
Equal inspiration in
Dimples of your cheek and chin,
And the golden atmosphere
Of your paintings, Kate, my dear!

Trying! Yes, at times it is,
To clink happy rhymes, and fling
On the canvas scenes of bliss,
When we are half famishing!—
When your "jersey" rips in spots,
And your hat's "forget-me-nots"
Have grown tousled, old and sear—
It is trying, Kate, my dear!

But—as sure—*some* picture sells,
And—sometimes—the poetry—
Bless us! How the parrot yells
His acclaims at you and me!
How we revel then in scenes
Or high banqueting!—sardines—
Salads—olives—and a sheer
Pint of sherry, Kate, my dear!

Even now I cross your palm
  With this great round world of gold!—
"Talking wild?" Perhaps I am—
  Then, this little five-year-old!—
    Call it anything you will,
    So it lifts your face until
    I may kiss away that tear
    Ere it drowns me, Kate, my dear.

MOON-DROWNED

'TWAS the height of the fête when we quitted
    the riot,
And quietly stole to the terrace alone,
Where, pale as the lovers that ever swear by it,
    The moon it gazed down as a god from his throne.
We stood there enchanted.—And O the delight of
    The sight of the stars and the moon and the sea,
And the infinite skies of that opulent night of
    Purple and gold and ivory!

The lisp of the lip of the ripple just under—
    The half-awake nightingale's dream in the yews—
Came up from the water, and down from the
        wonder
    Of shadowy foliage, drowsed with the dews,—
Unsteady the firefly's taper—unsteady
    The poise of the stars, and their light in the tide,
As it struggled and writhed in caress of the eddy,
    As love in the billowy breast of a bride.

The far-away lilt of the waltz rippled to us,
    And through us the exquisite thrill of the air:
Like the scent of bruised bloom was her breath, and
        its dew was
    Not honier-sweet than her warm kisses were.

We stood there enchanted.—And O the delight of
  The sight of the stars and the moon and the sea,
And the infinite skies of that opulent night of
  Purple and gold and ivory!

WHO SANTY CLAUS WUZ

JES' a little bit o' feller—I remember still,—
Ust to almost *cry* fer Christmas, like a young-
  ster will.
Fourth o' July's nothin' to it!—New-Year's ain't a
  smell:
Easter-Sunday—Circus-Day—jes' all dead in the
  shell!
Lordy, though! at night, you know, to set around
  and hear
The old folks work the story off about the sledge
  and deer,
And "Santy" skootin' round the roof, all wrapped
  in fur and fuzz—
Long afore
            I knowed who
                      "Santy Claus" wuz!

Ust to wait, and set up late, a week or two ahead:
Couldn't hardly keep awake, ner wouldn't go to bed:
Kittle stewin' on the fire, and Mother settin' here
Darnin' socks, and rockin' in the skreeky rockin'-
  cheer;

Pap gap', and wunder where it wuz the mcney went,
And quar'l with his frosted heels, and spill his lini-
    ment:
And me a-dreamin' sleigh-bells when the clock 'ud
    whir and buzz,
Long afore
        I knowed who
            "Santy Claus" wuz!

Size the fireplace up, and figger how "Old Santy"
    could
Manage to come down the chimbly, like they said he
    would:
Wisht that I could hide and see him—wundered
    what he'd say
Ef he ketched a feller layin' fer him thataway!
But I *bet* on him, and *liked* him, same as ef he had
Turned to pat me on the back and say, "Look here,
    my lad,
Here's my pack,—jes' he'p yourse'f, like all good
    boys does!"
Long afore
        I knowed who
            "Santy Claus" wuz!

Wisht that yarn wuz *true* about him, as it 'peared to
    be—
Truth made out o' lies like that 'un's good enough
    fer me!—
Wisht I still wuz so confidin' I could jes' go wild
Over hangin' up my stockin's, like the little child

Climbin' in my lap to-night, and beggin' me to tell
'Bout them reindeers, and "Old Santy" that she
     loves so well
I'm half sorry fer this little-girl-sweetheart of his—
Long afore
               She knows who
                         "Santy Claus" is!

TO MY GOOD MASTER

IN fancy, always, at thy desk, thrown wide,
  Thy most betreasured books ranged
        neighborly—
  The rarest rhymes of every land and sea
And curious tongue—thine old face glorified,—
Thou haltest thy glib quill, and, laughing-eyed,
  Givest hale welcome even unto me,
  Profaning thus thine attic's sanctity,
Briefly to visit, yet to still abide
Enthralled there of thy sorcery of wit
  And thy songs' most exceeding dear conceits.
  O lips, cleft to the ripe core of all sweets,
  With poems, like nectar, issuing therefrom,
  Thy gentle utterances do overcome
My listening heart and all the love of it!

CHAIRLEY BURKE'S IN TOWN

IT'S Chairley Burke's in town, b'ys! He's down
til "Jamesy's Place,"
Wid a bran'-new shave upon 'um, an' the fhwhusk-
ers aff his face;
He's quit the Section-Gang last night, an' yez can
chalk it down
There's goin' to be the divil's toime, since Chairley
Burke's in town.

Ye'll know 'um by the neck av 'um behind—the tan
an' fair
The barber left he overfilled before he mowed a
hair;
Ye'll know 'um by the ja'nty hat juist bought he's
wearin' now—
But Chairley—*He'll* not miss it in the mornin' ony-
how!

It's treatin' iv'ry b'y he is, an' poundin' on the bar
Till iv'ry man he's dhrinkin' wid musht shmoke a
foine cigar;
An' Missus Murphy's little Kate, that's coomin'
there for beer,
Can't pay wan cint the bucketful, the whilst that
Chairley's here!

He's joompin' oor the tops av shtools, the both for-
   ninsht an' back!
He'll lave yez pick the blessed flure, an' walk the
   straightest crack!
He's liftin' barrels wid his teeth, an' singin' "Garry
   Owen,"
Till all the house be shtrikin' hands, since Chairley
   Burke's in town.

He'll sink the glitther av his eye a-dancin' deep an'
   dim
The toime yez tie his hands behind an' thin lave go
   av him!—
An' fwhat's the knots av mortal man ag'insht the
   nimble twisht
An' shlim an' shlender soopleness that *he* have in
   his wrisht!

The Road-Yaird hands coomes dhroppin' in, an'
   niver goin' back;
An' there's two freights upon the switch—the wan
   on aither track—
An' Mr. Gearry, from The Shops, he's mad enough
   to shwear,
An' durstn't spake a word but grin, the whilst that
   Chairley's there!

Och! Chairley! Chairley! Chairley Burke! ye divil,
   wid yer ways
Av dhrivin' all the throubles aff, these dhark an'
   ghloomy days!

Ohone! that it's meself, wid all the graifs I have to
    dhrown,
Must lave me pick to resht a bit, since Chairley
    Burke's in town.

WAIT FOR THE MORNING

WAIT for the morning:—It will come,
    indeed,
As surely as the night hath given need.
The yearning eyes, at last, will strain their sight
No more unanswered by the morning light;
No longer will they vainly strive, through tears,
To pierce the darkness of thy doubts and fears,
But, bathed in balmy dews and rays of dawn,
Will smile with rapture o'er the darkness drawn.

Wait for the morning, O thou smitten child,
Scorned, scourged and persecuted and reviled—
Athirst and famishing, none pitying thee,
Crowned with the twisted thorns of agony—
No faintest gleam of sunlight through the dense
Infinity of gloom to lead thee thence.—
Wait for the morning:—It will come, indeed,
As surely as the night hath given need,

NOTES

NOTES

p. 1   A FRUIT-PIECE

Printed in *The Indianapolis Journal,* September
16, 1882; published in AFTERWHILES—1887, OLD-
FASHIONED ROSES—1888, THE LOCKERBIE BOOK—
1911.

p. 3   THE SOUTH WIND AND THE SUN

Printed in *The Indianapolis Journal,* September
23, 1882; published in AFTERWHILES—1887, OLD-
FASHIONED ROSES—1888, RHYMES OF CHILDHOOD—
1890 (first edition only), CHILD-RHYMES—1898,
THE LOCKERBIE BOOK—1911. Mr. Riley has always had a particular affection for this poem.

p. 10   WHERE-AWAY

Printed in *The Indianapolis Journal,* October 14,
1882; published in GREEN FIELDS AND RUNNING
BROOKS—1892, SONGS OF HOME—1910, THE LOCK-
ERBIE BOOK—1911.

p. 12   THE SMITTEN PURIST

Written in October, 1882; published in HOME-
FOLKS—1900. These verses, originally entitled *To
—Any Smith,* were written for Miss Anna Smith,
now Mrs. Robert A. Brown, of Franklin, Indiana.

Her sister's possession of the poem, *When Evening
Shadows Fall,* Vol. I, p. 234, furnished the occasion
for these lines, prompting her to write to Mr. Riley
and suggest that "original poems should be passed
around." He responded with the last two stanzas
of the poem. A third stanza was composed and
prefaced to the other verses when published in
HOME-FOLKS—1900.

p. 14   CHRISTINE BRAIBRY

Printed in *The Indianapolis Journal,* November
4, 1882; published in RHYMES OF CHILDHOOD—
1890, WHILE THE HEART BEATS YOUNG—1906,
CHILD-VERSE—1908. This poem, accompanied by
an introductory letter and a doll, was sent to the
Flower Mission Charity Fair, in Indianapolis, November 3, 1882, and was read by a member of the
committee at that time.

p. 18   DEAR HANDS

Printed in *The Indianapolis Journal,* November
4, 1882, with the title, *The Touches of Her Hands;*
published in PIPES O' PAN AT ZEKESBURY—1888,
LOVE-LYRICS—1899, THE LOCKERBIE BOOK—1911.

p. 19   WINTER FANCIES

Printed in *The Indianapolis Journal,* November
18, 1882, with the title, *It's a Cold Day;* published
in RHYMES OF CHILDHOOD—1890, CHILD-RHYMES
—1898, THE LOCKERBIE BOOK—1911.

p. 21   "A BRAVE REFRAIN"

Printed in *The Indianapolis Journal,* November
18, 1882; published in NYE AND RILEY'S RAILWAY

GUIDE—1888, HIS PA'S ROMANCE—1903, SONGS OF
HOME—1910. This had originally as its subtitle,
Imitated. It was an imitation merely in its form,
that of a French ballad.

Stanza 3, ll. 5-6: The reference is to the wooden
ceilings of years ago.

p. 23   AS I SIT IN THE SILENCE

Printed in *The Indianapolis Journal,* November
18, 1882; entitled *Envoy* in RHYMES OF CHILDHOOD
—1890, CHILD-RHYMES—1898, THE LOCKERBIE
BOOK—1911.

p. 25 LONGFELLOW'S LOVE FOR THE CHILDREN

Written in January, 1883; published in RHYMES
OF CHILDHOOD—1890, THE LOCKERBIE BOOK—1911.
These stanzas are a portion of a longer poem, now
lost, called, *At the Grave of Longfellow,* of which
the two stanzas in the text and the following alone
have been preserved:—

> Kindly and warm and tender,
>   He nestled each childish palm
> So close in his own that his touch was a prayer
>   And his voice a blessed psalm.

This poem referred to the author's second visit to
Boston in January, 1883. On December 31, 1881,
during his first visit to Boston and about three
months prior to Longfellow's death, Mr. Riley, accompanied by General Daniel McCauley, visited him
at Cambridge. By order of his physician, Longfellow was not at this time receiving visitors, but he
made an exception of Mr. Riley and greeted him,
after the long confinement of his illness, in a holiday
spirit of indulging himself. Mr. Riley recalls the
pleasure of first seeing the venerable poet,—"a man

of immaculate appearance, conspicuous for his long snow-white hair and for tender kindliness of expression." His greeting was the gentlest welcome in the world. And in turn Mr. Riley was able to address him, as he had always wished, in a poet's most affectionate praise, as his "Master."

p. 26 A SONG OF LONG AGO

Printed in *The Indianapolis Journal,* February 17, 1883; published in GREEN FIELDS AND RUNNING BROOKS—1892, LOVE-LYRICS—1899, FARM-RHYMES —1901, THE LOCKERBIE BOOK—1911, KNEE-DEEP IN JUNE AND OTHER POEMS—1912, A SONG OF LONG AGO—1913.

p. 28 UNLESS

Printed in *The Indianapolis Journal,* February 24, 1883; published in HIS PA'S ROMANCE—1903, SONGS O' CHEER—1905, THE LOCKERBIE BOOK—1911.

p. 30 WHEN EARLY MARCH SEEMS MIDDLE MAY

Printed in *The Indianapolis Journal,* March 3, 1883, entitled *When Knotted Horse-Tails Are Untied;* published in RHYMES OF CHILDHOOD— 1890, FARM-RHYMES—1901, THE LOCKERBIE BOOK —1911, WHEN THE FROST IS ON THE PUNKIN AND OTHER POEMS—1911. Mr. Riley dislikes the winter and assumes a new cheer with the first hint of spring.

p. 32 THE MUSKINGUM VALLEY

Printed in *Life,* March 8, 1883; published in ARMAZINDY—1894, SONGS OF SUMMER—1908, DOWN AROUND THE RIVER AND OTHER POEMS—

1911. This is one of the few summer poems that Mr. Riley wrote in the dead of winter, and there were curious circumstances surrounding its composition. Mr. Riley was on his way to fill a lecture engagement at McConnellsville, Ohio, in the Muskingum Valley. He says: "The cold was ferocious, and the usual communication with the town by boat was cut off in an unprecedented manner. I was, therefore, compelled to ride the entire distance in a hack, and a scabby old hack, too, with the glaze of its oilcloth cover frozen off in spots. We started from Zanesville at five o'clock in the morning, while it was still night, and drove and drove and drove, and about every two miles the hack became mired and we had to walk. I was so chilled and disheartened by that terrible journey when I reached McConnellsville at eight o'clock that night that I vowed I would rather live there than undertake the return drive. During the journey the cold was so trying that in reaction and for diversion I busied myself picturing the summer-time in the valley and the beauty of it. The poem took its source in these longings and imaginings."

p. 34   SERENADE—TO NORA

Printed in *Life,* March 8, 1883; published in AR-MAZINDY—1894.

p. 36   THE LITTLE WHITE HEARSE

Printed in *The Indianapolis Journal,* March 10, 1883; published in OLD-FASHIONED ROSES—1888, ARMAZINDY—1894, THE LOCKERBIE BOOK—1911.

p. 37   A GLIMPSE OF PAN

Written early in March, 1883, printed in *The*

Indianapolis Journal, May 12, 1883; published in
GREEN FIELDS AND RUNNING BROOKS—1890, AFT-
ERWHILES (not in first edition)—1898, SONGS OF
SUMMER—1908, DOWN AROUND THE RIVER AND
OTHER POEMS—1911, THE LOCKERBIE BOOK—1911.

p. 38   THE GREAT GOD PAN

Written early in March, 1883; printed in *The
Indianapolis Journal,* May 12, 1883; published in
MORNING—1908, THE LOCKERBIE BOOK—1911. In
the early version this poem formed the last three
stanzas of *A Glimpse of Pan,* the preceding poem.

The quotation at the head of the poem recalls the
fact that of all the English poets, Elizabeth Barrett
Browning is Mr. Riley's favorite.

p. 40   HER LIGHT GUITAR

Printed in *Life,* March 15, 1883; hitherto unpublished in book form.

p. 41   THE ALL-GOLDEN

Printed in *The Indianapolis Journal,* March 17,
1883; published in RHYMES OF CHILDHOOD—1890,
SONGS O' CHEER—1905, SONGS OF SUMMER—1908,
THE LOCKERBIE BOOK—1911, THE OLD SWIMMIN'-
HOLE AND OTHER POEMS—1912.

p. 43   THE WAY THE BABY CAME

Printed in *The Indianapolis Journal,* April 7,
1883; published in RHYMES OF CHILDHOOD—1890,
THE LOCKERBIE BOOK—1911. Originally this was
the first stanza of a longer poem entitled *The Baby,*
consisting of this and the two following poems.

p. 44   THE WAY THE BABY WOKE

Printed in *The Indianapolis Journal,* April 7, 1883, as stanza 2 of *The Baby;* published in RHYMES OF CHILDHOOD—1890, THE LOCKERBIE BOOK—1911. See previous note.

p. 45   THE WAY THE BABY SLEPT

Printed in *The Indianapolis Journal,* April 7, 1883, as stanza 3 of *The Baby;* published in RHYMES OF CHILDHOOD—1890, THE LOCKERBIE BOOK—1911. See previous two notes.

p. 46   WHEN MAIMIE MARRIED

Printed in *Life,* April 12, 1883; published in ARMAZINDY—1894.

p. 48   HER HAIR

Printed in *The Indianapolis Journal,* April 14, 1883; published in AFTERWHILES—1887, OLD-FASHIONED ROSES—1888, LOVE-LYRICS—1899, THE LOCKERBIE BOOK—1911.

p. 49   A VISION OF SUMMER

Printed in *The Indianapolis Journal,* April 21, 1883; published in POEMS HERE AT HOME—1893, THE LOCKERBIE BOOK—1911. This poem was always a favorite with its author. In a letter to Benj. S. Parker, May 10, 1883, he said of it:—

Your comments on my last published poem—*A Vision of Summer*—were particularly gratifying, and I thank you with all fervor. I had dared to anticipate that you would be pleased with parts of it at least, but feared that its

length and symmetry, considered as a whole, might meet
with less favor in your sight; and so, to find you liking
it in all respects, even as well as I do myself, warms me
through and through with a most tropical delight. And
you are right, I think, in your last comment—that no magazine of the first-class order but what would have hurled
it back at "my defenseless head" like a boomerang, had I
dared send it in their direction. All the same, however, my
regard for it is none the less,—nor yours—nor Dan Paine's
—and so it is "A secret laughter tickles all my soul!"

Mr. Riley was especially pleased recently when he
saw a translation of stanzas 8, 9, 10 and 23 of this
poem in a German newspaper [*Wächter und An-
zeiger,* Cleveland, Ohio, October 13, 1912]. Among
other poems translated into the German are *A Life
Lesson* [*Eine Lebensgeschichte,* by Arthur Thoms,
and also an unsigned version *Wächter und An-
zeiger,* Cleveland, Ohio, October 13, 1892] and *Out
to Old Aunt Mary's,* by Julius Gugler.

p. 54   WHILE CIGARETTES TO ASHES TURN

Printed in *Life,* May 3, 1883; published in NYE
AND RILEY'S RAILWAY GUIDE—1888.

p. 57   THE LITTLE RED RIBBON

Written May 9, 1883; printed in *The Indianapolis
Journal,* May 12, 1883; published in ARMAZINDY—
1894, SONGS OF SUMMER—1908, THE LOCKERBIE
BOOK—1911, A SUMMER'S DAY AND OTHER POEMS
—1911. These verses are reproduced in the author's letter to Benj. S. Parker, May 10, 1883, where
he says in introducing them :—

You must not forget that in the pecuniary aspect I present the picturesque outlines of the typical poet,—but
merry, thank God, at times, as Chispa describes the Ser-
enaders, who "enjoy hunger by day, and noise by night,"—
which reminds me of this bit of rhythmical tumult that I
sung myself to sleep with last night.

p. 58   THE MAN IN THE MOON

Printed in *The Indianapolis Journal,* May 12,
1883; published in NYE AND RILEY'S RAILWAY
GUIDE — 1888, RHYMES OF CHILDHOOD — 1890,
WHILE THE HEART BEATS YOUNG—1906, THE
RAGGEDY MAN—1907, CHILD-VERSE—1908. The
first version did not contain stanzas 1 and 5, and
consequently the reference to The Raggedy Man
was not incorporated until later,—not in fact until
the RHYMES OF CHILDHOOD—1890.

p. 61   A BAREFOOT BOY

Printed in *The Indianapolis Journal,* May 12,
1883, with the title, *Sonnet unto a Barefoot Boy;*
published in ARMAZINDY—1894.

p. 62   "THE PREACHER'S BOY"

Printed in *The Indianapolis Journal,* June 2,
1883; published in RHYMES OF CHILDHOOD—1890.

p. 66   WE TO SIGH INSTEAD OF SING

Printed in *The Indianapolis Journal,* June 2,
1883; published in GREEN FIELDS AND RUNNING
BROOKS—1890, AFTERWHILES (not in first edition)
—1898, SONGS O' CHEER—1905, THE LOCKERBIE
BOOK—1911.

p. 68   NOTHIN' TO SAY

Written early in June, 1883; printed in *The Cen-
tury Magazine,* August, 1887; published in AFTER-
WHILES — 1887, OLD-FASHIONED ROSES — 1888,
LOVE-LYRICS—1899, POEMS HERE AT HOME—1893.
This poem was accepted by *The Century Magazine*

in June, 1883, but was not published until August, 1887. In the interim Mr. Riley wrote to the editors asking what had become of the poem. They found that the manuscript had been lost and requested another copy. The letter of the editor, in which he accepts *Nothin' to Say* and returns a "serious" poem, is quoted as an example of the kind of estimate often made of serious verse because expressed in dialect form :—

> I am sorry that we thus seem to put a premium on humorous work as compared with serious, but we can't help it now. . . . We are doing our best to get out of arrears with verse this summer, but the light piece strikes us below the belt!

See *Dialect in Literature* and its note, Vol. VI.

p. 70   JACK-IN-THE-BOX

Printed in *The Indianapolis Journal,* June 2, 1883; published in RHYMES OF CHILDHOOD (not first edition)—1898, SONGS OF HOME—1910, THE LOCKERBIE BOOK—1911. Mr. Riley has a vivid memory of his grandfather, John Marine, sitting before the fireplace, smoking hour after hour and watching the smoke that he exhaled dip downward and then swoop up the chimney. This grandfather, who was a minister, looked up but seldom and then very likely only to pacify some impetuous child, most frequently the brother, Humboldt. On such occasions he took the child between his knees and told him stories from the Bible. But for the most part the grandfather sat lost in reverie, whetting the speculation and wonder of his observing grandchild.

p. 72   THE OLD TRUNDLE-BED

Printed in *Life*, June 14, 1883; published in AR-

MAZINDY—1894, SONGS OF HOME—1910, THE LOCKERBIE BOOK—1911. This poem is a childhood memory.

p. 74 MY MARY

Printed in *The Indianapolis Journal,* June 16, 1883; published in ARMAZINDY—1894, LOVE-LYRICS —1899.

p. 77 TWO SONNETS TO THE JUNE-BUG

Printed in *The Indianapolis Journal,* June 16, 1883; hitherto unpublished in book form.

p. 79 ONE AFTERNOON

Printed in *The Indianapolis Journal,* June 23, 1883; published in POEMS HERE AT HOME—1893, THE LOCKERBIE BOOK—1911.

p. 81 THE BEAUTIFUL CITY

Printed in *The Indianapolis Journal,* June 30, 1883; published in AFTERWHILES—1887, OLD-FASH-IONED ROSES—1888, THE LOCKERBIE BOOK—1911.

p. 83 A LIFE TERM

Printed in *The Indianapolis Journal,* June 30, 1883; published in POEMS HERE AT HOME—1893.

p. 84 McFEETERS' FOURTH

Printed in *The Indianapolis Journal,* July 5, 1883; published in NYE AND RILEY'S RAILWAY GUIDE — 1888, RHYMES OF CHILDHOOD — 1890,

Songs of Summer—1908, The Lockerbie Book—1911, A Summer's Day and Other Poems—1911.

p. 87 AT NINETY IN THE SHADE

Printed in *The Indianapolis Journal,* July 7, 1883; published in His Pa's Romance—1903, Songs of Summer—1908, The Old Swimmin'-Hole and Other Poems—1912.

p. 89 A SUDDEN SHOWER

Printed in *The Indianapolis Journal,* July 14, 1883; published in Rhymes of Childhood—1890, Child-Rhymes—1898, While the Heart Beats Young—1906, Child-Verse—1908, Songs of Summer—1908, The Lockerbie Book—1911, The Old Swimmin'-Hole and Other Poems—1912. The following five stanzas, originally preceding the others and forming the first part of the poem, have since been discarded :—

> The noon is tropical. The rose
> Leans like a yearning mouth to meet
> The kisses that the zephyr blows
> Full-flavored with the fragrant heat.

> The breezy maples seem to quaff
> The shade like wine, and, thrilled with glee,
> Toss up their leafy hands and laugh
> And lisp and whisper tipsily.

> As in the sight the air afloat
> The meadow glimmers on to us,
> A glamoured murmur, high, remote,
> Falls on the hearing tremulous :—

> The pent-up anger of the storm!
> The dust grows ashen, as with fright,
> And, rising, reels in phantom form,
> And passes in convulsive flight.

,With petulant and gusty breaths
  The winds come waltzing as they may,
,Till e'en the sunshine vanishes
  As it were whirled and blown away.

p. 91   **GOOD-BY ER HOWDY-DO**

Printed in *The Indianapolis Journal,* July 16, 1883; published in NYE AND RILEY'S RAILWAY GUIDE—1888, HIS PA'S ROMANCE—1903.

p. 92   **WITH THE CURRENT**

Printed in *The Indianapolis Journal,* July 21, 1883; published in RHYMES OF CHILDHOOD—1890, SONGS OF SUMMER—1908, THE LOCKERBIE BOOK —1911, THE OLD SWIMMIN'-HOLE AND OTHER POEMS—1912.

p. 94   **WET-WEATHER TALK**

Printed in *The Indianapolis Journal,* July 28, 1883; published in PIPES O' PAN AT ZEKESBURY— 1888, NEGHBORLY POEMS—1891, FARM-RHYMES— 1901, WHEN THE FROST IS ON THE PUNKIN AND OTHER POEMS—1911. These lines are written in the character of "Benj. F. Johnson of Boone."

p. 96   **A POOR MAN'S WEALTH**

Printed in *The Indianapolis Journal,* August 4, 1883; published in ARMAZINDY—1894, THE LOCKERBIE BOOK—1911.

p. 98   AUTOGRAPHIC

Written in the album of Miss Ettie Bowen at Delphi in late August, 1883; not hitherto printed.

p. 99 IN SWIMMING-TIME

Printed in *The Century Magazine,* September, 1883; published in RHYMES OF CHILDHOOD—1890, POEMS HERE AT HOME—1893, SONGS OF SUMMER—1908, DOWN AROUND THE RIVER AND OTHER POEMS —1911, THE LOCKERBIE BOOK—1911. The contribution of this poem furnished the occasion for the comment from the editor of *The Century Magazine,* which gave Mr. Riley much encouragement: "I must say that there is nobody at present writing who seems, to me, to get so much of genuine human nature into a short space, as you have."

p. 101 THE BEST IS GOOD ENOUGH

Printed in *The Indianapolis Journal,* September 8, 1883; published in HIS PA'S ROMANCE—1903, SONGS OF HOME—1910.

p. 102 HE CALLED HER IN

Printed in *The Indianapolis Journal,* September 22, 1883; published in RHYMES OF CHILDHOOD—1890, LOVE-LYRICS—1899, THE LOCKERBIE BOOK—1911.

p. 107 GIVE ME THE BABY

Printed in *The Indianapolis Journal,* October 13, 1883; published in POEMS HERE AT HOME—1893, THE LOCKERBIE BOOK—1911.

p. 109 AN AUTUMNAL TONIC

Printed in *The Indianapolis Journal,* October 23, 1883; published in MORNING—1907, THE LOCKERBIE BOOK—1911.

p. 110   OUT OF THE HITHERWHERE

Printed in *The Indianapolis Journal,* December 22, 1883; published in ARMAZINDY—1894, SONGS OF HOME—1910, THE LOCKERBIE BOOK—1911.

p. 111   A TINKLE OF BELLS

Printed in *The Indianapolis Journal,* January 12, 1884; published in HIS PA'S ROMANCE—1903, THE LOCKERBIE BOOK—1911.

p. 113   THE OLD MAN

At a banquet of The Indianapolis Literary Club, February 18, 1884, Mr. Riley read this poem, introducing it with the prose sketch, *The Old Man* (Vol. VI); both printed in *The Indianapolis Journal,* February 20, 1884; and published in THE BOSS GIRL—1885, SKETCHES IN PROSE—1891; the poem alone published in OLD-FASHIONED ROSES—1888, NEGHBORLY POEMS (not in first edition)—1897. In the last mentioned volume it appears as a *Salutation to Benj. F. Johnson.*

p. 118   OUR KIND OF A MAN

Printed in *The Indianapolis Journal,* March 5, 1884; published in AFTERWHILES—1887, OLD-FASHIONED ROSES—1888, SONGS OF HOME—1910, THE LOCKERBIE BOOK—1911. The inspiration of the poem was the author's dear friend, the Rev. Myron W. Reed, and the verses are a faithful portrayal of his character. Of him Mr. Riley once said [interview in *The Indianapolis News,* January, 30, 1899]:—

He was intellectually and as a man distinctively marked by a great human sympathy. He was at times sympathetic to an extreme, but it took such a man to be the true champion of his fellows. Eight years ago [1891] we took together a trip to England and Scotland. His interest in the Burns country was particular. It was to me a liberal education to be along with such a man. Though it was his second or third visit to Scotland, he seemingly knew the places he visited by heart. Yet he always found in each place a new interest, a delight which was unending, as he turned up newer testimony in matters not in written history regarding the real personal character of such men as Burns and Carlyle. He liked especially well the testimony he found regarding Burns as a citizen of Dumfries, for this showed that the Scotch poet was a man of dual character, that while he was a dreamer and a singer, he was no less a practical man, whose judgment was of value in matters of public interest.

Mr. Reed was a man who enjoyed "the harvest of the quiet eye," as I think it is Wordsworth calls it. He was eternally seeing and reading the book of life as it was opened before him. He had a rare gift of discernment.

See *The Onward Trail,* Vol. V, p. 88, and its note.

p. 120 **THE LITTLE COAT**

Printed in *The Indianapolis Journal,* March 8, 1884; published in RHYMES OF CHILDHOOD—1890, CHILD-RHYMES—1898.

p. 122 **AN IMPROMPTU ON ROLLER SKATES**

Printed in *The Indianapolis Journal,* March 29, 1884; hitherto unpublished in book form. The writing of the lines was actually accomplished by the author in impromptu manner at the old Indianapolis roller-skating rink.

p. 123 ME AND MARY

Printed in *The Indianapolis Journal,* March 29,

1884; published in Pipes o' Pan at Zekesbury— 1888, Nye and Riley's Railway Guide—1888, His Pa's Romance—1903, Songs of Summer—1908, Down around the River and Other Poems— 1911.

p. 125

WRITTEN IN BUNNER'S "AIRS FROM ARCADY"

Printed in *The Indianapolis Journal,* April 5, 1884; hitherto unpublished in book form. Henry C. Bunner, editor of *Puck,* and a friend of Mr. Riley, published at this time a small volume with the title, *Airs from Arcady.* He presented a copy to Mr. Riley, who thereupon composed and inscribed this poem on its fly-leaf. A few months previous to this, Mr. Riley gave his friend a first edition of The Old Swimmin'-Hole and 'Leven More Poems, then just issued, upon the fly-leaf of which Mr. Bunner wrote the following :—

> When the red back-log sags and sinks,
> And every little ember winks,
> And winks, and winks, and winks, and sleeps—
> The drowsy vigil Fancy keeps
> In softer sleep may fade away,
> And waken in a summer day,
> Where cattle swish their burry tails,
> Near creeks where water-spiders skip,
> And dragon-flies do *whizz* and *zip!*
> And every thicket, all alive,
> Is humming like a lazy hive,
> And one small boy it somehow seems
> We used to know in old-time dreams
> Is jabbing earthworms on his hook—
>
> —If Fancy's book has been *this* book.
> > attest
> > > H. C. Bunner.

New York, January 19, 1884.

p. 126 A SONG

Printed in *The Indianapolis Journal*, April 5, 1884; published in Afterwhiles—1887, Old-Fashioned Roses—1888, Songs o' Cheer (title, first line)—1905, Songs of Summer—1908, The Lockerbie Book—1911.

p. 128 NEVER TALK BACK

Printed in *The Indianapolis Journal*, April 5, 1884; published in Nye and Riley's Railway Guide—1888, Green Fields and Running Brooks —1892, His Pa's Romance—1903.

p. 129 MY FRIEND

Printed in *The Indianapolis Journal*, April 12, 1884; published in Green Fields and Running Brooks—1892, Songs of Home—1910, The Lockerbie Book—1911.

p. 130 THE LITTLE FAT DOCTOR

Printed in *The Indianapolis Journal*, April 12, 1884; published in Green Fields and Running Brooks—1892.

p. 132 THE STRANGE YOUNG MAN

Printed in *The Indianapolis Journal*, April 12, 1884, with the title, *Nonsense Jingles;* published in *Spirk and Wunk Rhymes, Rounds and Catches* in The Flying Islands of the Night—1898.

p. 134 SCOTTY

Printed in *The Chicago Current*, April 19, 1884; published in Poems Here at Home—1893.

p. 136 ON THE SUNNY SIDE

Printed in *The Indianapolis Journal,* April 19, 1884; published in Rhymes of Childhood—1890, Child-Rhymes—1898, Songs of Summer—1908, The Lockerbie Book—1911, The Old Swimmin'-Hole and Other Poems—1912.

p. 138 THE HARPER

Printed in *The Indianapolis Journal,* April 26, 1884; published in Afterwhiles—1887, Old-Fashioned Roses—1888, Songs o' Cheer—1905, The Lockerbie Book—1911. The poem is one of Mr. Riley's favorites.

p. 139 THE BLOSSOMS ON THE TREES

Printed in *The Indianapolis Journal,* May 10, 1884; published in Afterwhiles—1887, Green Fields and Running Brooks—1892, Songs o' Cheer—1905, The Lockerbie Book—1911.

p. 140 LAUGHTER HOLDING BOTH HIS SIDES

Printed in *The Indianapolis Journal,* May 10, 1884; published in Afterwhiles—1887, Old-Fashioned Roses—1888, Songs of Home—1910, The Lockerbie Book—1911. The following lines originally completed this poem:—

> Tiptoe up and pour thy mirth
> Sloshingly around the earth
> For a wallow-slough for thee
> To swash round in—Hi! whoop-ee!
> Throughout all eternity.

The title is from Milton's *L'Allegro,* l. 32.

p. 141   IN STATE

Printed in *The Indianapolis Journal*, May 17,
1884; published in His Pa's Romance—1903, The
Lockerbie Book—1911. Originally this poem con-
sisted of the first and second stanzas, followed by
the three stanzas which now appear with the title,
The Dead Lover. See the following poem.

p. 143   THE DEAD LOVER

Printed in *The Indianapolis Journal*, May 17,
1884; published in Afterwhiles—1887, The
Lockerbie Book—1911. See preceding note.

p. 144   THE KIND OLD MAN

Printed in *The Indianapolis Journal*, May 24,
1884; published in Poems Here at Home—1893.

p. 145   A SCRAWL

Printed in *The Indianapolis Journal*, May 24,
1884; published in Afterwhiles—1887, Old-
Fashioned Roses—1888, Songs of Home—1910,
The Lockerbie Book—1911.

p. 146   AWAY

Printed in *The Indianapolis Journal*, May 31,
1884; published in Afterwhiles—1887, Old-
Fashioned Roses—1888, Songs o' Cheer—1905,
The Lockerbie Book—1911, Away—1913. The
early version had the subtitle, *In Memoriam Gen.
W. H. H. Terrell*. General William H. H. Terrell
was born in Kentucky in 1827 and died at Indianapolis, May 16, 1884. During the Civil War he

rendered distinguished service in connection with Governor Morton by devising a plan that afforded the speedy and accurate transmission of bandages and supplies to the soldiers from Indiana. At the close of the war he was appointed adjutant general. Mr. Riley "loved the man dearly," as did all who came in contact with his kindly nature.

p. 148 A MONUMENT FOR THE SOLDIERS

Printed in *The Indianapolis Journal,* June 12, 1884; published in GREEN FIELDS AND RUNNING BROOKS—1892, THE LOCKERBIE BOOK—1911. This poem was written in sympathy with a patriotic movement to erect what eventually became the Soldiers' and Sailors' Monument at Indianapolis. On the occasion of this monument's dedication, May 15, 1902, Mr. Riley read his poem, *The Soldier,* Vol. V, p. 179.

p. 150 OUT TO OLD AUNT MARY'S

Printed in *The Indianapolis Journal,* June 14, 1884; published in AFTERWHILES—1887, OLD-FASHIONED ROSES—1888, CHILD-RHYMES—1898, OUT TO OLD AUNT MARY'S (Christy Edition)—1904, THE LOCKERBIE BOOK—1911. The early version of the poem was composed of six stanzas (1, 3, 5, 8, 10, 20) and entitled *Old Aunt Mary's.* When it was published in AFTERWHILES (Homestead Edition)—1898, two new stanzas (11 and 18 in this version) were inserted just preceding the last. In the special edition (1904) twelve new stanzas (2, 4, 6, 7, 9, 12, 13, 14, 15, 16, 17, and 19) were added and the title changed to its present form.

This last version contains a dedication "To Robert J. Burdette, with all gratefulness and affection,"

to whom is addressed the following introductory
stanza :—

> You who have journeyed the wide world through—
> Knowing the Old world as the New,—
> Cruise or pilgrimage or shrine,
> Found you ever so all-divine
> A haven as first was yours and mine
> Out to old Aunt Mary's?

**This poem was one of Mr. Riley's favorite public
readings.**

The author says :—

My boys and girls are town boys and girls, not children
living in the country. They touch the country but are not
actually of it. Were they country boys and girls, they
would not, as I take it, see any novelty in country life.

Out to Old Aunt Mary's was written in the form of a
letter to my brother, who was far out west at the time.
The experience portrayed in the poem is a composite one
and there was no particular Old Aunt Mary. In a vague
way I did have in mind a visit paid to Mooresville and
Martinsville, Indiana, when "Cousin Rufus," Judge W. R.
Hough, of Greenfield, and my mother drove there with
my brother and me and my sister Elva, then a child in
mother's arms. My brother and I sat on a seat that un-
folded from the dashboard in the manner of old-fashioned
vehicles of that date. It was a joyous journey, for "Cousin
Rufus" was the jolliest, cheeriest young man that ever
lived and there was always a song on his lips. We drove
from Greenfield to Indianapolis, where we stopped for a
midday meal. At Mooresville we visited Uncle James and
Aunt Ann Marine, and at Martinsville, Uncle Charles and
Aunt Hester Marine. The simple child-felt joy of these
visits is as warm in my memory to-day as when we jogged
back on the dusty road to Greenfield.

Then again, when I think of the poem, the old house is
very vivid to my fancy with its gourds growing up over
the little clapboard roof which extended out over the doorway. It is no particular house that I can remember, and
yet in my mind it is a very vivid scene.

p. 155 **IN THE AFTERNOON**

Printed in *The Indianapolis Journal,* June 28, 1884; published in NYE AND RILEY'S RAILWAY GUIDE—1888.

p. 157 UNINTERPRETED

Printed in *The Indianapolis Journal,* July 12, 1884; published in RHYMES OF CHILDHOOD (not in first edition)—1898, THE LOCKERBIE BOOK—1911. The following appeared as fifth and sixth stanzas of the early version:—

Could I but delve out the deeper sublimity
  Hid in the lily that smiles as I write—
Ah! my good friends, how in glad unanimity
  You should read rhymes writ in fragrance and white!

Or could I translate the sweet song of merriment
  Spilled from the wicker-cage hung in the hall,
How you should chuckle to hear what canary meant
  By his wild tangle of twitter and call!

p. 158 BILLY'S ALPHABETICAL ANIMAL SHOW

Printed in *The Indianapolis Journal,* July 26, 1884; published in the prose sketch, *The Gilded Roll,* in PIPES O' PAN AT ZEKESBURY—1888.

p. 164 THE PIXY PEOPLE

Printed in *Wide-Awake,* August, 1884, with the title, *Little Pixy People;* published in RHYMES OF CHILDHOOD—1890, CHILD-RHYMES—1898, WHILE THE HEART BEATS YOUNG—1906, CHILD-VERSE—1908, THE LOCKERBIE BOOK—1911.

p. 167   THE TOWN KARNTEEL

Printed in *The Indianapolis Journal,* August 2, 1884; published in Afterwhiles—1887.

p. 169   DONN PIATT OF MAC-O-CHEE

Printed in *The Indianapolis Journal,* August 16, 1884; published in Green Fields and Running Brooks—1892, The Lockerbie Book—1911. Donn Piatt, journalist, soldier, judge and poet, was born at Cincinnati, Ohio, June 29, 1819, and died at Cleveland, November 12, 1891. Laura Ream, of Indianapolis, incidentally brought about the visit described in the poem when she sent a copy of The Old Swimmin'-Hole and 'Leven More Poems to Donn Piatt, who in reply extended a hearty invitation through her to Mr. Riley. Miss Ream thus described his visit:—

The writer of dialect verses, unknown to fame, bashful as a child and as warm-hearted and impulsive as a woman, found at Mac-o-chee delights that he had hardly dared to hope for. Donn Piatt, infinite in resource and illimitable in versatility, the terror of snobs and a free-lance to frauds, had in him, too, a delicacy of sentiment and the chivalric graces of temperament to enchant the young poet. Riley told me not long ago, speaking of that visit of years before: "I can not imagine two men more different in every respect than Piatt as his writings led me to picture him and the man as I found him. He won my heart quickly and completely."

And Mac-o-chee in itself is an inspiration. Its tall gray towers and sharp Flemish gables, nestling in among smoothly rounded, wooded hills, and the winding little valley cut into two graceful slopes by the sparkling stream that seems to sing always of that time long ago when the lovers trysted on its banks—"When the bloom was on the alder and the tassel on the corn"—make up a vision and a charm as beautiful as any dreamer's fantasy.

p. 172   HERR WEISER

Written at Delphi, Indiana, August 18, 1884;
printed in *The Indianapolis Journal,* August 24,
1884; published in AFTERWHILES—1887, OLD-
FASHIONED ROSES—1888, THE LOCKERBIE BOOK—
1911. Mr. Riley and his friend Dr. Wyckliffe Smith
visited Herr Weiser at his thickly wooded farm
near Delphi, Indiana, where, among fragrant or-
chards and bloomy gardens, they met this kindly
man. "He was indeed 'a hale white rose of his
countrymen' as he greeted us there, standing before
us without a hat and in his shirt-sleeves, reflecting
the sunshine."—J. W. R.

p. 174   FROM DELPHI TO CAMDEN

Printed in *The Indianapolis Journal,* August 24,
1884; published in NYE AND RILEY'S RAILWAY
GUIDE—1888, HOME-FOLKS—1900, THE LOCKERBIE
BOOK—1911. The "master and commander" was
Dr. Wyckliffe Smith, of Delphi, one of Mr. Riley's
most loved friends. Outwardly he was a very
plain-spoken man of uncompromising opinions, but
beneath this exterior there was, as one of his towns-
men testified, "a largeness of heart that spread its
good spirit throughout Carroll County." His generous deeds were unnumbered. Mr. Riley met Dr.
Smith at Camden in 1882 at the conclusion of one
of his readings and a firm friendship sprang into
being immediately. In the summer of 1883 and
frequently thereafter, he visited Dr. Smith and
rode horseback with him through Carroll County
or fished there "on the banks o' Deer Crick." See
On the Banks o' Deer Crick, p. 290, and its note,
and the above note on *Herr Weiser.*
In December, 1899, during the course of a pro-

fessional visit, Dr. Smith was killed at a railroad crossing. In memory of his friend Mr. Riley wrote *The Noblest Service,* Vol. V, p. 99.

p. 176   A NOON INTERVAL

Printed in *The Indianapolis Journal,* August 24, 1884, with the title, *Noon;* published in HIS PA'S ROMANCE (entitled *A Midday in Midsummer* in Homestead Edition)—1903, SONGS O' CHEER—1905, SONGS OF SUMMER—1908, THE LOCKERBIE BOOK—1911.

p. 177   AT MADAME MANICURE'S

Printed in *The Indianapolis Journal,* August 24, 1884; hitherto unpublished in book form.

p. 179   JOHN McKEEN

Printed in *The Indianapolis Journal,* August 31, 1884; published in GREEN FIELDS AND RUNNING BROOKS—1892, AFTERWHILES (not in first edition) —1898, SONGS OF HOME—1910, THE LOCKERBIE BOOK—1911.

p. 181   THE BOY-FRIEND

Written in Clarence A. Hough's album September 12, 1884, with the title, *To Clarence A. Hough;* printed in *The Indianapolis Journal,* September 14, 1884; published in NYE AND RILEY'S RAILWAY GUIDE—1888, RHYMES OF CHILDHOOD—1890, THE LOCKERBIE BOOK—1911. Clarence A. Hough is the older son of Judge W. R. Hough, of Greenfield, Mr. Riley's cousin. "He was one of the best boys that ever lived, wholesome and cheery and jovial, just

as his father was when a boy; and he had the un-
usual boyish virtue of being always at work, shin-
ing harness in the barn if no other task presented
itself, and ever whistling away, accomplishing some
usefulness every minute. He wrote very well, too,
and used to imitate Irving with great success. I remember in particular his little sketch called 'The
Cheese-monger of Antwerp.' 'The Bold Dragoon,'
which I mentioned in my verses, is one of Irving's
characters, and the air of the name being fitting, I
called him that."—J. W. R.

p. 183   WHEN BESSIE DIED

Printed in *The Indianapolis Journal,* September
14, 1884; published in AFTERWHILES—1887, OLD-
FASHIONED ROSES—1888, THE LOCKERBIE BOOK—
1911. The quotation heading the verses is from
Tired Mothers, by May Riley Smith.

p. 185 THE RIVALS; OR THE SHOWMAN'S RUSE

Printed in *The Indianapolis Journal,* September
14, 1884; published in GREEN FIELDS AND RUNNING
BROOKS—1892. See *Billy Miller's Circus-Show,*
Vol. V, p. 288.

p. 189   THE CHRIST

Printed in *The Indianapolis Journal,* September
14, 1884; published in HOME-FOLKS—1900, THE
LOCKERBIE BOOK—1911.

p. 190   TO HEAR HER SING

Printed in *The Indianapolis Journal,* September
21, 1884; published in GREEN FIELDS AND RUNNING

Brooks—1892, Love-Lyrics—1899, The Lockerbie Book—1911. Written to Miss Belle Wells, of
Cincinnati, a visitor at Greenfield.

FROM THE HEADBOARD OF A GRAVE IN PARA-GUAY

p. 192

Printed in *The Indianapolis Journal,* September
21, 1884; published in Afterwhiles—1887, The
Lockerbie Book—1911. The queer title was con-
trived as befitting the strangeness of the poem.

p. 193   A CANARY AT THE FARM

Printed in *The Indianapolis Journal,* September
21, 1884; published in Afterwhiles—1887, Farm-
Rhymes—1901, Knee-Deep in June and Other
Poems—1912.

p. 195   SEPTEMBER DARK

Printed in *The Indianapolis Journal,* September
28, 1884, with the title, *December Dark;* published
in Green Fields and Running Brooks—1892,
Afterwhiles (not in first edition)—1898, Farm-
Rhymes—1901, The Lockerbie Book—1911,
When the Frost Is on the Punkin and Other
Poems—1911. Many changes in the original version have been made. The last stanza, formerly
the second, read:—

> In stratas gray
> And level lay
> The mists across the face of day,
> At foot and head
> Above the dead
> The dews weep on uncomforted.

p. 196 ANSELMO

Printed in *The Indianapolis Journal,* October 18, 1884; published in AFTERWHILES—1887, THE LOCKERBIE BOOK—1911. Father Anselmo is a characteristic name, not a historical one.

p. 197 TIME OF CLEARER TWITTERINGS

Printed in *The Indianapolis Journal,* October 19, 1884, with the title, *October;* published in RHYMES OF CHILDHOOD—1890, CHILD-RHYMES—1898, THE LOCKERBIE BOOK—1911.

p. 200 THE BOYS

Printed in *The Indianapolis Journal,* October 19, 1884; published in RHYMES OF CHILDHOOD—1890, SONGS OF HOME—1910, THE LOCKERBIE BOOK— 1911.

p. 201 LINCOLN

Printed in *The Indianapolis Journal,* October 26, 1884; published in HOME-FOLKS—1900, THE LOCKERBIE BOOK—1911. Many minor deviations from the original form have been made.

In connection with Mr. Riley's love of Lincoln, it is of interest to quote a letter from his brother John, in which the latter relates a vivid incident of their childhood in referring to their father :—

Perhaps the occasion on which we have most reason to be proud of him, was his presence as delegate at large at the Chicago convention when he helped to nominate Abraham Lincoln for the first time. I remember it was in the middle of the night when he got back home, and we all sat up in bed or got up and dressed to hear him describe the thrilling incidents of the nomination, and how the West was victorious over the East in the defeat of Seward, who was their candidate.

p. 203   THE BLIND GIRL

Printed in *The Indianapolis Journal,* November 1, 1884; published in ARMAZINDY—1894, THE LOCKERBIE BOOK—1911.

p. 206   THE KING

Printed in *The Indianapolis Journal,* November 2, 1884; published in AFTERWHILES—1887, SONGS OF SUMMER—1908, THE LOCKERBIE BOOK—1911.

p. 208   A LIZ-TOWN HUMORIST

Printed in *The Indianapolis Journal,* November 2, 1884; published in AFTERWHILES—1887. Elizabeth City, Indiana, a small place, is sometimes called "Liz-Town."

p. 210   LIKE HIS MOTHER USED TO MAKE

Printed in *The Indianapolis Journal,* December 14, 1884; published in AFTERWHILES—1887, OLD-FASHIONED ROSES—1888. The subtitle ascribes the poem to "Uncle Jake's Place, St. Joe, Missouri, 1874," where, according to a newspaper sketch which Mr. Riley read, a certain restaurant bore the sign, "Come in and get some coffee like your mother used to make." As he thought upon this suggestive phrase the poem made itself, narrating how the boy, who had been away for years, was returning homeward, seeking his parents who were searching for him at the same time, and how they were happily brought together.

p. 212   A GOLDEN WEDDING

Dated December 23, 1884; published in MORNING
—1907. These lines were written for the fiftieth
anniversary of the marriage of Mr. and Mrs. Hugh
B. Wilson, celebrated Tuesday, December 23, 1884,
when the verses were read by a granddaughter,
Mrs. B. E. Hays. The husband, affectionately
known in Greenfield as "Father Wilson," had been
a faithful elder in the Presbyterian church for more
than twenty years and was seldom known to "neglect the Lord." He was the father of Mrs. Julia
W. Riley, the author's sister-in-law.

p. 215   HIS CHRISTMAS SLED

Printed in *The Indianapolis Journal,* December
25, 1884; published in NYE AND RILEY'S RAILWAY
GUIDE—1888, RHYMES OF CHILDHOOD (not in first
edition)—1898, THE LOCKERBIE BOOK—1911.

p. 217   A NEW YEAR'S TIME AT WILLARDS'S

Printed in *The Indianapolis Journal,* January 1,
1885; published in AFTERWHILES—1887.

p. 224   WHATEVER THE WEATHER MAY BE

Printed in *The Indianapolis Journal,* January 18,
1885, with the title, *Says He;* published in the prose
sketch, *A Wild Irishman,* in PIPES O' PAN AT
ZEKESBURY—1888, NYE AND RILEY'S RAILWAY
GUIDE—1888, SONGS O' CHEER—1905.

p. 226   A LEAVE-TAKING

Printed in *The Indianapolis Sentinel,* February 1,

1885; published in PIPES O' PAN AT ZEKESBURY—
1888, THE LOCKERBIE BOOK—1911.

p. 227   DOWN ON WRIGGLE CRICK

Printed in *The Indianapolis Journal*, March 8,
1885; published in AFTERWHILES—1887. "With so
many creeks as there are wriggling in and around
the underbrush," says Mr. Riley, "I have always
wondered why there never came to be such a name
for stream or town,—hence the Wriggle Crick of
the poem."

p. 230   LORD BACON

Dated April 10, 1885, printed in *The Indianapolis
Journal*, April 12, 1885, signed "Amos J. Walker";
hitherto unpublished in book form. Under the title
originally appeared a bracket: *Ignatius Donnelly, as
a Student of Cryptography, Claims to Have Found
Absolute Proof of Bacon's Authorship of Shakespeare.* Mr. Walker, to whom these high and mighty
verses were ascribed as a joke, had no vestige of
poetry about him. He was a great practical joker
and entered into Mr. Riley's prank immediately
upon its appearance, saying in great seriousness
when questioned by surprised friends, "Oh, Riley
got me into that. I was showing him my manu-
scripts the other evening and he took a particular
fancy to this poem and said, 'By jove, Walker, you
ought to publish some of these verses.' And so I
let him have that sonnet."

p. 231   MY FIRST WOMERN

Printed in *The Indianapolis Journal*, April 12,
1885; published in NYE AND RILEY'S RAILWAY
GUIDE—1888.

p. 233 THE QUEST

Printed in *The Indianapolis Journal,* April 12, 1885; published in *Spirk and Wunk Rhymes, Rounds and Catches* in THE FLYING ISLANDS OF THE NIGHT—1898, SONGS OF HOME—1910, THE LOCKERBIE BOOK—1911.

p. 234 TO AN IMPORTUNATE GHOST

Printed in *The Indianapolis Journal,* April 12, 1885; published in GREEN FIELDS AND RUNNING BROOKS—1890, THE LOCKERBIE BOOK—1911.

p. 235 WHO BIDES HIS TIME

Printed in *The Indianapolis Journal,* April 12, 1885; published in AFTERWHILES—1887, OLD-FASHIONED ROSES—1888, SONGS O' CHEER—1905, SONGS OF HOME—1910, THE LOCKERBIE BOOK—1911.

p. 237 AS WE READ BURNS

Printed in *The Indianapolis Herald,* April 18, 1885; hitherto unpublished in book form. On June 9, 1891, Mr. Riley, in company with William P. Fishback and Myron Reed, visited Dumfries and thus described the visit in a letter to Mr. Henry Eitel:—

Have to-day visited the house Burns *first* occupied upon his coming here, and also the house in which he died—something better than the first, I was glad to note,—this latter bearing the newly-printed placard above the door, "Burns' House—To Rent." I could have cried. Some time later we were persistently fortunate enough to find the young man who seemed to have this house in charge, and by him were admitted and shown through it,

I think all three of us did quite a quantity of hard breathing and thinking as we reverently moved from room to room.—Main room and kitchen parallel below—then at back a narrow, winding, stone stairway above, and—the room in which the last work of the great poet's pen was done,—most exquisite, tender, loving, human *songs,* that clamber still and twine and bloom about all hearts; and, no less, the *prose* appeals, wrenched from him for a pitiful pound or so of *loan,* to provide against the commonest household necessities.

p. 238   WHEN JUNE IS HERE

Printed in *The Indianapolis Journal,* April 19, 1885; published in PIPES O' PAN AT ZEKESBURY— 1888, SONGS OF SUMMER—1908, THE LOCKERBIE BOOK—1911, A SUMMER'S DAY AND OTHER POEMS —1911.

p. 239   AT NOON—AND MIDNIGHT

Printed in *The Indianapolis Journal,* April 19, 1885; published in PIPES O' PAN AT ZEKESBURY— 1888, THE LOCKERBIE BOOK—1911.

p. 240   TO JAMES NEWTON MATTHEWS

Printed in *The Indianapolis Herald* about April 19, 1885, with the title, *Par Nobile Fratrum;* hitherto unpublished by Mr. Riley. This poem, with the reply, is found in James Newton Matthews' volume of poems, *The Lute of Life.* See *When We Three Meet,* p. 301; *In Days to Come,* p. 384; and *Three Singing Friends,* Vol. IV, p. 273; and their notes.

p. 241   SPIRITS AT HOME

Printed in *The Indianapolis Journal,* April 26, 1885; published in NYE AND RILEY'S RAILWAY GUIDE—1888, HIS PA'S ROMANCE—1903.

p. 244 ART AND LOVE

Printed in *The Indianapolis Journal,* April 26, 1885; published in AFTERWHILES—1887, THE LOCKERBIE BOOK—1911.

p. 245 SONG

Printed in *The Indianapolis Journal,* April 26, 1885; hitherto unpublished in book form.

p. 247 PAP'S OLD SAYIN'

Printed in *The Indianapolis Journal,* May 3, 1885; published in NEGHBORLY POEMS (not in first edition)—1897.

THE WILLOW

This was the next poem to appear, printed in *The Indianapolis Journal,* May 3, 1885. It is included in *A Child-World* in Vol. IV, p. 363.

p. 249 GRANNY

Printed in *The Indianapolis Journal,* May 10, 1885; published in AFTERWHILES—1887, RHYMES OF CHILDHOOD (first edition only with title, *Granny's Come to Our House*)—1890, SONGS O' CHEER —1905, WHILE THE HEART BEATS YOUNG—1906, CHILD-VERSE—1908. The poem is in harmony with Mr. Riley's own happy childhood. His grandmother, Margaret Slick Riley, was a genuine lover of children and always welcomed them and made them feel "at home" in her house at Greenfield. As a consequence her home became a playground and her appearance was always greeted with childhood ecstasies. Wade and Silas Walker, little

Orphant Annie, and the others were veritable play-mates of the author and the stories they listened to so greedily are enumerated faithfully in the poem.

p. 251   BECALMED

Printed in *The Indianapolis Journal,* May 10; 1885; published in AFTERWHILES (not first edition) —1898, THE LOCKERBIE BOOK—1911.

p. 253   GRIGGSBY'S STATION

Printed in *The Indianapolis Journal,* May 17, 1885, with the title, *Back Where They Used To Be;* published in AFTERWHILES—1887, OLD-FASHIONED ROSES—1888, FARM-RHYMES—1901, WHEN THE FROST IS ON THE PUNKIN AND OTHER POEMS— 1911. The wife is talking and calls her husband "Pap" as the children address him.

p. 256   FESSLER'S BEES

Dated May, 1885, printed in *The Indianapolis Journal,* May 31, 1885; published in POEMS HERE AT HOME—1893. See the picture of Bee Fessler drawn by Mr. Riley the day after the poem appeared in *The Journal,* and reproduced in this volume.

p. 264   JONEY

Printed in *The Indianapolis Journal,* June 7, 1885; published in AFTERWHILES—1887.

p. 267   KNEE-DEEP IN JUNE

Printed in *The Indianapolis Journal,* June 14, 1885, with the title, *Long About Knee Deep in*

June; published in AFTERWHILES—1887, OLD-FASHIONED ROSES—1888, FARM-RHYMES—1901, SONGS OF SUMMER—1908, KNEE-DEEP IN JUNE AND OTHER POEMS—1912.

p. 272   THE LAW OF THE PERVERSE

Printed in *The Indianapolis Journal,* June 28, 1885; published in HIS PA'S ROMANCE—1903.

In harmony with the feeling of this poem is the apt comment of Mr. Riley in a letter to Kate Douglas Wiggin, March 30, 1891:—

Did you ever hear of *"The Miggses"?* Years and years ago, The Danbury News Man struck those beautiful, lovely, poverty-ridden people, and my eyes are like this moist unpleasant weather outside as I think of them.—"Little *Tommy* Miggs"—ragged, tousle-headed, and awfully restless through morning session of school—communicates, by divers signs, to a favorite schoolmate, that his Ma told him to come straight home at noon—they were going to have strawberry shortcake. And can't you see him on his way there—like a letter X in the air—and the sudden nameless apprehension, seeing from afar the sad-faced group of little brothers and sisters at the gate, wistfully awaiting him with the intelligence in bated breath,—*"Company's Come!"* And I recall that among the visiting gorillas was "Uncle Richard," with his sweaty old smile and his big fat hairy hands, whose unctuous caresses Tommy so indignantly repulsed, as he headed the little exiles to "go out and *play*" in the back yard during dinner. Then at the backdoor steps where they listen, with white faces and clenched fists, at the havoc at the dinner table—clean on up to where "Uncle Richard"—the ungodly old hog!—says "I don't keer if I do," and swipes in the *last—lone—only—orphan* slice of the shortcake!—— Then the stars—and the schoolroom again—and *Tommy.* . . . "Books" is called, and all bright —cheery—happy—expectant—but Tommy. His favorite schoolmate funnels his hand—not guessing Tommy's real condition, but *glad,* remembering Tommy's promised rapture,—and whispers gleefully across.—*"Tommy! Say, Tommy; how was the shortcake?"* And then the lips tremble and crumble and the little face drops over into the ragged sleeves on the desk top. . . . And when the teacher's hand is laid an instant later on the little tow-head, and a voice asks kindly, "What's the matter with my little boy?"—it is just altogether too much—and the sobs take and shake the little martyr—till the inspired reader wants to just rise up in his might and fare forth, with a dog-iron or an old rusty pair of steelyards, and brain all the "Uncle Richards" in the Universe! ! !

p. 274   OUT OF NAZARETH

Printed in *The Indianapolis Journal,* July 12, 1885; published in AFTERWHILES—1887, GREEN FIELDS AND RUNNING BROOKS—1892, THE LOCKERBIE BOOK—1911. Many changes in the original version have been made. The following lines formerly completed the last stanza:

> So he slept, and, even so,
>   Sleeping in the robber's tent,
> Morning came at last, and lo,
>   He had not a single cent,
> Nor a thought but—pure content.

p. 276   TIME

The two sonnets here combined were originally printed separately. The first, with the title, *A Mood,* appeared in *The Indianapolis Journal,* November 29, 1880; the second, with the title, *The Smell of Bruised Grass,* appeared in *The Indianapolis Journal,* July 12, 1885. They were published combined in AFTERWHILES—1887, THE LOCKERBIE BOOK—1911, with the title, *Time.*

p. 278   IKE WALTON'S PRAYER

Printed in *The Indianapolis Journal,* July 26, 1885, published in AFTERWHILES—1887, OLD-FASHIONED ROSES—1888, LOVE-LYRICS—1899, THE LOCKERBIE BOOK—1911. The prayer was ascribed to Ike Wal-

ton because he was a character in full accord with
the simplicity of the ideals expressed.

This poem in two reminiscent lines recalls a
favorite early recitation of Mr. Riley's—*Brave
Love,* by Mary Kyle Dallas, designated by him, "a
perfect poem" :—

> He'd nothing but his violin,
>   I'd nothing but my song,
> But we were wed when the skies were blue
>   And summer days were long.
> And when we rested by the hedge
>   The robins came and told
> How they had dared to woo and win
>   When early Spring was cold.
> We sometimes supped on dewberries,
>   Or slept among the hay,
> But oft the farmers' wives at eve
>   Came out to hear us play
> The rare old songs—the dear old tunes—
>   We could not starve for long
> While my man had his violin
>   And I my sweet love-song.
>
> The world has aye gone well with us,
>   Old man, since we were one—
> Our homeless wandering down the lanes—
>   It long ago was done.
> But those who wait for gold or gear,
>   For houses and for kine,
> Till youth's sweet spring grows brown and sear,
>   And love and beauty tine,
> Will never know the joy of hearts
>   That met without a fear,
> When you had but your violin
>   And I a song, my dear.

p. 281   THE WAY IT WUZ

Printed in *The Indianapolis Journal,* August 2,
1885, with the notation, *Elizabeth City, Ind., 1884*;
published in PIPES O' PAN AT ZEKESBURY—1888,
NEGHBORLY POEMS (not first edition)—1897. Mr.

Riley never saw Elizabeth City, but knew it to be a typical early-Hoosier town. He actually heard the strange dialectic expression used at the end of each stanza.

p. 284   CURLY LOCKS

Printed in *The Indianapolis Journal,* August 2, 1885; published in NYE AND RILEY'S RAILWAY GUIDE — 1888, OLD-FASHIONED ROSES — 1888, RHYMES OF CHILDHOOD—1890, CHILD-RHYMES—1898, THE LOCKERBIE BOOK—1911. The quotation is from the old nursery ballad.

p. 286   GRANT

Printed in *The Indianapolis Journal,* August 8, 1885; published in AFTERWHILES (not in first edition)—1898, THE LOCKERBIE BOOK—1911. The last stanza and the one following were printed in *The Indianapolis Journal,* July 26, 1885, with the title, *The Dead Leader:*—

> Soldiers! look on his face the last,
>   With never a tremble of lip or lid;
> Look on the hero, as you file past,
>   And front his foe as your leader did—
> For still you may see, in the deepest dole
>   And the darkest night of your discontent,
> The great white light of his loyal soul
>   Ablaze in the midmost firmament.

p. 290   ON THE BANKS O' DEER CRICK

Printed in *The Delphi Times,* August 16, 1885; published in GREEN FIELDS AND RUNNING BROOKS —1890, SONGS OF SUMMER—1908, A SUMMER'S DAY AND OTHER POEMS—1911. These lines are reminiscent of pleasant fishing trips with Dr. Wyckliffe Smith near Delphi, Indiana, where the poem was written. See *Herr Weiser,* p. 172; *From Delphi to Camden,* p. 174; *The Noblest Service,* Vol. V, p. 99.

p. 292   BILLY COULD RIDE

Printed in *The Indianapolis Journal,* September 13, 1885, with the title, *The Way That Billy Could Ride;* sections II, III, and IV, except ll. 13-21, section IV, published in RHYMES OF CHILDHOOD (not in first edition)—1898, THE LOCKERBIE BOOK—1911. The poem entire is here published in book form for the first time.

p. 299   DAVE FIELD

Printed in *The Indianapolis Journal,* September 27, 1885; published in HIS PA'S ROMANCE (Homestead Edition)—1908, THE LOCKERBIE BOOK—1911. Dave Field, an amateur artist of ability, was an early friend of Mr. Riley.

p. 301   WHEN WE THREE MEET

Printed in *The Indianapolis Journal,* October 11, 1885, with the title *M. C. R.;* hitherto unpublished in book form. The initials refer to Dr. James Newton Matthews, Dr. W. C. Cooper, and Mr. Riley, all fast friends in mutual poetical interests and endeavors. See *To James Newton Matthews,* p. 240; *In Days to Come,* p. 384; and *Three Singing Friends,* Vol. IV, p. 273; and their notes.

p. 302   JOSH BILLINGS

Printed in *The Indianapolis Journal,* October 18, 1885; hitherto unpublished in book form. Mr.

Riley had always a grateful regard for the humorist, who was kind to him in his early days on the platform. Josh Billings then wrote:—

Deer Publik: I take extreem delite in introdusing 2 your imediate notis mi yung and handsum frend, Mr. James Whitkum Riley, who is a phunny man of purest ray sereen. He is the only man i kno that plays his own hand, or, in wurds less profeshonal, the only man that gives his own produxions, and not other folks'. He is phunnier than tung kan tell.   Yures without a struggle,
JOSH BILLINGS.

p. 304   THE LAND OF THE THUS-AND-SO

Printed in *The Indianapolis Journal,* October 25, 1885; published in RHYMES OF CHILDHOOD—1890, WHILE THE HEART BEATS YOUNG—1906, THE RUNAWAY BOY—1908, THE LOCKERBIE BOOK—1911.

p. 307   THE HOSS

Printed in *The Indianapolis Journal,* November 1, 1885; signed "Benj. F. Johnson of Boone"; published in NEGHBORLY POEMS—1891.

p. 311   A OLD PLAYED-OUT SONG

Printed in *The Indianapolis Journal,* November 8, 1885, with the title, *Lines on A' Old Played-Out Song,* signed "Benj. F. Johnson of Boone"; published in PIPES O' PAN AT ZEKESBURY—1888, NEGHBORLY POEMS—1891, LOVE-LYRICS—1899, DO THEY MISS ME—1913. S. M. Grannis is the composer of the old song, *Do They Miss Me at Home.*

p. 313   LITTLE ORPHANT ANNIE

Printed in *The Indianapolis Journal,* November 15, 1885, with the title, *The Elf Child;* published in The Boss Girl—1885; Old-Fashioned Roses—1888, Rhymes of Childhood—1890, Sketches in Prose—1891, Afterwhiles (Homestead Edition only)—1898, Child-Rhymes—1898, While the Heart Beats Young—1906, The Runaway Boy—1908, The Orphant Annie Book—1908, Ef You Don't Watch Out—1911. "Little Orphant Annie" was a real character and is described in the prose sketch, *Where Is Mary Alice Smith?* [Vol. VI]. The poem was once entitled *Little Orphant Allie.* She was a slender, elfish, little girl, an orphan, apparently not more than ten years of age though said to be fourteen, and she came to the Riley home one winter, clad in black and wearing a summer hat. She was brought there by a reputed uncle, whose home she was leaving to become a servant. This little girl had a great power of mysterious description, a wonderful skill of imitating other people, and a singular ability to amuse herself, probably developed through neglect. She cared little whether the children of the house played with her or not, and while washing dishes in the kitchen she used to carry on imaginative conversations between several other people and herself for her own amusement. Mr. Riley has a vivid remembrance of her going up the stairs, leaning down and patting each step affectionately and naming it, while the children of the house stood around in awe. She would finally disappear around the corner of the winding stairway, calling back in mysterious voice: "Some time you'll say, 'Where —is—Mary—Alice—Smith?' and the answer will

come, 'Oh—she—has—gone—home!' And then
ever'thing'll be all still ag'in, and you'll be afeard
to holler any more—and you durstn't play—and you
can't laugh, and yer throat'll thist hurt and hurt,
like you been a-eatin' too much calamus-root er
somepin'!"

In the story of *Where Is Mary Alice Smith?* this
little orphan falls in love with a soldier boy who is
killed, after which misfortune she dies of grief.
Actually she married a country boy, left Greenfield
and was lost to view.

Little Orphant Annie was always one of Mr.
Riley's most popular readings and children fre-
quently mention it in their letters to him, as did one
little fellow who asked, "Did you stop to think, Mr.
Riley, where that little boy went in "Little Orphant
Annie'?"

p. 317   A DOS'T O' BLUES

Printed in *The Indianapolis Journal,* November
22, 1885, signed "Benj. F. Johnson"; published in
Pipes o' Pan at Zekesbury—1888, Nye and
Riley's Railway Guide—1888, Neghborly Poems
—1897.

p. 319   THE TRAIN-MISSER

Printed in *The Indianapolis Journal,* December
20, 1885; published in Afterwhiles—1887. This
was written after actually missing a train at the
Union Station, Indianapolis. On this occasion
Mr. Riley made his appearance a half-hour before train-time on his way to Hamilton, Ohio,
where he was to give a reading. "I waited,"
he said, "until I saw a traveling man with whom
I was acquainted come in, told him about my

train, and how I was invariably hoodooed. 'There will be no trouble this time, Riley,' he said, 'for the Cincinnati, Hamilton & Dayton always makes up on the track right in front of us, and I am going on it myself. You can't miss it.' I waited there, never taking my eyes off that track until the train was three minutes past due and then I remonstrated with him. 'By George, that's queer,' he said, and turning to an official learned that the train had made up outside of the station—the first time in twenty years. Then it put on its rubbers and slipped inside, and tiptoed out of that station without my knowing it and just because I wanted to go on it, I suppose. And so I had to wait there for the next train and go via Cincinnati and transfer. In making the transfer I missed the next train and lost my engagement for that night."

On another occasion Mr. Riley started out for State Line, Warren County, Indiana, and brought up at State Line, Clark County, Illinois. By a lucky combination of trains he was able to retrace his way and reach the lecture about two hours late. When he returned home he informed his friends that he had found a new state line.

p. 321   THE PLAINT HUMAN

Printed in *The Indianapolis Journal,* January 18, 1886; published in GREEN FIELDS AND RUNNING BROOKS—1892, SONGS OF HOME—1910, THE LOCKERBIE BOOK—1911.

p. 322   WHICH ANE

Printed in *The Indianapolis Journal,* January 21, 1886; hitherto unpublished in book form.

p. 325   REGARDIN' TERRY HUT

Printed in *The Indianapolis Journal,* February 28, 1886; published in AFTERWHILES—1887. Terre Haute, county seat of Vigo County, Indiana, possessed at the time one of the most remarkable groups of men the country afforded. It included all except one of the characters mentioned in the poem. As talkers these men would have distinguished any gathering in the nation. First of all, there was Daniel Wolsey Voorhees, popularly called "the Tall Sycamore of the Wabash," Democratic politician and famous orator, who was United States Senator from 1877 to 1885. There was Thomas Henry Nelson, a noted diplomat and a leader of the Whig party, afterward a founder of the Republican party, who, when minister to Chili in 1864, won international popularity by saving numerous lives in the Santiago cathedral fire. Richard Wigginton Thompson, another member, was Secretary of the Navy in President Hayes' cabinet and was long prominent nationally in Republican politics. Occasionally William Riley McKeen joined the group. His distinguished service to the country was a loan negotiated during the Civil War, at a crisis encountered by Governor Morton, of Indiana. Mr. McKeen was president of the Vandalia Railroad Company from 1870 to 1896, was always prominent as a banker and well known in Republican politics, state and nation wide.

Eugene Debs, lecturer and organizer, has for many years been prominent as a leader of the Socialist party, and was the presidential candidate of this organization in 1904, 1908 and 1912.

p. 328   A TALE OF THE AIRLY DAYS

Printed in *The Indianapolis Journal,* March 7, 1886, signed "Benj. F. Johnson"; published in

AFTERWHILES — 1887, OLD-FASHIONED ROSES — 1888, NEGHBORLY POEMS—1891, FARM-RHYMES— 1901, THE PRAYER PERFECT AND OTHER POEMS— 1912.

p. 330   THE ROSSVILLE LECTUR' COURSE

Printed in *The Indianapolis Journal*, March 28, 1886, with the subtitle, *Rossville, Mich., March, '86;* printed in NYE AND RILEY'S RAILWAY GUIDE—1888, NEGHBORLY POEMS (not in first edition)—1897. The theme itself is a fancy suggested by the two towns named Rossville, one in Michigan and one in Indiana. Mr. Nye and Mr. Riley were then on the lecture platform, and, in the helpless way characteristic of them both, were struggling with the perplexities of railroad travel. The "hoodoo" that gave constant attendance to their endeavors was always a subject of jest between them. See *The Train Misser,* p. 319; *Another Ride from Ghent to Aix,* Vol. II, p. 343.

p. 333   HER BEAUTIFUL EYES

Printed in *The Indianapolis Journal,* April 4, 1886; published in GREEN FIELDS AND RUNNING BROOKS—1892, LOVE-LYRICS—1899, THE LOCKER-BIE BOOK—1911, HER BEAUTIFUL EYES—1913.

p. 334   WANT TO BE WHUR MOTHER IS

Printed in *The Indianapolis Journal,* April 4, 1886; published in PIPES O' PAN AT ZEKESBURY— 1888.

p. 336   BABE HERRICK

Printed in *The Indianapolis Journal,* April 4, 1886, with the title, *In the Manner of Herrick—To a Babe Sleeping;* published in RHYMES OF CHILD-HOOD—1890. See two following poems.

p. 337 **TO A JILTED SWAIN**

Printed in *The Indianapolis Journal,* April 4, 1886; published in ARMAZINDY—1894, THE LOCK-ERBIE BOOK—1911. In the manner of Herrick. See preceding and following poem.

p. 338 KNEELING WITH HERRICK

Printed in *The Indianapolis Journal,* April 4, 1886, with the title, *A Prayer for Content with Simple Store;* published in PIPES O' PAN AT ZEKESBURY—1888, SONGS OF HOME—1910, THE LOCKERBIE BOOK—1911. "In its title the poem refers to Robert Herrick, intimating that he is of a simple and humble disposition. It is the kind of supplication he would make, of course."—J. W. R.

p. 340 IN THE SOUTH

Printed in *The Indianapolis Journal,* April 11, 1886; published in PIPES O' PAN AT ZEKESBURY—1888, SONGS OF SUMMER—1908, THE LOCKERBIE BOOK—1911. The last two stanzas were used as a proem to LOVE-LYRICS—1899.

p. 342 THE HAPPY LITTLE CRIPPLE

Printed as a part of the sketch, *At Zekesbury,* which bore the title, *A Waste of Genius at Zekesbury,* in *The Chicago Current,* April 24, 1886; published in RHYMES OF CHILDHOOD—1890, CHILD-RHYMES—1898. Stanza 5 was not added until 1898 in a second edition of RHYMES OF CHILDHOOD.

"The idea of the poem," Mr. Riley once said, "was suggested by a rough, rugged man that I met on one of my tours. I had been lecturing in a little interior town, and had to get up at daylight one cold morning to ride to the nearest railway station. The man who drove me over was one of those hardy characters you meet in the rural regions,—one of those men who deem sentimentality a weakness and tears something to be ashamed of. As we rode along over the creaking snow he said: 'I heard you talk last night.' I remarked: 'Indeed! I hope you enjoyed it.' 'Yes,' said he, 'fust rate. My little girl was there. She likes that sort o' thing. She's great on po'try. You may hev' seen her. She set on the front row. She's a little girl, not very tall. You must 'a' noticed her.' I told him that I did not recall having seen her, and he continued: 'She ain't very big. She don't weigh more'n fifty pound. You see, she's got curv'ture of the spine. Her mother died when she was a little thing and havin' no one to look out fer her as a mother can, she fell down-stairs one day an' hurt herse'f. She never got over it. I hev' took care o' her the best I know'd how, but she's never growed. Sometimes I think she'll never be no bigger.' The tears welled to his eyes as he talked. He was ashamed to show the evidences of his grief and turned aside his head. Seeing that I was looking at him and had discovered his emotion, he dashed away the moisture from his eyes with one of the heavy leather mittens he wore and said: 'I dunno what's the matter with my eyes. One o' my hosses is lame, an' I put some liniment on his leg this morning. I must 'a' got some of it on this yer mitten o' mine.' "

For Mr. Riley's experience with the poem on the lecture platform, see Vol. I, p. 382. The following note was appended to the verses when published:—

The word "thist," as used in the foregoing lines, is an occasional childish pronunciation evolved from the word "just" —a word which in child vernacular has manifold supplanters,—such as "jus," "jes," "des," "jis," "dis," "jist," "dist," "ist," and even "gist," with hard *g*. In "thist," as above, sound "th" as in the word "the."

p. 346   HAS SHE FORGOTTEN

Printed in *The Indianapolis Journal*, May 23, 1886; printed in PIPES O' PAN AT ZEKESBURY— 1888, LOVE-LYRICS—1899, THE LOCKERBIE BOOK— 1911.

p. 348   ILLILEO

Printed in *The Indianapolis Journal*, July 25, 1886; published in AFTERWHILES—1887, OLD-FASHIONED ROSES—1888, LOVE-LYRICS—1899, THE LOCKERBIE BOOK—1911. The name is fanciful.

p. 350   **THE JOLLY MILLER**

Written and sent to William C. Edgar, editor of *The Northwestern Miller*, August 21, 1886; printed in the Christmas number of that paper, 1886; published in RHYMES OF CHILDHOOD—1890, CHILD-RHYMES — 1898. Compare Isaac Bickerstaff's *"There Was a Jolly Miller."*

p. 353   HE COMETH IN SWEET SENSE

Printed in *The Indianapolis Journal*, August 22, 1886; published in HIS PA'S ROMANCE (not in first edition)—1908, THE LOCKERBIE BOOK—1911.

p. 354   KINGRY'S MILL

Written and sent to William C. Edgar, editor of *The Northwestern Miller*, August 23, 1886; printed in the Christmas number of that paper, 1886, published in AFTERWHILES—1887. The mill stood on Brandywine Creek about a mile down stream from "the old swimmin'-hole."

p. 358 THE EARTHQUAKE

Printed in *The Indianapolis Journal,* September 5, 1886, dated September 1, 1886; hitherto unpublished in book form. The heading, *The Earthquake,* originally included the poems which follow, *A Fall-Crick View of the Earthquake* and *When the World Bu'sts Through.* The subtitle for this sonnet was *Charleston.* The earthquake of September, 1886, shook a tract of country extending from the Atlantic seaboard to the Mississippi Valley and from the heart of Georgia and Alabama as far north as Lake Michigan. The shocks continued for thirty-six hours. Numerous lives were lost and there was great destruction of property.

p. 359
A FALL-CRICK VIEW OF THE EARTHQUAKE

Printed in *The Indianapolis Journal,* September 5, 1886, dated September 1, 1886; published in NYE AND RILEY'S RAILWAY GUIDE—1888, HIS PA'S ROMANCE—1903. See preceding note.

p. 361 WHEN THE WORLD BU'STS THROUGH

Printed in *The Indianapolis Journal,* September 5, 1886, dated September 1, 1886; published in RHYMES OF CHILDHOOD—1890. See two preceding poems and their notes.

p. 363   THE OLD RETIRED SEA-CAPTAIN

Printed in *The Indianapolis Journal,* September 12, 1886; published in GREEN FIELDS AND RUNNING BROOKS—1892, THE LOCKERBIE BOOK—1911.

p. 365   JIM

Printed in *The Indianapolis Journal,* September 26, 1886; published in AFTERWHILES—1887, SONGS OF HOME—1910. The lore of the shoeshop in this poem is absolutely accurate, and is reminiscent of young Riley's days of observation in "old Tom Snow's" shop at Greenfield. "A 'jour,' pronounced 'jer,'" says Mr. Riley, "was a journeyman. Such a fellow, according to the old custom, had to complete his time as a journeyman before he became a regular shoemaker. We would often see such a man tramp up to the doorway of the shop, stick his head in and say: 'Any occasion,' which was the trade form of inquiry for work. If it was denied him he would say in the shoeman's vernacular, 'Well then, I'll jes' side up the pike.' The man Wigger, in the poem, did the exacting sewed work in the shop, and after the completion of a task might sit around the remainder of the day resting and feeling highly satisfied with himself. He would, therefore, imagine the Deity behaving in the manner ascribed to Him."

p. 368   OLD OCTOBER

Printed in *The Indianapolis Journal,* October 24, 1886, with the title, *Sompin' Strange About October;* published in AFTERWHILES—1897, FARM-RHYMES—1901, KNEE-DEEP IN JUNE AND OTHER POEMS—1912.

p. 370 JUDITH

Printed in *The Indianapolis Journal,* October 31, 1886; published in GREEN FIELDS AND RUNNING BROOKS—1892, LOVE-LYRICS—1899, THE LOCKERBIE BOOK—1911.

p. 371 THE LEGEND GLORIFIED

Printed in *The Indianapolis Journal,* November 14, 1886; published in PIPES O' PAN AT ZEKESBURY —1888, THE LOCKERBIE BOOK—1911. "I deem that God is not disquieted" is the fifteenth line of Swinburne's *The Two Dreams* (from Boccaccio).

p. 372 ON A FLY-LEAF

Printed in *The Indianapolis Journal,* December 12, 1886, with the title, *Written in John Boyle O'Reilly's "In Bohemia";* published in HOME-FOLKS—1900, THE LOCKERBIE BOOK—1911. John Boyle O'Reilly, editor of *The Boston Pilot,* was Mr. Riley's first literary friend of the East, and was, with Dr. Franc A. Harris, his host at the banquet given by the Papyrus Club of Boston in January, 1882. See *John Boyle O'Reilly,* Vol. IV, p. 83.

p. 373 OLD MAN'S NURSERY RHYME

Printed in *The Indianapolis Journal,* December 19, 1886; published in PIPES O' PAN AT ZEKESBURY —1888, RHYMES OF CHILDHOOD—1890, FARM-RHYMES—1901, THE PRAYER PERFECT AND OTHER POEMS—1912.

p. 375 LEWIS D. HAYES

Printed in *The Indianapolis Journal,* December 30, 1886; hitherto unpublished in book form. These

verses, in the manner of Longfellow, were written
on the death of Lewis D. Hayes, a friend and asso-
ciate of Mr. Riley's on *The Indianapolis Journal*.
He possessed a marked facility and talent as an edi-
torial writer.

p. 377   A LOCAL POLITICIAN FROM AWAY BACK

Printed in *The Indianapolis Journal*, January 30,
1887; published in HIS PA'S ROMANCE—1903. At
this time the currency was the subject of debate in
Congress and silver certificates of very small de-
nominations were proposed.

p. 381   THE MUTE SINGER

Printed in *The Indianapolis Journal*, February 6,
1887; published in HIS PA'S ROMANCE—1903, THE
LOCKERBIE BOOK—1911.

p. 382   THE CYCLONE

Printed in *The Indianapolis Journal*, March 13,
1887; published in GREEN FIELDS AND RUNNING
BROOKS—1892, THE LOCKERBIE BOOK—1911.

p. 384   IN DAYS TO COME

Printed in *The Indianapolis Journal*, March 20,
1887; hitherto unpublished in book form. This
poem was preceded by the following stanzas, with
the same title, written by Mr. Riley's friend, Dr.
James Newton Matthews.

> In days to come, when you and I
> Wax faint and frail, and heartfires die,
> And tinkling rhymes no more obey
> The wooing lips of yesterday,

How slowly will the hours go by!
When we have drained our song-cups dry.
My comrade, shall we sit and sigh,
　Childlike, o'er joys too sweet to stay
　　In days to come?

Nay! nay! we'll give old time the lie,
And, thatched with three score years, we'll try
　A roundeau or a roundelay
　As long as any lute string may
To our light touches make reply—
　　In days to come.

See *To James Newton Matthews,* p. 240; *When We Three Meet,* p. 301; *Three Singing Friends,* Vol. IV, p. 273; and their notes.

p. 385　　　　　THE STEPMOTHER

Printed in *The Indianapolis Journal,* March 27, 1887; published in Pipes o' Pan at Zekesbury—1888, Rhymes of Childhood (first edition only)—1890.

p. 386　WHEN MY DREAMS COME TRUE

Printed in *The Chicago Current,* April 2, 1887; published in Pipes o' Pan at Zekesbury—1888, Love-Lyrics—1899, The Lockerbie Book—1911, When My Dreams Come True—1913.

p. 388
THE CHANT OF THE CROSS-BEARING CHILD

Printed in *The Indianapolis Journal,* April 24, 1887; published in Green Fields and Running Brooks—1892. The inspiration came from a sanctimonious old darky, Ed Tyler, a servant of Mr. Harry S. New, of Indianapolis. He proclaimed himself a "cross-bearin' child."

p. 390 THREE DEAD FRIENDS

Printed in *The Indianapolis Journal,* May 15, 1887; published in PIPES O' PAN AT ZEKESBURY— 1888, THE LOCKERBIE BOOK—1911. "The poem is fanciful as to characters though veritable as to experience. There were numberless soldiers like this one, who were both fighters and poets, and similarly the other circumstances are veritable; yet the poem represents no particularities."—J. W. R.

p. 394 WHEN SHE COMES HOME

Printed in *The Indianapolis Journal,* June 5, 1887; published in AFTERWHILES (first edition only)—1887, OLD-FASHIONED ROSES—1888, POEMS HERE AT HOME—1893, LOVE-LYRICS—1899, THE LOCKERBIE BOOK—1911.

p. 395 LUTHER A. TODD

Printed in *The Indianapolis Journal,* August 7, 1887; hitherto unpublished in book form. Luther A. Todd, an Indianapolis pharmacist and a friend of Mr. Riley, was on his way westward in search of health at the time of his death. He died alone and unattended in his room in a Kansas City hotel.

p. 398 WHEN OLD JACK DIED

Printed in *The Indianapolis Journal,* August 7, 1887; published in PIPES O' PAN AT ZEKESBURY— 1888.

p. 400 WHEN THE HEARSE COMES BACK

Printed in *The Indianapolis Journal,* August 14, 1887; published in AFTERWHILES—1887.

p. 403 NESSMUK

Printed in *The Indianapolis Journal,* August 21, 1887; published in GREEN FIELDS AND RUNNING BROOKS — 1892, THE LOCKERBIE BOOK — 1911. These lines were addressed to the poet, George W. Sears, of Williamsport, West Virginia, a contributor to *Forest and Stream,* who adopted the name of "Nessmuk" from an old Indian who had taught him woodcraft. The issue of *Forest and Stream* for April 26, 1913, prints a characteristic picture of the hunter and says of him :—

Up to the time of Nessmuk's death, May 1, 1890, of all the contributors to *Forest and Stream* none ever won quite the place in the affectionate regard of readers that belonged to "Nessmuk." Into his writings was put not alone the lore of the woods—nature's secrets, revealed to such a woods haunter as he had been—but there was more than this —the philosophy and sentiment and wit and wisdom of a shrewd, observant, keen and penetrating student of human nature. A 'wonderful knowledge of the woodlands and of the ways of the woodland creatures was his, and a remarkable knowledge of his fellow men as well. Some one else might have written *Woodcraft* and another pen have contributed *Forest Runes,* but the "Nessmuk" who could write them both may be found not once in a century.

p. 404 BACK FROM A TWO-YEARS' SENTENCE

Printed in *The Indianapolis Journal,* August 28, 1887; published in AFTERWHILES (not in first edition)—1898.

p. 406 TO ROBERT LOUIS STEVENSON

Printed in *The World* (New York), December 11, 1887, dated September, 1887; published in HOME-FOLKS—1900, THE LOCKERBIE BOOK—1911. Mr. Riley found Stevenson's works particularly congenial reading. See *On a Youthful Portrait of Stevenson,* Vol. V, p. 14, and its note.

p. 408   THEM FLOWERS

Written in September, 1887; published in PIPES O' PAN AT ZEKESBURY (not in first edition)—1898, SONGS OF SUMMER—1908. The poem was written while Mr. Riley was ill and confined to his bed. Eugene Debs brought him the flowers that furnished the inspiration of these verses.

p. 410   THE ROBINS' OTHER NAME

Written in the fall of 1887; published in RHYMES OF CHILDHOOD—1890. "Bessie" and "Winnie" were the little daughters of Edgar Wilson Nye, at whose home Mr. Riley was visiting when the poem was suggested. Winifred always called robins after the name of her sister, "Bessie-birds."

p. 411   THE RAIN

Printed in *The World* (New York), October 23, 1887; published in PIPES O' PAN AT ZEKESBURY— 1888, THE LOCKERBIE BOOK—1911. This poem is one of Mr. Riley's favorites.

p. 413   TO EDGAR WILSON NYE

Written about November 26, 1887; published in ARMAZINDY—1894, THE LOCKERBIE BOOK—1911. The hearty friendship between Mr. Riley and Mr. Nye began in the fall of 1885, when they met at Indianapolis. Mr. Nye, who had gained prominence as a humorist on *The Laramie Boomerang,* had just been employed to contribute a weekly

article to *The Sunday World* (New York). The
meeting resulted in an arrangement for a short
reading tour under the management of Amos J.
Walker, and for the three following seasons dates
were made in Indiana, Illinois, Ohio and Michigan.
In the fall of 1888 Major J. B. Pond arranged the
first of their two enormously successful seasons, by
a tour through the East and Central West. The following season (1889-90) they made a still more ex-
tensive schedule. "The blithe companionship" developed through these associations became a deep-
rooted friendship. See Vol. I, pp. 380-81; *The
Rossville Lectur' Course,* p. 330; *The Artemus of
Michigan,* Vol. IV, p. 4; *Edgar Wilson Nye,* Vol.
IV, p. 348.

p. 414   A DISCOURAGING MODEL

Written prior to December, 1887; published in
AFTERWHILES (not in first edition)—1898, LOVE-
LYRICS—1899, RILEY ROSES—1909, THE LOCKERBIE
BOOK—1911.

p. 415   THE SERENADE

Printed in *The Cosmopolitan,* December, 1887;
published in OLD-FASHIONED ROSES—1888, AFTER-
WHILES (not in first edition)—1898, THE LOCKER-
BIE BOOK—1911.

p. 416   DOC SIFERS

Printed in *The World* (New York), December
11, 1887; published in PIPES O' PAN AT ZEKESBURY
—1888. In introducing this poem at a banquet of
the Indiana State Medical Society, June 5, 1888, at
Indianapolis, Mr. Riley said:— "I have . . . simply a sketch of the country physician or of a country doctor, as viewed by a denizen of the interior

country, who is speaking in perhaps a rather biased way of my friend, Doc Sifers, and the virtues of the country physician."

The character of Doc Sifers is founded on the author's observation of many country doctors, and is a composite picture. And yet, if influenced by any one in particular, Mr. Riley says, he has kept in mind the qualities of his own father. Captain Riley, though a lawyer by profession, took a natural interest in medicine, and was noted among his neighbors for his skill in old-fashioned remedies. As the case with many country doctors, he combined with curative skill a love for devising mechanical things and for diversified knowledge. Some of the incidents told in this poem and in its sequel, the *Rubáiyát of Doc Sifers,* refer to Captain Riley.

In an interview reported by *The Indianapolis News,* September 9, 1907, Mr. Riley said:—

When I say that Doc Sifers does not represent any particular person I don't mean that he is not true to human nature, for he is just as true as I could make him, and as I made him myself I ought to know. Every trait that I have attributed to him I have encountered in somebody, sometime and somewhere. All the incidents in which he figures were real incidents, too, and if they didn't happen to Doc Sifers they happened to somebody else. So you see, in the last analysis it's all true. If it isn't as true as gospel it's as true as human nature.

Mr. Riley found the work on Doc Sifers so congenial and absorbing that he continued it and produced the *Rubáiyát of Doc Sifers* in similar verse form and spirit. See *Rubáiyát of Doc Sifers,* Vol. V, p. 15.

p. 421   AFTERWHILES

Written as the proem for and published in the

first edition of AFTERWHILES—1887, OLD-FASHIONED ROSES—1888, THE LOCKERBIE BOOK—1911.

p. 424   A HOME-MADE FAIRY TALE

Published in AFTERWHILES—1887, RHYMES OF CHILDHOOD—1890, CHILD-RHYMES—1898.

p. 426   A VOICE FROM THE FARM

Published in AFTERWHILES—1887, SONGS OF SUMMER—1908, THE LOCKERBIE BOOK—1911.

p. 427   THE OLD HOME BY THE MILL

Printed in *The Northwestern Miller,* Christmas number, 1887, with the title, *At the Old Home by the Mill;* published in PIPES O' PAN AT ZEKESBURY—1888, NEGHBORLY POEMS (not in first edition)—1897.

p. 429   THE OLD MAN AND JIM

First read January 18, 1888, at a testimonial entertainment to Mr. Riley at The Grand Opera House, Indianapolis; published in POEMS HERE AT HOME—1893, GOOD-BYE, JIM (Christy Edition)—1913.

Line 7—"When the army broke out": "I have heard this phrase a hundred times. It is not fanciful, but genuine."—J. W. R.

"Cap. Bigler" and "Camp Ben Wade" are characteristic names, the latter having its source in the Ben Wade of Lincoln's cabinet. The poem was one of Mr. Riley's most favored recitations, and in introducing it he sometimes said:—

Among the many unwritten deeds of heroism brought out by the late war is one that occurred in an Indiana homestead. The old farmer was too old to enlist, but he was of that tough fiber that is truly genuine, and so he permitted to go his favorite son, a boy as much too young as his father was too old. It would seem that he made a fairly good soldier, too. At least, if we may judge from the story as told by a comrade.

p. 432   OUR OLD FRIEND NEVERFAIL

Printed in *The Indianapolis Journal,* January 22, 1888; hitherto unpublished in book form.

p. 434   DAN O'SULLIVAN

Printed in *The Indianapolis Journal,* January 22, 1888; hitherto unpublished in book form. Mr. Riley's friend, Dan O'Sullivan, of Louisville, Kentucky, journalist, poet, lawyer, was formerly the editor of *Truth,* a weekly in that city.

p. 436   AT "THE LITERARY"

Printed in *The Century Magazine,* February, 1888; published in POEMS HERE AT HOME—1893.

p. 440   SHE "DISPLAINS" IT

Printed in *St. Nicholas,* February, 1888; published in RHYMES OF CHILDHOOD—1890.

p. 441   DEAD, MY LORDS

Dated February 20, 1888, printed in *The Indianapolis Journal,* February 26, 1888; published in POEMS HERE AT HOME—1893, THE LOCKERBIE BOOK—1911. These lines were suggested by a suicide at the Denison Hotel, Indianapolis. The body lay in the room for a day and a night before it was discovered. With the body was found a note in which were these words: "Here is a man who has got just sense enough to be a fool."

p. 442   A MAN BY THE NAME OF BOLUS

Printed in *The World* (New York), April 8, 1888; published in POEMS HERE AT HOME—1893. The story is an actual fact even to the detail of the ice dropped down the dying man's collar, except that the author imagined the explanatory letter, and arbitrarily selected the name Bolus. No one ever knew the stranger's name or the cause of his act.

p. 445   THE TRAVELING MAN

Written for and read at a convention of The Indiana Commercial Travelers, at Evansville, April 13, 1888; published in HOME-FOLKS—1900.

p. 447   THE ABSENCE OF LITTLE WESLEY

Printed in *The Century Magazine,* May, 1888; published in POEMS HERE AT HOME—1893.

p. 449
WHEN THE GREEN GITS BACK IN THE TREES

Printed in *The World* (New York), May 13, 1888; published in PIPES O' PAN AT ZEKESBURY— 1888, NEGHBORLY POEMS (not in first edition)— 1898, FARM-RHYMES—1901, SONGS OF SUMMER— 1908, KNEE-DEEP IN JUNE AND OTHER POEMS— 1912.

p. 451   HOW IT HAPPENED

Printed in *The Pittsburgh Bulletin* just prior to May 20, 1888; published in PIPES O' PAN AT ZEKES-

BURY—1888, NEGHBORLY POEMS (not in first edition)—1898, LOVE-LYRICS—1899. This poem is in
the style and orthography of "Benj. F. Johnson, of
Boone."

p. 454   GLADNESS

Printed in *The Century Magazine,* July, 1888;
published in POEMS HERE AT HOME—1893.

p. 457   THE WIFE-BLESSED

Printed in *The Indianapolis Journal,* August 19,
1888, with the title, *The Wife;* published in GREEN
FIELDS AND RUNNING BROOKS—1892, LOVE-LYRICS
—1899, THE LOCKERBIE BOOK—1911.

p. 458   ROBERT BURNS WILSON

Dated October 30, 1888, printed in *The Critic,*
November 24, 1888, with the title, *To Robert Burns
Wilson;* published in GREEN FIELDS AND RUNNING
BROOKS—1892, THE LOCKERBIE BOOK—1911. Rob-
ert Burns Wilson (1850-1902), who made his home
at Frankfort, Kentucky, was "both a real artist and
a real poet," says Mr. Riley. He began painting por-
traits for a livelihood at the age of nineteen and ex-
hibited landscapes and other work at the Louisville
Exposition, 1883, and at the New Orleans Exposi-
tion, 1888. His poems were chiefly contributed to
Harper's Magazine. He was the author of *Life and
Love* (poems) and a novel, *Until the Day Breaks.*
Mr. Riley's personal regard for Mr. Wilson was
expressed in a letter to the editor of *The West
Virginia School Journal* in the summer of 1889:
"Your contributors' list is blessed with lovely char-
acters—none lovelier or nobler than Robert Burns
Wilson."

p. 459 'MONGST THE HILLS O' SOMERSET

Printed in *The Century Magazine,* November, 1888; published in POEMS HERE AT HOME—1893. Although there are Somerset Hills in Indiana, Mr. Riley did not know it when he wrote this poem in Hoosier dialect. The idea was suggested in the office of *The Pittsburgh Bulletin* during the course of a random conversation with the editor, John W. Black. The latter relates that "he alluded to the trout fishing in Somerset County, among other things, and had incidentally used the expression 'mongst the hills o' Somerset' in describing the picturesque nooks of that near-by locality, when Riley was observed suddenly to fidget about in his chair, then to rub his hands, then to roll his eyes in a state of intense pleasure at something, and finally was heard to break out with the joyful ejaculation: 'I'll make a poem about that!' And he did, literally building the poem up, idea and all, within the next few hours, on the basis of one line then suggested. . . . The dialect of the verses doesn't apply to Somerset County at all, it being simply the same old Hoosier idiom that Riley has made famous in all his poems; whereas the dialect of the Somerset Mountains is notoriously the most homely Pennsylvania Dutch in Pennsylvania! However, the question of anachronism is of no consequence, for, so far as the poem is concerned, it might apply to any other hills of Somerset that the broad topography of all America may be noted for."

It is interesting to note that Somerset County, Pennsylvania, is a portion of what was the original Bedford County, where Mr. Riley's father was born and where his grandparents were born and where they lived before they came to Indiana.

p. 462   A PASSING HAIL

Printed in *The Home Magazine,* December, 1888, with the title, *Rest;* published in Rhymes of Childhood—1890, Songs o' Cheer—1905, The Lockerbie Book—1911.

p. 464   "LAST CHRISTMAS WAS A YEAR AGO"

Printed in *The Century Magazine,* December, 1888; published in Poems Here at Home—1893.

p. 471   LITTLE JOHNTS'S CHRIS'MUS

Printed in *The Book Buyer,* December, 1888; published in Rhymes of Childhood—1890, While the Heart Beats Young—1906, The Runaway Boy—1908.

p. 476   THAT-AIR YOUNG-UN

Printed in *The 'Northwestern Miller,* Christmas number, 1888; published in Rhymes of Childhood —1890. Mr. T. P. O'Conner, in *The London Sunday Sun* of April 10, 1892, described this poem with his rare insight and sympathy :—

It is the story of a curious, dreamy, weird child, told by its father,—a child to whom everything in nature had voices. The wistfulness of childhood comes home to you in some of these lines with startling distinctness, and the infinite pathos of a parent love, apprehensions and final loss are visible through the grim control of phrase and feeling which are characteristic of the Yankee . . . Again and again, the child returns to this problem—what is the water talking of? He can interpret every sound in animal nature, . . . but that voice of the running water—with that mysterious melody which has puzzled more boyish ears—remains still unintelligible. . . . Finally is the story of the child's death, and of nature's service over her young lover.

p. 480   THE PIPES O' PAN

Written as the proem for and published in the first edition of PIPES O' PAN AT ZEKESBURY—1888.

p. 481   DOWN AROUND THE RIVER

Published in PIPES O' PAN AT ZEKESBURY—1888, RHYMES OF CHILDHOOD—1890, CHILD-RHYMES— 1898, SONGS OF SUMMER—1908, DOWN AROUND THE RIVER AND OTHER POEMS—1911.

p. 484   HIS MOTHER

Published in PIPES O' PAN AT ZEKESBURY—1888.

p. 485   IN BOHEMIA

Published in PIPES O' PAN AT ZEKESBURY—1888, THE LOCKERBIE BOOK—1911.

p. 488   MOON-DROWNED

Published in PIPES O' PAN AT ZEKESBURY—1888, THE LOCKERBIE BOOK—1911. A favorite poem of Mr. Riley's.

p. 490   WHO SANTY CLAUS WUZ

Published in PIPES O' PAN AT ZEKESBURY—1888, with the title, *Long Afore He Knowed Who Santy Claus Wuz,* RHYMES OF CHILDHOOD (first edition only)—1890, CHILD-RHYMES—1898.

p. 493   TO MY GOOD MASTER

Published in PIPES O' PAN AT ZEKESBURY—1888, THE LOCKERBIE BOOK—1911. "This is fanciful and means no particular old master, though the conception is very vivid in my mind."—J. W. R.

p. 494   CHAIRLEY BURKE'S IN TOWN

Published in the prose sketch, *A Wild Irishman,* in PIPES O' PAN AT ZEKESBURY—1888; published separately in HIS PA'S ROMANCE (not Homestead Edition)—1903. Stanzas 2 and 5 were not in the first version.

p. 497   WAIT FOR THE MORNING

Published in PIPES O' PAN AT ZEKESBURY, 1888, THE LOCKERBIE BOOK—1911.